PLAY AND SCENE PREPARATION

A Workbook for Actors and Directors

Harry E. Stiver, Jr.
California State University,
Long Beach

Stanley Kahan
California State University,
Long Beach

ALLYN AND BACON, INC.
Boston   London   Sydney   Toronto

Portions of this book first appeared in *A Director's Workbook* by Stanley
Kahan and Harry E. Stiver, Jr. Copyright © 1974 by Allyn and Bacon, Inc.

Library of Congress Cataloging in Publication Data

Stiver, Harry E., Jr.
    Play and scene preparation.

    Bibliography: p.
    1. Acting.   2. Theater—Production and direction.
3. Drama—Collections.   I. Kahan, Stanley, 1931-
II. Title.
PN2080.S75   1984   792′.028   84–421
ISBN 0-205-08150-9

Printed in the United States of America
10   9   8   7   6   5   4   3   2   88   87   86

CREDITS

Illustrations on pages 83, 85, 86, 89 and 90 are by B. J. Skalka.

Scenes from plays are reprinted by permission of the publishers:

From *All My Sons* by Arthur Miller in *Arthur Miller's Collected Plays*. Copyright © 1947, 1957, © renewed 1975 by Arthur Miller. Reprinted by permission of Viking
Penguin Inc., and by permission of International Creative Management.
Caution: All rights, including professional, amateur, motion picture, recitation, lecturing, public reading, radio broadcasting, and television are strictly reserved. Inquiries on all rights should be addressed to: International Creative Management, 40 W. 57th St., NY, NY 10019.

From *Death of a Salesman* by Arthur Miller. Copyright © 1949, © renewed 1977 by Arthur Miller. Reprinted by permission of Viking Penguin Inc., and by permission
of International Creative Management.
Caution: All rights, including professional, amateur, motion picture, recitation, lecturing, public reading, radio broadcasting, and television are strictly reserved. Inquiries on all rights should be addressed to: International Creative Management, 40 W. 57th St., NY, NY 10019.

From *Of Mice and Men* by John Steinbeck. Copyright © 1937, © renewed 1965 by John Steinbeck. Reprinted by permission of Viking Penguin Inc., and by permission
of McIntosh and Otis, Inc.

From *Come Back, Little Sheba* by William Inge. Copyright © 1950 by William Inge. Reprinted by permission of Random House, Inc., and by permission of
International Creative Management.
Caution: All rights, including professional, amateur, motion picture, recitation, lecturing, public reading, radio broadcasting, and television are strictly reserved. Inquiries on all rights should be addressed to: Random House, Inc. Alfred A. Knopf, Inc., 201 East 50th St., NY, NY 10022.

From *Inherit the Wind* by Jerome Lawrence and Robert E. Lee. Copyright as an unpublished work 1951 by Jerome Lawrence and Robert E. Lee. Copyright © 1955 by
Jerome Lawrence and Robert E. Lee. Reprinted by permission of Random House, Inc., and by permission of Harold Freedman Brandt & Brandt Dramatic Department,
Inc. All rights reserved. All inquiries should be addressed to Harold Freedman Brandt & Brandt Dramatic Department, Inc., 1501 Broadway, New York, NY 10036.
Caution: All rights, including professional, amateur, motion picture, recitation, lecturing, public reading, radio broadcasting, and television are strictly reserved. Inquiries on all rights should be addressed to: Random House, Inc. Alfred A. Knopf, Inc., 201 East 50th St., NY, NY 10022.

Credits continue on page 350.

Contents

PART THREE
Appendices

 **Preface**

The purposes of this book are to help train actors and directors in the analysis and preparation of play scripts and provide them with a variety of scenes for execution. It has been designed to serve the needs of those who, regardless of their process or approach, realize that careful preparation of the text is essential before the play (or scene) is placed on stage. It is intended that the beginning and continuing student of acting and/or directing will find the contents useful in individual or special classroom situations. Also, those numerous workshops in which the actor and director work together should benefit from direct application of the included materials.

In Part One, Preparation: The Actor's/Director's Analyses, a series of exercises have been included to illustrate several major considerations which either the actor or director should undertake in his/her "initial coming to grips" with the text. For the purpose of consistency, Arthur Miller's *Death of a Salesman* has been used throughout to provide illustrative examples for these exercises. As a major and well-known American play, it serves to make distinctions between the actor's and director's problems and concerns more readily apparent. Therefore, each of the exercises is preceded by a sample exercise already completed using *Death of a Salesmen* as the specific "problem-solving" illustration. The suggested answers are hardly to be considered definitive; rather, they serve as one means of suggesting how a particular scene or play might be approached.

In Part Two, Execution: The Scenes, major scenes have been selected from three categories of dramatic periods and types:

1. Modern Realistic Scenes
2. Modern Non-Realistic Scenes
3. Pre-Twentieth Century Period Scenes

Over forty scenes in these categories have been chosen to provide diversity and challenge to the actor/director. An introduction has been prepared for each.

Preceding these scenes, a sample scene from *Death of a Salesman* has been included with thorough script notations indicated from two divergent points of view. The external or technical approach is counterpointed with notations as they might be rendered by what can be called the internal or subjective psychological method. These approaches, illustrated for both the actor and director, represent two extremes that may be modified, altered, or blended depending on the individual needs or techniques of the actor/director involved. What is important is an understanding of the diversity of approaches available and finding the approach most compatible for the individual's work and the particular production involved. Also included in this section are original "ground plans" for the director, with selective blocking notations illustrated.

The final portion of the book includes helpful appendices and exercises, such as developing a rehearsal schedule, a list of major play companies, and a bibliography of recommended readings.

It is hoped that this book will prove useful to the beginning and continuing student of acting and/or directing, regardless of fundamental approach or previous experience. It has been carefully designed to be compatible with a diversity of methodologies in acting and directing. Its wide margins permit the actor or director to include extensive blocking and psychological or interpretive character notes; its "tear out" pages allow for the extraction of scenes or exercises. The real value of this volume, however, ultimately depends on the extent to which the actor/director applies himself/herself to the preparation and execution of scenes.

PART ONE

PREPARATION
The Actor's/Director's Analyses

A. General Explanation: ACTING
   1. Exercise for the study of APPROACH AND STYLE
   2. Exercise for the study of BUSINESS AND MOVEMENT
   3. Exercise for the study of CHARACTERIZATION
   4. Exercise for the study of DIALOGUE AND LANGUAGE

B. General Explanation: DIRECTING
   1. Exercise for the study of PRODUCTION APPROACH AND STYLE
   2. Exercise for the study of PICTURIZATION AND MOVEMENT
   3. Exercise for the study of CHARACTERIZATION
   4. Exercise for the study of LANGUAGE AND DIALOGUE

The exercises may be extracted without damage to the book.

A General Explanation: ACTING

The actor works to create a role, in keeping with the general tone of the production, which is revealing of all the nuances and subtleties inherent in the text. The actor examines the entire play, at first for the pleasure to be derived from a good piece of theatre, limited of course to its verbal context. How does the plot work out, who are the major characters, and how do they relate to each other are some questions the actor asks. Only after a general reading of the play should the actor go back and analyze the work in depth.

Often, for the purpose of stretching the acting muscles, the actor works on short scenes taken out of context from the complete work. This section of the book includes four important aspects which the actor should consider when working either on a scene or on the complete play. Clearly, any scene taken out of context can easily become distorted or erroneous in its treatment. Therefore the exercises have been developed to help the actor undertake a full and appropriate study of his or her character in relation to the *entire play*. The following four categories are the ones discussed in this section, although clearly a full examination of a character might include even more details than are suggested here. These basic areas of consideration are:

1. Approach and Style
2. Business and Movement
3. Characterization
4. Dialogue and Language

Several questions are included in each section, with appropriate space provided for succinct answers. Although one may be tempted to write more than the space permits, try to get to the marrow of the question and pinpoint the important parts that will directly affect the playing of the role.

Specific examples have been written as illustrations to show hypothetically how the exercises might be approached. The play chosen is *Death of a Salesman* by Arthur Miller, and the role is that of Willy Loman, the central character of the play. The same play and role are used in all of the examples to provide continuity. In each of the exercise sections, it is recommended that *one* character and *one* play be used in order to examine all of the potential considerations the actor must undergo in the preparation of a role. Three sets of each exercise are provided, permitting the analysis of three different characters and the factors that will affect the creation of each role.

1. Exercise for the study of APPROACH AND STYLE

The purpose of this exercise is to help the actor see his or her role in relation to the totality of the play. No performance can, or rather should, exist in isolation from the meaning of the play. A "solo" performance isolated from fellow performers and total concept is artistically dishonest and usually shallow. The actor should see his or her character in relation to the main idea of the playwright, the genre of the play (be it comedy, tragedy, melodrama, etc.), and the playing style that might be required depending upon the period of composition, the historical setting of the piece, or the qualities of national culture that might be inherent parts of the play. The actor should examine the role in relation to the intent of the play in order to determine if the character has been honestly drawn or is self-serving for the playwright's limited ends. A thorough search of the text (dialogue) of the role is often useful in relating the role to the central core or idea of a play. Often, critical decisions about the ultimate approach or style of a play are made by the director, but the director cannot accomplish that without the cooperation and concurrence by the cast who honestly commit themselves to that view.

2. Exercise for the study of BUSINESS AND MOVEMENT

Although basic movement patterns in a play are frequently decided by the director, few actors want to react as mere automatons at the whim of a stage director. Movement and stage business (the little details of physical action) are often integral parts of the character and the means of revealing motivation. The reaction of one character to another, to objects, furniture, or stage areas and the revelation of the character's state of mind are frequently tied to the actor's choices of the kinds of movement and business to be employed.

This exercise asks the actor to examine the text and character to ascertain such external factors as the mood, style, and period of the play, and the environment, climate, and costume worn, to determine their individual and collective influences on the type of movement and business used. Additionally, analysis of certain aspects of the role being performed will be important factors in stage movement. The character's age, status, education, and state of health should be considered. Taken together, these obvious factors of character and the "milieu" of the play should help the actor understand the elements that should go into a fundamental approach to the development of business and movement.

3. Exercise for the study of CHARACTERIZATION

The actor grapples with the most fundamental questions in this section. How does he or she go about the problem of building a character in the theatre from the words on a printed page? The questions raised in this section ask the actor to look at basic motivation (Why am I in this play?—What do I want?—Can I get what I want?)

and begin to determine that motivation. Most often this can be revealed by what the character says about himself or herself, what others say about the character, and what the playwright may suggest in preliminary or interior notes to the play. Then the actor is asked to look at specific details of the character, the easily discovered factors such as occupation or dress which touch on the obvious externals of the character's social existence. These should serve as touchstones to other questions of external evidence, i.e., age, education, friends, or beliefs, which the actor must be aware of in any thorough preparation of a character. Answering thoughtfully the questions in this section should serve the actor as a useful device for developing facility in knowing how to deal with the critical questions of character.

4.   Exercise for the study of DIALOGUE AND LANGUAGE

The purpose of this section is for the actor to deal with the dialogue that he or she must speak in the guise of the character. The actor is asked to examine his or her personal text from the viewpoint of its distinctness from the text of other characters. Often the subtlest distinctions in dialogue may reveal the most vital bits of information about how to develop a character. Additionally, an understanding of the character will help to determine how the dialogue might be presented during the performance of the role. Such factors as regional expressions, accents, age, health, and social status are all revealed by the actor's handling of the dialogue. Therefore, after working on this section, the actor should be able to visualize how a study of the language and dialogue works both as a means and an end in character projection. First, the dialogue helps the actor to analyze the role, and secondly, it serves as an important means of clarifying aspects of that character to the audience.

Name *B. Anne Actor*   Date *1/1/00*

1. THE ACTOR: Sample exercise for the study of APPROACH AND STYLE

Play *Death of a Salesman*   Author *Arthur Miller*

Name of Character *Willy Loman*

Analysis

1. What is the basic or central idea (spine) set forth in the play?

It is important for an individual to live his life according to his abilities and talents and not be turned away from fulfilling his potential because of false ideals, even if these seem to be a part of the so-called American dream. Also, a "little" man can attain tragic dignity in trying to fight against the circumstances of his environment.

2. How does your character contribute to the central idea of the play?

Willy is central to the play, as the title suggests. Willy became a salesman (probably not a very good one, either) although he was happiest working with his hands, putting up a ceiling, or working on the front steps of his house. His name, Loman, suggests the little (low) man whose life takes on tragic meaning in his attempt to attain human dignity.

3. Is the character honestly drawn, or has he or she been distorted in order to affect the overall intent of the play?

Willy, unfortunately, is an all-too-recognizable character. He is honestly but piteously drawn. Although he may seem blind to us, he is shown by the playwright to follow remorselessly the ideals and the code that identify him throughout the play.

4. Indicate selected illustrations of action and/or dialogue of your character that help to reveal the thematic idea of the play.

Willy (Act II) to Howard: "I realized that selling was the greatest career a man could want! Cause what could be more satisfying than to be able to go—into twenty or thirty different cities, and pick up the phone, and be remembered. . . ." Willy (Act II) to Biff: "I am not a dime a dozen! I am Willy Loman, and you are Biff Loman." Willy comments throughout the play that it is important to be "well-liked"—his superficial view of success. He encourages his sons to cheat or steal a little if it will help them on the road to success.

5. Does the character appropriately fit into the genre (tragedy, comedy, melodrama, etc.) chosen by the playwright?

Arthur Miller intended the play as a tragedy. His essay "Tragedy and the Common Man" written after Salesman *opened suggests much of what he wrote in the play. Willy is his version of an American tragic hero, and despite Willy's lack of classic tragic stature, he is perfectly suited to Miller's view of modern tragedy. There are some comic touches in Willy that should not be missed which help to heighten the tragic feeling.*

6. How does the style of the play affect the manner in which your role should be performed?

Although the play mixes symbolism and expressionistic dream sequences, most of the play and its dialogue are realistic. Willy must be played realistically and honestly. Much of the impact of the play is created because we recognize Willy and men like him, and it is important to develop this portrayal in a realistic manner.

1. THE ACTOR: Exercise for the study of APPROACH AND STYLE

Play ————————————————— Author —————————————————

Name of Character ——————————————————————————————

Analysis

1. What is the basic or central idea (spine) set forth in the play?

   ——

   ——

   ——

   ——

   ——

   ——

2. How does your character contribute to the central idea of the play?

   ——

   ——

   ——

   ——

   ——

   ——

3. Is the character honestly drawn, or has he or she been distorted in order to affect the overall intent of the play?

   ——

   ——

   ——

   ——

   ——

4. Indicate selected illustrations of action and/or dialogue of your character that help to reveal the thematic idea of the play.

_____

_____

_____

_____

_____

_____

_____

5. Does the character appropriately fit into the genre (tragedy, comedy, melodrama, etc.) chosen by the playwright?

_____

_____

_____

_____

_____

_____

_____

6. How does the style of the play affect the manner in which your role should be performed?

_____

_____

_____

_____

_____

_____

_____

1. THE ACTOR: Exercise for the study of APPROACH AND STYLE

Play _____ Author _____

Name of Character _____

Analysis

1. What is the basic or central idea (spine) set forth in the play?

_____

_____

_____

_____

_____

_____

2. How does your character contribute to the central idea of the play?

_____

_____

_____

_____

_____

_____

3. Is the character honestly drawn, or has he or she been distorted in order to affect the overall intent of the play?

_____

_____

_____

_____

_____

_____

4. Indicate selected illustrations of action and/or dialogue of your character that help to reveal the thematic idea of the play.

_____

_____

_____

_____

_____

_____

_____

5. Does the character appropriately fit into the genre (tragedy, comedy, melodrama, etc.) chosen by the playwright?

_____

_____

_____

_____

_____

_____

_____

6. How does the style of the play affect the manner in which your role should be performed?

_____

_____

_____

_____

_____

_____

_____

1. THE ACTOR: Exercise for the study of APPROACH AND STYLE

Play _____ Author _____

Name of Character _____

Analysis

1. What is the basic or central idea (spine) set forth in the play?

_____

_____

_____

_____

_____

_____

2. How does your character contribute to the central idea of the play?

_____

_____

_____

_____

_____

_____

3. Is the character honestly drawn, or has he or she been distorted in order to affect the overall intent of the play?

_____

_____

_____

_____

_____

_____

4. Indicate selected illustrations of action and/or dialogue of your character that help to reveal the thematic idea of the play.

_____

_____

_____

_____

_____

_____

_____

5. Does the character appropriately fit into the genre (tragedy, comedy, melodrama, etc.) chosen by the playwright?

_____

_____

_____

_____

_____

_____

_____

_____

6. How does the style of the play affect the manner in which your role should be performed?

_____

_____

_____

_____

_____

_____

2. THE ACTOR: Sample exercise for the study of BUSINESS AND MOVEMENT

Play ___Death of a Salesman___ Author ___Arthur Miller___

Name of Character ___Willy Loman___

Analysis

1. How does the style and/or period of the play affect the type of movement to be used in the play?

The play is realistic, set in the late 20s and the late 40s. Movement should not be affected seriously because of period or style. America in the mid-20s and 40s poses no major variation from modern movement.

2. How do such factors as the character's age, social status, education, and health suggest the type of movement to be used in the play?

Willy is seen both in his present (i.e., the 1940s) and flashbacks twenty years earlier. In the 1940s, he is sixty-three, exhausted and a failure. Movement should highlight the enthusiastic and hopeful Willy in early middle age and the exhausted Willy twenty years later. Movement will help to pinpoint age and varying professional success.

3. How do such factors as physical environment, climate, and familiarity with surroundings suggest the movement to be used in certain scenes or the play as a whole?

The scenes in which Willy appears, i.e., home, office, restaurant, hotel room, are part of his normal life. Willy should seem to fit comfortably into most of the surroundings, except in Howard's office where he is obviously ill at ease. Otherwise he should seem to be "at one" with his environment.

4. How does the mood of the play affect the type of movement to be used in the play?

The play is a modern tragedy, a depressing view of the modern common man. Willy's isolation and feelings of being lost and having "no place to go" should be reflected in the slow, almost bewildered tempo of his movement.

5. How do the demands of costume affect the type of movement to be used in the play?

Willy will be wearing a three-piece business suit, with the coat on or off through most of the play. This should create few problems, although I rarely wear a suit for everyday use, and therefore I have to avoid a normal

attitude towards lounging and informality.

6. Does the playwright indicate any necessary movement or business which must be incorporated into the character? If so, what does it suggest about playing the role?

Other than pointing out at the beginning of the play that Willy's "exhaustion is apparent," the playwright has

indicated no necessary business that will have a major impact on the character. However, it must be remembered

that Willy is constantly "selling" and that this activity is a part of his total being.

7. Are there any critical pieces of furniture or props which will affect movement and business? Can they be used to sharpen the character?

The kitchen table serves not only as a focal point in the action but as a psychological reminder of the Lomans as

"family" and of the countless meals they have eaten together in the past. It is a place of refuge and

remembrance, particularly for Willy.

2. THE ACTOR: Exercise for the study of BUSINESS AND MOVEMENT

Play _____ Author _____

Name of Character _____

Analysis

1. How does the style and/or period of the play affect the type of movement to be used in the play?

_____

_____

_____

_____

_____

2. How do such factors as the character's age, social status, education, and health suggest the type of movement to be used in the play?

_____

_____

_____

_____

_____

3. How do such factors as physical environment, climate, and familiarity with surroundings suggest the movement to be used in certain scenes or the play as a whole?

_____

_____

_____

_____

_____

4. How does the mood of the play affect the type of movement to be used in the play?

_____

_____

_____

_____

5. How do the demands of costume affect the type of movement to be used in the play?

_____

_____

_____

_____

6. Does the playwright indicate any necessary movement or business which must be incorporated into the character? If so, what does it suggest about playing the role?

_____

_____

_____

_____

7. Are there any critical pieces of furniture or props which will affect movement and business? Can they be used to sharpen the character?

_____

_____

_____

_____

2. THE ACTOR: Exercise for the study of BUSINESS AND MOVEMENT

Play _____ Author _____

Name of Character _____

Analysis

1. How does the style and/or period of the play affect the type of movement to be used in the play?

_____

_____

_____

_____

_____

2. How do such factors as the character's age, social status, education, and health suggest the type of movement to be used in the play?

_____

_____

_____

_____

_____

3. How do such factors as physical environment, climate, and familiarity with surroundings suggest the movement to be used in certain scenes or the play as a whole?

_____

_____

_____

_____

_____

4. How does the mood of the play affect the type of movement to be used in the play?

_____

_____

_____

_____

_____

5. How do the demands of costume affect the type of movement to be used in the play?

_____

_____

_____

_____

_____

6. Does the playwright indicate any necessary movement or business which must be incorporated into the character? If so, what does it suggest about playing the role?

_____

_____

_____

_____

_____

7. Are there any critical pieces of furniture or props which will affect movement and business? Can they be used to sharpen the character?

_____

_____

_____

_____

_____

2. THE ACTOR: Exercise for the study of BUSINESS AND MOVEMENT

Play _____ **Author** _____

Name of Character _____

Analysis

1. How does the style and/or period of the play affect the type of movement to be used in the play?

_____

_____

_____

_____

2. How do such factors as the character's age, social status, education, and health suggest the type of movement to be used in the play?

_____

_____

_____

_____

_____

3. How do such factors as physical environment, climate, and familiarity with surroundings suggest the movement to be used in certain scenes or the play as a whole?

_____

_____

_____

_____

_____

4. How does the mood of the play affect the type of movement to be used in the play?_____

_____

_____

_____

_____

5. How do the demands of costume affect the type of movement to be used in the play?

_____

_____

_____

_____

_____

6. Does the playwright indicate any necessary movement or business which must be incorporated into the character? If so, what does it suggest about playing the role?

_____

_____

_____

_____

_____

7. Are there any critical pieces of furniture or props which will affect movement and business? Can they be used to sharpen the character?

_____

_____

_____

_____

_____

3. THE ACTOR: Sample exercise for the study of CHARACTERIZATION

Play _Death of a Salesman_   Author _Arthur Miller_

Name of Character _Willy Loman_

Analysis

1. What is the major motivation (motive) of the character in the play?

To achieve success for himself through salesmanship and, failing that, to buy success for his son, Biff, even at the expense of his own life. Willy desperately wants to be "well-liked" by his colleagues and loved by his sons.

2. What significant comments does the character make about himself or herself that reveal aspects of the characterization?

Willy calls himself "foolish to look at." He defends Biff when he finds out Biff "borrowed" a football—"He's gotta practice with a regulation ball. . . ." Willy sadly notes that now "no one knows me anymore." This reveals his basic insecurity, the hope of finding success through his son, and his realization that at the end of his life he has failed to find success or security.

3. What significant comments are made about the character by other characters in the play?

Willy's wife Linda says, "A man who never worked a day but for your [Biff's] benefit." She also tells us Willy is sixty-three years old and worked for one company for thirty-six years. Biff points out that Willy is a "drummer who landed in an ash can" and that he had "the wrong dreams." Charley points out that "he was a happy man with a batch of cement" and that "a salesman has got to dream. . . . It comes with the territory."

4. What does the playwright say about the character in the notes?

Most of our knowledge of Willy comes from the dialogue. However, Miller notes when we first meet Willy that "his exhaustion is apparent." Linda loves him, notes the playwright, despite "his mercurial nature, his temper, his massive dreams and little cruelties. . . ."

5. What is the character's occupation?

He is a traveling salesman, working in New England. What he sells is never made clear—perhaps lingerie.

6. How does the character dress?

Quietly. Most likely a three-piece, medium-priced business suit.

7. What obstacles exist which prevent the character from achieving his or her goals?

His absolute belief in the wonders of salesmanship prevent him from seeing his own shortcomings and those of the system for which he is unsuited. He is sixty-three and should be ready for a peaceful retirement, but he must still work and has been put on a straight commission, as if he were a beginner. In the second act he is finally fired. His sons have not lived up to his expectations—Happy is "a philandering bum" and Biff has been wandering around the country, winding up in jail for stealing. Now Willy is simply exhausted.

8. How does the character deal with the obstacles that confront him or her?

We see Willy near the end of his life. Much of what we learn about how Willy reached his unhappy state comes from flashbacks. He is a dreamer who has deluded himself and his sons as well. We should not be surprised that Willy has reached this state in life. At the end he commits suicide, hoping his insurance money will put Biff on top again—clearly a last futile dream similar to all the dreams we've seen earlier.

3. THE ACTOR: Exercise for the study of CHARACTERIZATION

Play _____ Author _____

Name of Character _____

Analysis

1. What is the major motivation (motive) of the character in the play?

_____

_____

_____

_____

_____

2. What significant comments does the character make about himself or herself that reveal aspects of the characterization?

_____

_____

_____

_____

_____

3 What significant comments are made about the character by other characters in the play?

_____

_____

_____

_____

_____

4. What does the playwright say about the character in the notes?

_____

_____

_____

_____

_____

5. What is the character's occupation?

_____

6. How does the character dress?

_____

_____

7. What obstacles exist which prevent the character from achieving his or her goals?

_____

_____

_____

_____

_____

8. How does the character deal with the obstacles that confront him or her?

_____

_____

_____

_____

_____

3. THE ACTOR: Exercise for the study of CHARACTERIZATION

Play _____ Author _____

Name of Character _____

Analysis

1. What is the major motivation (motive) of the character in the play?

_____

_____

_____

_____

_____

2. What significant comments does the character make about himself or herself that reveal aspects of the characterization?

_____

_____

_____

_____

_____

_____

3. What significant comments are made about the character by other characters in the play?

_____

_____

_____

_____

_____

4. What does the playwright say about the character in the notes?

_____

_____

_____

_____

5. What is the character's occupation?

_____

6. How does the character dress?

_____

_____

7. What obstacles exist which prevent the character from achieving his or her goals?

_____

_____

_____

_____

_____

8. How does the character deal with the obstacles that confront him or her?

_____

_____

_____

_____

_____

3. THE ACTOR: Exercise for the study of CHARACTERIZATION

Play _____ Author _____

Name of Character _____

Analysis

1. What is the major motivation (motive) of the character in the play?

_____

_____

_____

_____

2. What significant comments does the character make about himself or herself that reveal aspects of the characterization?

_____

_____

_____

_____

_____

3. What significant comments are made about the character by other characters in the play?

_____

_____

_____

_____

_____

4. What does the playwright say about the character in the notes?

_____

_____

_____

_____

_____

5. What is the character's occupation?

_____

6. How does the character dress?

_____

_____

7. What obstacles exist which prevent the character from achieving his or her goals?

_____

_____

_____

_____

_____

8. How does the character deal with the obstacles that confront him or her?

_____

_____

_____

_____

_____

4. THE ACTOR: Sample exercise for the study of DIALOGUE AND LANGUAGE

Play _____Death of a Salesman_____ **Author** _____Arthur Miller_____

Name of Character _____Willy Loman_____

Analysis

1. Are there differences in language from one character to another which tend to clarify characterization?

The characters essentially talk in the rhythm of middle-class New York speech. Willy has become part of this environment and used this regional dialect, unlike his brother Ben who broke away and now uses a different rhythm and idiom.

2. Is your character's dialogue similar to that of the other characters? What does it reveal about your particular character?

Although there are distinct similarities between the major characters in their idiomatic dialogue, Willy often expresses himself in the "pitch" of the salesman, even when speaking to his sons, and frequently reveals his own basic naiveté when he comments "Isn't that remarkable."

3. Does your character speak with any dialect or use particular regionalisms in his or her speech? Explain.

The major characters all speak in the rhythm of a big Eastern city—obviously New York—although not as heavily as New York speech is sometimes caricatured. Inasmuch as the playwright was brought up in New York, he has an accurate "feel" for that quality of language. Willy's manner of speaking also suggests the city-bound aspects of his life. He even still seems to yearn for the independence of his family, who were pioneers, and of his brother Ben, who was an adventurer (in a symbolic sense).

4. Are there any long speeches or passages which need to be planned or "scored" for performance?

There are no long passages in the scene I am performing. However, earlier when Willy is talking to Howard, he expresses feelings at length about his family and about the incident when he met Dave Singleman which motivated him to become a salesman. That sequence would need careful scoring.

5. Are there any factors in the character's age, social status, education, or health that will require a change from your "normal" speaking voice? Explain.

Willy has the following characteristics that may create some problems for me at this stage of my work. 1. He is over sixty years of age and exhausted. 2. He comes from New York, specifically Brooklyn. 3. He is a man of very little education. 4. He is given to sudden fits of anger which soon pass. 5. Basically he is not very intelligent or perceptive.

6. Are there any vocal exercises or preparations you must undergo in order to create this character?

I will need to work on my voice to "get the feeling" of age and also study New York dialects in order at least to suggest something of Willy's environmental background.

4. THE ACTOR: Exercise for the study of DIALOGUE AND LANGUAGE

Play _____ Author _____

Name of Character _____

Analysis

1. Are there differences in language from one character to another which tend to clarify characterization?

_____

_____

_____

_____

2. Is your character's dialogue similar to that of the other characters? What does it reveal about your particular character?

_____

_____

_____

_____

_____

3. Does your character speak with any dialect or use particular regionalisms in his or her speech? Explain.

_____

_____

_____

_____

_____

4. Are there any long speeches or passages which need to be planned or "scored" for performance?

_____

_____

_____

_____

_____

_____

5. Are there any factors in the character's age, social status, education, or health that will require a change from your "normal" speaking voice? Explain.

_____

_____

_____

_____

_____

_____

_____

6. Are there any vocal exercises or preparations you must undergo in order to create this character?

_____

_____

_____

_____

_____

_____

4. THE ACTOR: Exercise for the study of DIALOGUE AND LANGUAGE

Play _____ Author _____

Name of Character _____

Analysis

1. Are there differences in language from one character to another which tend to clarify characterization?

_____

_____

_____

_____

_____

2. Is your character's dialogue similar to that of the other characters? What does it reveal about your particular character?

_____

_____

_____

_____

_____

_____

3. Does your character speak with any dialect or use particular regionalisms in his or her speech? Explain.

_____

_____

_____

_____

_____

_____

4. Are there any long speeches or passages which need to be planned or ''scored'' for performance?

_____

_____

_____

_____

_____

_____

5. Are there any factors in the character's age, social status, education, or health that will require a change from your ''normal'' speaking voice? Explain.

_____

_____

_____

_____

_____

_____

_____

6. Are there any vocal exercises or preparations you must undergo in order to create this character?

_____

_____

_____

_____

_____

_____

_____

4. THE ACTOR: Exercise for the study of DIALOGUE AND LANGUAGE

Play _____ Author _____

Name of Character _____

Analysis

1. Are there differences in language from one character to another which tend to clarify characterization?

_____

_____

_____

_____

2. Is your character's dialogue similar to that of the other characters? What does it reveal about your particular character?

_____

_____

_____

_____

_____

3. Does your character speak with any dialect or use particular regionalisms in his or her speech? Explain.

_____

_____

_____

_____

4. Are there any long speeches or passages which need to be planned or "scored" for performance?

_____

_____

_____

_____

_____

_____

5. Are there any factors in the character's age, social status, education, or health that will require a change from your "normal" speaking voice? Explain.

_____

_____

_____

_____

_____

_____

_____

6. Are there any vocal exercises or preparations you must undergo in order to create this character?

_____

_____

_____

_____

_____

_____

_____

B General Explanation: DIRECTING

The director cannot begin work with the cast until after thoroughly analyzing the play and developing an interpretation and concept of production. The two fundamental considerations, then, which are related to the director's interpretative concept are determining (1) an approach and (2) a style for production. All other aspects of analysis must naturally support and directly correspond with these.

This section presents a basic format that will help the director arrive at an approach and style treatment as well as formats for the other essentials of preparation. For determining the director's overall interpretation, the following listed categories are vital. It should be clear, however, that it is not always simple to isolate each category to the point where one is not related to the other. Obviously, interrelationships exist among all aspects of the final work of art. Nor is the order of listing necessarily mandatory for the treatment of different plays. However, for the purpose of analysis, the following categories, where appropriate, in the order shown, will be helpful in preparing a thorough study of the play.

1. Production Approach and Style
2. Picturization and Movement
3. Characterization
4. Language and Dialogue

From a thorough investigation of these factors, the director will be prepared for the final step, recording the interpretation in the director's prompt script. For purposes of illustrating this step, a scene from *Death of a Salesman* has been selected and included in Part Two. Two different methods, among the multitude used by differing directors, have been indicated by proper blocking and/or interpretative notations on the scene.

To provide continuity the same play has been used to illustrate how each of the exercises in Part One might be approached; each exercise is directly preceded by the example. In that each step in the development of the director's interpretation is provided for in these exercises, it is recommended that *one* play be used for a consistent analysis in each of the four exercise sections. Three sets of each exercise are provided, permitting the analysis of three different plays in all of their aspects. Because different directors use different terms, the terms used in these exercises are purposely general in nature. However, other prevalent corresponding terms are listed in parentheses.

1. Exercise for the study of PRODUCTION APPROACH AND STYLE

The purpose of this exercise is for the director to analyze the play in terms of its genre, structure, and meaning in order to arrive at a specific concept for the production. Obviously, in order to do this, one must be familiar with the conventional classification of plays by genre (type), such as tragedy or comedy, and be able to recognize the basic type of play one is dealing with even though it may have elements of other types within it. An analysis of the structure of the play will illuminate essential information, such as where minor climaxes occur, where the major climax is in terms of the overall conflict within the play, where the resolution (dénouement) is, and how the play can be divided into the directorial units (beats, motivational units, French scenes). Often the discovery of the central conflict will lead to a clarification of the meaning (theme, central idea) of the play. Each of these points should help the director arrive at a valid statement about his or her selected production approach and style.

2. Exercise for the study of PICTURIZATION AND MOVEMENT

The purpose of this exercise is to analyze the play in terms of its basic action, picturization (meaningful visualization), movement (including business), and groundplan requirements. Essential to these considerations is the recognition by the director that it is through motivated movement that one is able to make stage pictures which are not only aesthetically pleasing but which have appropriate centers of attention and focus on the meaningful physical or psychological action. The director would do well to remember that movement is important not only to modify stage pictures but is an essential factor in communicating action, meaning, and character. Recognizing that a ground plan must be creatively developed for each fresh production of a play, the director must also keep in mind that his or her basic concept, visualization of essential picturizations, and preliminary ideas concerning action and movement will dictate many of his or her requirements for the ground plan.

3. Exercise for the study of CHARACTERIZATION

The purpose of this exercise is to analyze one major character in depth from a selected play. Obviously in the preparation of a play for production, the director must have a thorough knowledge of all of the characters in the play being directed. Perhaps the subtlest and most intricate facet of stage direction is the establishment of CHARACTER in the play and communicating to and extracting from the actor the concept developed by the director, especially as related to the entire play and other characters in it. Here the interplay of the individual actors and the relationship of one character to another in the play call for careful balance and the director's full talents as interpreter and psychologist. Although the director's initial concept of characters is determined in the way shown in this exercise, actors have their "homework" to do as well. They most certainly should have their own ideas to contribute. It therefore becomes the director's function not to avoid doing the character "homework" but to prepare an analysis that will deal with essentials and help maintain the integrity of the scene and his or her concept of the play without stifling the actors. The questions in this exercise should serve as a framework to accomplish this.

4.   Exercise for the study of LANGUAGE AND DIALOGUE

The purpose of this exercise is to analyze the play through its language to determine how effectively the playwright has used dialogue. The director should be fully aware that not only can the dialogue indicate an appropriate approach and style for production, but the more highly selective, memorable, and expressive the dialogue is, the more it will enhance these aspects. One should not necessarily consider all dialogue problems as weaknesses, for most gifted playwrights have created challenges by using rhythm, color, the poetry of everyday speech, dialect, or other special embellishments which demand strong directorial perception and treatment. Especially if changes or deletions must be made in the script, the director should have valid reasons for doing so. Although rhythm and tempo are found in other aspects of a play as well, they are frequently established by better playwrights in the dialogue. The language selected also frequently helps to establish the proper mood and atmosphere inherent in a play. Through attempting to answer the questions in this exercise, a director should at least become more conscious of some of the special problems in dealing with dialogue.

A. THE DIRECTOR: Sample exercise for the study of PRODUCTION APPROACH AND STYLE

Play *Death of a Salesman*   **Author** *Arthur Miller*

Analysis

1. What generic approach (tragedy, comedy, melodrama, etc.) has the playwright chosen to express the play's meaning?

Arthur Miller intended the play as a modern tragedy. His essay, "Tragedy and the Common Man," written after

Salesman opened, supports this intent. Linda's line, "A small man can be just as exhausted as a great man," is a

direct statement in the play supporting Miller's argument for Willy's tragic nature.

2. Describe the major climax and the resolution of the play.

(These occur in the scene included in this workbook.) The major climax appears in Act II in the final

confrontation between Willy and Biff, as a result of which Willy discovers that Biff really loves him. The

resolution (dénouement) follows immediately when Willy decides to sacrifice himself by committing suicide.

3. What is the basic theme or central idea set forth in the play?

It is important for an individual to live his life according to his abilities and talents and not be turned away from

his potential because of false ideals, even if these are part of the so-called American dream. Biff (in

the Requiem): "He [Willy] had the wrong dreams. All, all wrong. . . . He never knew who he was."

4. Select a major directorial unit in the play and describe how this unit relates to the basic theme.

(The scene from Salesman included in this workbook is from Act II, beginning with Willy's line: "Where the

hell is that seed?" and running through Linda's line: "He loves you, Willy." This particular scene may be con-

sidered to be a directing unit unto itself and can be further broken down into acting units.) This scene requires

the characters at last to confront the truth about their various abilities, talents, and potentialities and for Willy

especially to come to some realization of his false ideals.

5. Describe your particular directorial approach to the production and the production style you have selected in order to articulate this approach to an audience.

The universal theme in this play is revealed primarily through characterization and character interrelationships at

each given instant. Therefore, the directorial approach will emphasize these, and they will motivate all other

aspects of the production. The style of the play is eclectic, moving from 1940s realism into 1920s symbolic

dream sequences and almost expressionistic scenes with Uncle Ben. Although all of these styles are necessary, the

emphasis will be on realism and especially on believability throughout the production.

1. THE DIRECTOR: Exercise for the study of PRODUCTION APPROACH AND STYLE

Play _____ Author _____

Analysis

1. What generic approach (tragedy, comedy, melodrama, etc.) has the playwright chosen to express the play's meaning?

_____

_____

_____

_____

_____

_____

2. Describe the major climax and the resolution of the play.

_____

_____

_____

_____

_____

_____

3. What is the basic theme or central idea set forth in the play?

_____

_____

_____

_____

_____

_____

4. Select a major directorial unit in the play and describe how this unit directly relates to the basic theme.

_____

_____

_____

_____

_____

_____

_____

_____

_____

_____

5. Describe your particular directorial approach to the production and the production style you have selected in order to articulate this approach to an audience.

_____

_____

_____

_____

_____

_____

_____

_____

_____

_____

Name _____ Date _____

1. THE DIRECTOR: Exercise for the study of PRODUCTION APPROACH AND STYLE

Play _____ Author _____

Analysis

1. What generic approach (tragedy, comedy, melodrama, etc.) has the playwright chosen to express the play's meaning?

_____

_____

_____

_____

_____

_____

2. Describe the major climax and the resolution of the play.

_____

_____

_____

_____

_____

_____

3. What is the basic theme or central idea set forth in the play?

_____

_____

_____

_____

_____

_____

4. Select a major directorial unit in the play and describe how this unit directly relates to the basic theme.

_____

_____

_____

_____

_____

_____

_____

_____

_____

_____

5. Describe your particular directorial approach to the production and the production style you have selected in order to articulate this approach to an audience.

_____

_____

_____

_____

_____

_____

_____

_____

_____

_____

1. THE DIRECTOR: Exercise for the study of PRODUCTION APPROACH AND STYLE

Play _____ Author _____

Analysis

1. What generic approach (tragedy, comedy, melodrama, etc.) has the playwright chosen to express the play's meaning?

_____

_____

_____

_____

_____

2. Describe the major climax and the resolution of the play.

_____

_____

_____

_____

_____

_____

3. What is the basic theme or central idea set forth in the play?

_____

_____

_____

_____

_____

_____

4. Select a major directorial unit in the play and describe how this unit directly relates to the basic theme.

_____

_____

_____

_____

_____

_____

_____

_____

5. Describe your particular directorial approach to the production and the production style you have selected in order to articulate this approach to an audience.

_____

_____

_____

_____

_____

_____

_____

_____

_____

_____

_____

B.   THE DIRECTOR: Sample exercise for the study of PICTURIZATION AND MOVEMENT

Play   *Death of a Salesman*   Author   *Arthur Miller*

Analysis

1. How does the basic action of the play support the production approach and style you have selected?

The action of the play centers on Willy's character and his relationship with others. (Miller originally conceived the action as occurring within Willy's mind.) Obviously the flashbacks are seen through Willy's stream of consciousness. They merge with the scenes set in the present to illustrate Willy's quest for success and his failures. Thus the action must be shown primarily through character, especially Willy's character interrelationships, and stylistic changes, predominantly between the 1920s flashbacks and the 1940s present-day scenes.

2. Describe what element or elements you intend to emphasize in your use of "picturization" for this production.

Because of the "back and forth" episodic nature of the action, the specific relationships between characters must be established visually immediately at the beginning of each scene. Also, pictorial emphasis should usually either be put on Willy or arranged in relationship to his thinking, feeling, and actions. The final picturization of each unit must appropriately provide the actors with easy, smooth-flowing access into the next scene.

3. How does the style and/or period of the play affect the type of movement to be used in the play?

The play's eclectic style presents no special movement problems except for possibly the expressionistic scenes where some distinction from the basic realistic approach as seen through Willy might visually enhance the meaning. Retaining the play's setting in the late 1920s and 1940s should not alter the use of modern realistic movement.

4. What are you emphasizing as the basic motivation for the development of movement?

Movement should essentially be motivated by character in order to fit in with the basic approach. Movement should especially be dictated by Willy's character in all of its aspects and should help the audience to visualize Willy's interpersonal relationships at each given moment. The story must visually be told through the precise movements, but primarily told through Willy's character.

5. What are the major requirements necessary in the "ground plan" in order to achieve the picturization and movement you want?

The "ground plan" must provide possibilities for a continuous flow of action from scene to scene, even though the play has little continuity in time and space. Another key part of the plan is Willy's house with at least three major interior areas: kitchen; boy's bedroom; Willy and Linda's bedroom. The house should be established as being a New York "lower class" environment; multilevels, freeflowing entrances and exits, and isolation spaces will be used. Simultaneous scenes and movements should be possible. An unlocalized area which can accommodate dream sequences and/or exterior scenes is required. Only properties functional to the action are necessary.

2. THE DIRECTOR: Exercise for the study of PICTURIZATION AND MOVEMENT

Play _____ Author _____

Analysis

1. How does the basic action of the play support the production approach and style you have selected?

_____

_____

_____

_____

_____

_____

2. Describe what element or elements you intend to emphasize in your use of "picturization" for this production.

_____

_____

_____

_____

_____

_____

3. How does the style and/or period of the play affect the type of movement to be used in the play?

_____

_____

_____

_____

_____

_____

4. What are you emphasizing as the basic motivation for the development of movement?

_____

_____

_____

_____

_____

_____

_____

_____

_____

_____

5. What are the major requirements necessary in the "ground plan" in order to achieve the picturization and movement you want?

_____

_____

_____

_____

_____

_____

_____

_____

_____

_____

2. THE DIRECTOR: Exercise for the study of PICTURIZATION AND MOVEMENT

Play _____ Author _____

Analysis

1. How does the basic action of the play support the production approach and style you have selected?

_____

_____

_____

_____

_____

2. Describe what element or elements you intend to emphasize in your use of ''picturization'' for this production.

_____

_____

_____

_____

_____

3. How does the style and/or period of the play affect the type of movement to be used in the play?

_____

_____

_____

_____

_____

4. What are you emphasizing as the basic motivation for the development of movement?

_____

_____

_____

_____

_____

_____

_____

_____

_____

5. What are the major requirements necessary in the "ground plan" in order to achieve the picturization and movement you want?

_____

_____

_____

_____

_____

_____

_____

_____

_____

_____

2. THE DIRECTOR: Exercise for the study of PICTURIZATION AND MOVEMENT

Play _____ Author _____

Analysis

1. How does the basic action of the play support the production approach and style you have selected?

_____

_____

_____

_____

_____

_____

2. Describe what element or elements you intend to emphasize in your use of "picturization" for this production.

_____

_____

_____

_____

_____

_____

3. How does the style and/or period of the play affect the type of movement to be used in the play?

_____

_____

_____

_____

_____

_____

4. What are you emphasizing as the basic motivation for the development of movement?

_____

_____

_____

_____

_____

_____

_____

_____

_____

5. What are the major requirements necessary in the "ground plan" in order to achieve the picturization and movement you want?

_____

_____

_____

_____

_____

_____

_____

_____

_____

_____

C.   THE DIRECTOR: Sample exercise for the study of CHARACTERIZATION (Select *one* major character even though you would apply this to all characters.)

Play   *Death of a Salesman*   Author   *Arthur Miller*

Name of Character   *Willy Loman*

Analysis

1.   How may the character be treated in order to support the production approach and style you have selected?

Inasmuch as the directorial approach is concentrated on character, with Willy the central character in the production and realism the basic style, it is essential that the director and the actor portraying this role work together to develop a thoroughly believable Willy Loman—one who is not only a universal, fully dimensional "common man" but who represents theatrically the essence of this play.

2.   What is the character's basic dramatic function?

To serve as the major character in the play from whose actions all other actions occur.

3.   What is the character's major motivation?

To achieve "success" (materialistically) and be "loved" (well-liked). To Willy "success" is essential to being "loved."

4.   Essentially how does the character relate to the other principal characters?

He is constantly in conflict with his son, Biff, his chief antagonist, who eventually confronts Willy with the truth and gives him a new insight about love. Although Willy's wife, Linda, understands the true meaning of love and fiercely defends him against their sons, Willy is too physically and psychologically exhausted to relate in a meaningful way to her. His relationship with his other son, Happy, who personifies some of Willy's less attractive traits, is almost nonexistent. Uncle Ben represents Willy's ideal, materialistic success, while Charley and Bernard represent success in love and other humanitarian aspects of life which Willy doesn't understand.

5. Select personality and physical traits essential to the character.

63 years old; a salesman; exhausted; "mercurial"; desperate; insecure; a dreamer; suicidal; a "common man"; passionate; a "road man"; "a drummer"; confused; macho; New Yorker; an almost heroic determination at times; sensitive; "a happy man with a batch of cement"; insatiable desire to "succeed" and to be "well-liked"; a "father"; a materialist.

3. THE DIRECTOR: Exercise for the study of CHARACTERIZATION (Select *one* major character even though you would apply this to all characters.)

Play _____ Author _____

Name of Character _____

Analysis

1. How may the character be treated in order to support the production approach and style you have selected?

_____

_____

_____

_____

_____

_____

2. What is the character's basic dramatic function?

_____

_____

_____

_____

_____

3. What is the character's major motivation?

_____

_____

_____

_____

_____

_____

4. Essentially how does the character relate to the other principal characters?

_____

_____

_____

_____

_____

_____

_____

_____

_____

_____

5. Select personality and physical traits essential to the character.

_____

_____

_____

_____

_____

_____

_____

_____

_____

3. **THE DIRECTOR: Exercise for the study of CHARACTERIZATION** (Select *one* major character even though you would apply this to all characters.)

Play _____ Author _____

Name of Character _____

Analysis

1. How may the character be treated in order to support the production approach and style you have selected?

_____

_____

_____

_____

_____

_____

2. What is the character's basic dramatic function?

_____

_____

_____

_____

_____

3. What is the character's major motivation?

_____

_____

_____

_____

_____

_____

4. Essentially how does the character relate to the other principal characters?

_____

_____

_____

_____

_____

_____

_____

_____

_____

_____

5. Select personality and physical traits essential to the character.

_____

_____

_____

_____

_____

_____

_____

_____

_____

_____

3. THE DIRECTOR: Exercise for the study of CHARACTERIZATION (Select *one* major character even though you would apply this to all characters.)

Play _____ **Author** _____

Name of Character _____

Analysis

1. How may the character be treated in order to support the production approach and style you have selected?

_____

_____

_____

_____

_____

_____

2. What is the character's basic dramatic function?

_____

_____

_____

_____

3. What is the character's major motivation?

_____

_____

_____

_____

_____

4. Essentially how does the character relate to the other principal characters?

_____

_____

_____

_____

_____

_____

_____

_____

_____

_____

5. Select personality and physical traits essential to the character.

_____

_____

_____

_____

_____

_____

_____

_____

_____

D.   THE DIRECTOR: Sample exercise for the study of LANGUAGE AND DIALOGUE

Play   *Death of a Salesman*   Author   *Arthur Miller*

Analysis

1.   How does the language of the play support the production approach and style you have selected?

Arthur Miller, born in New York and reared in Brooklyn, has given his characters a selective poetic realism in their language which enhances the basic realistic approach chosen for this production. Each character's language immediately identifies the nature of that character. Even the more expressionistic lines of Uncle Ben grow out of the reality of the type of character Ben is and his environment.

2.   Describe any special dialogue problems which the language of the play presents.

Gratefully, I see that rather than having to overcome any dialogue problems or weaknesses in the script, the director's challenge in this play will be to take advantage of the diverse possibilities which Miller's dialogue offers. Moving from colloquial to symbolic reality with ease will be necessary, as well as establishing a basic New York dialect.

3.   Are any textual changes necessary for this production? If so, why? What are these changes?

Inasmuch as this production will adhere to the intent and the time and place created for the original production, no textual changes are anticipated.

4.   How may the rhythm and tempo of this production be affected by the dialogue?

The rhythm of each character's speech has been carefully scored by the playwright for purposes of identification and expression. For example, Ben's staccato dialogue, "His flute. He played his flute." differs considerably from Linda's colloquially fluid dialogue, "He's not to be allowed to fall into his grave like an old dog." The overall Eastern/New York rhythm is also important. The tempo variations are especially noteworthy in the dialogue during the various emotional climaxes and at the beginning and end of each unit and/or scene, as Miller has provided definite potentialities for changes.

5. Will the mood and atmosphere of this production be affected by the dialogue? How?

Mood and atmosphere are sensitively affected by the dialogue, especially in moving from scene to scene. Each

succeeding scene immediately sets its own mood according to how the opening word or words are attacked. Yet

each scene must fit within the overall structural mood of tragedy and precipitate especially the final

"Requiem," a mood piece unto itself.

4. THE DIRECTOR: Exercise for the study of LANGUAGE AND DIALOGUE

Play _____ Author _____

Analysis

1. How does the language of the play support the production approach and style you have selected?

_____

_____

_____

_____

_____

_____

2. Describe any special dialogue problems which the language of the play presents.

_____

_____

_____

_____

_____

3. Are any textual changes necessary for this production? If so, why? What are these changes?

_____

_____

_____

_____

_____

_____

_____

_____

4. How may the rhythm and tempo of this production be affected by the dialogue?

_____

_____

_____

_____

_____

_____

_____

_____

_____

_____

5. Will the mood and atmosphere of this production be affected by the dialogue? How?

_____

_____

_____

_____

_____

_____

_____

_____

_____

_____

4. THE DIRECTOR: Exercise for the study of LANGUAGE AND DIALOGUE

Play _____ Author _____

Analysis

1. How does the language of the play support the production approach and style you have selected?

_____

_____

_____

_____

_____

_____

2. Describe any special dialogue problems which the language of the play presents.

_____

_____

_____

_____

_____

3. Are any textual changes necessary for this production? If so, why? What are these changes?

_____

_____

_____

_____

_____

_____

_____

4. How may the rhythm and tempo of this production be affected by the dialogue?

_____

_____

_____

_____

_____

_____

_____

_____

_____

5. Will the mood and atmosphere of this production be affected by the dialogue? How?

_____

_____

_____

_____

_____

_____

_____

_____

_____

4. THE DIRECTOR: Exercise for the study of LANGUAGE AND DIALOGUE

Play _____ Author _____

Analysis

1. How does the language of the play support the production approach and style you have selected?

_____

_____

_____

_____

_____

_____

2. Describe any special dialogue problems which the language of the play presents.

_____

_____

_____

_____

_____

3. Are any textual changes necessary for this production? If so, why? What are these changes?

_____

_____

_____

_____

_____

_____

_____

4. How may the rhythm and tempo of this production be affected by the dialogue?

_____

_____

_____

_____

_____

_____

_____

_____

_____

_____

5. Will the mood and atmosphere of this production be affected by the dialogue? How?

_____

_____

_____

_____

_____

_____

_____

_____

_____

_____

PART
TWO

EXECUTION
The Scenes

The scenes may be extracted without damage to the book.

A Explanation: ACTOR'S/DIRECTOR'S SCRIPT NOTATIONS

After the actor or director has thoroughly studied and analyzed the play, he or she is prepared to record notations in the script and, of course, begin rehearsals. For these purposes, this section of the book contains a large number of carefully selected scenes representing a diversity of types, styles, and problems. Although the actor or director should be thoroughly familiar with the entire play, a brief introduction to each scene has been included as an aid to selection and understanding. These same scenes may be used for the exercises in Part One and may easily be removed from the book for notations and rehearsals.

The scene from Act II of *Death of a Salesman* has again been chosen as an example. Script notations for both a typical director and a typical actor utilizing two different methods or approaches have been indicated. One approach may be arbitrarily called external, objective, or technical in contrast to the other approach, which may be referred to as internal, subjective, or perhaps emotional. In order to distinguish these, the scene appears with the annotations of one approach on the left and the other on the right of the printed text.

The left-hand margin for both the actor and director illustrates the more external approach, the selection of meaningful theatrical devices in order to make the scene work. Such a technique might indicate exact places for the actor to move, precise ways to use the body, specific associations with images such as animals or objects, specific physical relationships to stage properties or other actors, and specific types or patterns of stage movement and vocal qualities. These choices are made, of course, both by the director for all of the characters and by the individual actor.

The right-hand margin contains examples of the more internal approach, notations more concerned with the motivations of the characters and the reasons they are thinking and reacting as they are to the situation or to the other characters. Not many specific indications as to stage business or movement are suggested; rather the notes imply that the actor and/or director will work toward having the movement and picturization grow organically out of the inner meaning of the play and from the characters. Some of the insights therefore suggest statements that an actor might make about his or her character and in some cases a type of shorthand that the actor might use in quoting the character. Sometimes this is in slang; sometimes it is a key phrase that succinctly states what is in the character's mind.

It needs to be emphasized that these two approaches represent two extremes. Many actors and directors work in a method that combines both approaches so that, for example, stage movement and business notations would be a very proper out-growth of notations on the play's inner meaning. There are numerous ways to work and the relatively inexperienced actor/director would do well to explore as many as possible. The best method of working develops over a period of time as one finds the most effective means for expressing the creative impulses of each individual and for performing each type and style of production.

In the following examples it may appear that perhaps too much detail has been noted. This should be thought of, however, as primarily a guide or structure for future development as one discovers the method that is most useful for his or her own rehearsals.

It will be noticed that adequate margins for notations have been allowed on both the left and right sides of all of the printed scenes. In the *Death of a Salesman* scene examples, whenever a line is drawn through a stage direction or playwright's comment, it is an indication that the actor/director has chosen to reinterpret that particular part; naturally, those directions without a line through them have been retained for the current production.

The director's example includes an original "ground plan" for the setting opposite each page of script for blocking purposes. Rather than cluttering the ground plan and making it difficult to read by including every movement for each character, only selected positions and movements have been recorded in order to show one method or approach. A capital-letter initial has been used for each character.

Conventional symbols have been used in the scripts to indicate crosses and other stage terminology. Movements are recorded in the script at exactly the place each movement is to occur.

Actor's Script Notations

External   *Internal*

Willy crawls R on hands and knees. Keep animal image of tired bear through scene.

Willy [~~suddenly conscious of~~ **Biff**, ~~turns and looks up at him, then begins picking up the packages of seeds in confusion~~]: Where the hell is that seed? [*Indignantly.*] You can't see nothing out here! They boxed in the whole goddam neighborhood!

(Willy in confusion tries to avoid Biff's scrutiny and any confrontation. He cannot bear to look at Biff—"Leave me alone.")

Willy stays there, looking for seeds; business of planting and don't look at Biff.
Pick at ground.
Focus down.

Biff: There are people all around here. Don't you realize that?

Willy: I'm busy. Don't bother me.

(Willy still doesn't have anything in the ground.)

Biff [*taking the hoe from* **Willy**]: I'm saying good-bye to you, Pop. [**Willy** *looks at him, silent, unable to move.*] I'm not coming back any more.

Look sharply at Biff, disgruntled.

Willy: You're not going to see Oliver tomorrow?

Biff: I've got no appointment, Dad.

Willy: He put his arm around you, and you've got no appointment?

Biff: Pop, get this now, will you? Everytime I've left it's been a fight that sent me out of here. Today I realized something about myself and I tried to explain it to you and I—I think I'm just not smart enough to make any sense out of it for you. To hell with whose fault it is or anything like that. [*He takes* **Willy's** *arm.*] Let's just wrap it up, heh? Come on in, we'll tell Mom. [*He gently tries to pull* **Willy** *to left.*]

(Challenges Biff through his disappointment.)

Willy remains still—don't relax; don't give control to Biff.

Willy [*frozen, immobile, with guilt in his voice*]: No, I don't want to see her.

Biff: Come on! [*He pulls again, and* **Willy** *tries to pull away.*]

Willy [*highly nervous*]: No, no, I don't want to see her.

Biff [*tries to look into* **Willy's** *face, as if to find the answer there*]: Why don't you want to see her?

Willy [*more harshly now*]: Don't bother me, will you?

Biff: What do you mean, you don't want to see her? You don't want them calling you yellow, do you? This isn't your fault; it's me, I'm a bum. Now come inside! [**Willy** *strains to get away.*] Did you hear what I said to you?

(Willy can't face Linda and leave his hold on the past. He can't bear the thought of saying good-bye to Biff.)

Willy X angrily to kitchen below Biff.

[Willy *pulls away and quickly goes by himself into the house.* **Biff** *follows.*]

Linda [*to* **Willy**]: Did you plant, dear?

Biff [*at the door, to* **Linda**]: All right, we had it out. I'm going and I'm not writing any more.

Linda [~~going to **Willy** in the kitchen~~]: I think that's the best way, dear. 'Cause there's no use drawing it out, you'll just never get along.

[**Willy** *doesn't respond.*]

Biff: People ask where I am and what I'm doing, you don't know, and you don't care. That way it'll be off your mind and you can start brightening up again. All right? That clears it, doesn't it? [**Willy** *is silent, and* **Biff** *goes to him.*] You gonna wish me luck, scout! [*He extends his hand.*] What do you say?

(Willy must get away—now.)

Willy X D to R of Linda. Reject Biff. He seems not to want to listen.

External   *Internal*

Linda: Shake his hand, Willy.

Willy [*turning to her, seething with hurt*]: There's no necessity to mention the pen at all, y'know.

Biff [*gently*]: I've got no appointment, Dad.

Accuse Biff. Strong here. Show him how it was. **Willy** [*erupting* *fiercely*]: He put his arm around . . .?

(Willy isn't listening. "Isn't there something we can salvage? Why is this happening to me?")
(Still committed to the reality of his fantasy.)

Biff: Dad, you're never going to see what I am, so what's the use of arguing? If I strike oil I'll send you a check. Meantime forget I'm alive.

Willy [*to Linda*]: Spite, see?

Biff: Shake hands, Dad.

Willy: Not my hand.

Biff: I was hoping not to go this way.

Willy: Well, this is the way you're going. Goodbye.

[**Biff** *looks at him a moment, then turns sharply and goes to the stairs.*]

("You're doing this to me deliberately, because you caught me in the hotel room. You've been doing it ever since.")
(This is Willy's solution to a parting.)

Show anger and tension. X to Biff. **Willy** [*stops him with*]: May you rot in hell if you leave this house!

Biff [*turning*]: Exactly what is it that you want from me?

(Willy can't contain himself; all his pride, hurt and love erupt simultaneously.)

Willy: I want you to know, on the train, in the mountains, in the valleys, wherever you go, that you cut down your life for spite!

Biff: No, no.

Willy: Spite, spite, is the word of your undoing! And when you're down and out, remember what did it. When you're rotting somewhere beside the railroad tracks, remember, and don't you dare blame it on me!

Biff: I'm not blaming it on you!

Willy slumps in chair. Avoid looking at Biff! **Willy:** I won't take the rap for this, you hear?

[**Happy** *comes down the stairs and stands on the bottom step, watching.*]

(Willy removes himself from the confrontation. He reverses the blame, placing it on Biff.)

Biff: That's just what I'm telling you!

Willy [*sinking into a chair at the table, with full accusation*]: You're trying to put a knife in me—don't think I don't know what you're doing!

(Willy tries to raise Biff's feeling of guilt.)

Biff: All right, phony! Then let's lay it on the line.

[*He whips the rubber tube out of his pocket and* *puts* *it on the table.*]

Freezes—speech is halting, choppy. Eyes glassy. Voice low. Mumbles.

Happy: You crazy—

Linda: Biff! [*She moves to grab the hose, but* **Biff** *holds it down with his hand.*]

Biff: Leave it there! Don't move it!

Willy [*not looking at it*]: What is that?

Biff: You know goddam well what that is.

Willy [*caged, wanting to escape*]: I never saw that.

Biff: You saw it. The mice didn't bring it into the cellar! What is this supposed to do, make a hero out of you? This supposed to make me sorry for you?

Willy: Never heard of it.

Biff: There'll be no pity for you, you hear it? No pity!

(Willy's world collapses. Guilt, shame, pain, shock, fear, numbing, numbing. It takes time for Willy to recover. It carries through. He sits there with those emotions going through him as Biff and Happy confront each other.)

Show anger despite pain in body. Voice rises. **Willy** [*to* **Linda**]: You hear the spite!

Biff: No, you're going to hear the truth—what you are and what I am!

External   *Internal*

Linda: Stop it!

Willy: Spite!

Happy [*coming down toward* **Biff**]: You cut it now!

Biff [*to* Happy]: The man don't know who we are! The man is gonna know! [*To* **Willy.**] We never told the truth for ten minutes in this house!

Happy: We always told the truth!

Biff [*turning on him*]: You big blow, are you the assistant buyer? You're one of the two assistants to the assistant, aren't you?

Happy: Well, I'm practically—

Biff: You're practically full of it! We all are! And I'm through with it. [*To* **Willy.**] Now hear this, Willy, this is me.

Retorts sharply. **Willy:** Ⓘ know you!

Biff: You know why I had no address for three months? I stole a suit in Kansas City and I was in jail. [*To* **Linda,** *who is sobbing.*] Stop crying. I'm through with it.

[**Linda** *turns away from them, her hands covering her face.*]

(Willy finally hears something, but doesn't really understand.)

Still sharply. **Willy:** Ⓘ suppose that's my fault!

Biff: I stole myself out of every good job since high school!

Willy: And whose fault is that?

Biff: And I never got anywhere because you blew me so full of hot air I could never stand taking orders from anybody! That's whose fault it is!

Willy: I hear that!

Linda: Don't, Biff!

Biff: It's goddam time you heard that! I had to be boss big shot in two weeks, and I'm through with it!

Vocally sharp here. **Willy:** Ⓣⓗⓔⓝ hang yourself! For spite, hang your-
Physically rigid. self!

(Willy is still trying to place the blame. He still thinks it is because Biff wants revenge.)

Biff: No! Nobody's hanging himself, Willy! I ran down eleven flights with a pen in my hand today. And suddenly I stopped, you hear me? And in the middle of that office building, do you hear this? I stopped in the middle of that building and I saw— the sky. I saw the things that I love in this world. The work and the food and time to sit and smoke. And I looked at the pen and said to myself, what the hell am I grabbing this for? Why am I trying to become what I don't want to be? What am I doing in an office, making a contemptuous, begging fool of myself, when all I want is out there, waiting for me the minute I say I know who I am! Why can't I say that, Willy? [*He tries to make* **Willy** *face him, but* **Willy** *pulls away and moves to the left.*]

(Willy is hearing the wrong things. He still doesn't under-stand.)

Move to Biff. Raises his voice **Willy** [~~with hatred, threateningly~~]: Ⓣⓗⓔ door of your
again. Try to outshout Biff. life is wide open!

Biff: Pop! I'm a dime a dozen, and so are you!

Willy [*turning on him now in an uncontrolled out-burst*]: I am not a dime a dozen! I am Willy Loman, and you are Biff Loman!

(Willy can't accept this. "Why did I raise a son in the first place. We are something and my son is something special.")

(Willy confronts Biff. His pride will not permit this assessment of his life.)

[**Biff** *starts for* **Willy**, *but is blocked by* **Happy**. *In his fury,* **Biff** *seems on the verge of attacking his father.*]

Biff: I am not a leader of men, Willy, and neither are you. You were never anything but a hard-working drummer who landed in the ash-can like all the rest of them! I'm one dollar an hour, Willy! I tried seven states and couldn't raise it. A buck an hour! Do you gather my meaning? I'm not bringing home any prizes any more, and you're going to stop waiting for me to bring them home!

Willy X away.
Almost shouting, hoarse.

Willy [~~directly to Biff~~: (You) vengeful, spiteful mutt!

[**Biff** *breaks from* **Happy**. **Willy**, *in fright, starts up the stair.* **Biff** *grabs him.*]

Biff [*at the peak of his fury*]: Pop, I'm nothing! I'm nothing, Pop. Can't you understand that? There's no spite in it any more. I'm just what I am, that's all.

[**Biff**'s *fury has spent itself, and he breaks down, sobbing, holding on to* **Willy**, *who dumbly fumbles for* **Biff**'s *face.*]

(Willy is repeating himself. What else can he say—he rejects Biff's view.)

("What's happening here?")

Willy sit. Much of the tension is going. Keep bear image in mind. The warm father returns.

Willy [*astonished*]: What're you doing? What're you doing? [*To* **Linda**.] Why is he crying?

Biff [*crying, broken*]: Will you let me go, for Christ's sake? Will you take that phony dream and burn it before something happens? [*Struggling to contain himself, he pulls away and moves to the stairs.*] I'll go in the morning. Put him—put him to bed. [*Exhausted,* **Biff** *moves up the stairs to his room.*]

("How can he cry if he hates me? Could he love me? How can this be?")

Take long pause. Physically and vocally, Willy becomes younger and prouder and gains stature. Watch posture here.

Willy [(*after*) *a long pause, astonished, elevated*]: Isn't that—isn't that remarkable? Biff—he likes me!

Linda: He loves you, Willy!

(For the first time since the hotel episode Willy senses Biff's true love. A major beat change for Willy. Very critical for Willy here. Determines future decisions.)

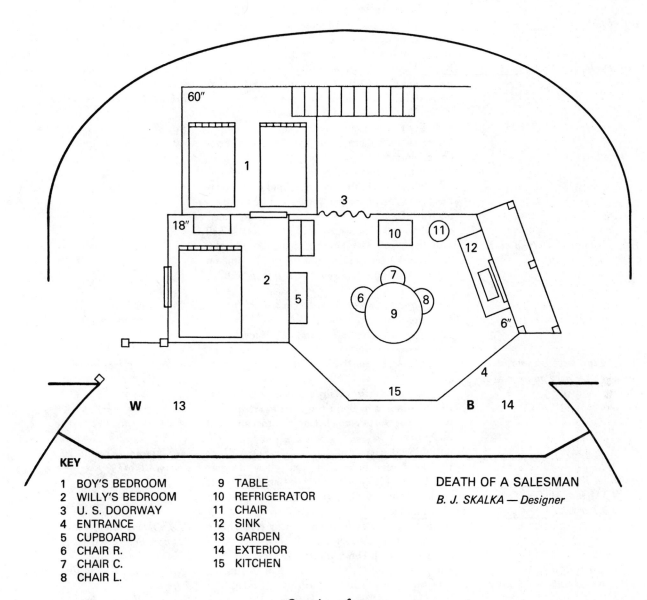

KEY

1 BOY'S BEDROOM
2 WILLY'S BEDROOM
3 U. S. DOORWAY
4 ENTRANCE
5 CUPBOARD
6 CHAIR R.
7 CHAIR C.
8 CHAIR L.
9 TABLE
10 REFRIGERATOR
11 CHAIR
12 SINK
13 GARDEN
14 EXTERIOR
15 KITCHEN

DEATH OF A SALESMAN
B. J. SKALKA — Designer

Opening of scene

Director's Script Notations

External   *Internal*

Willy [~~suddenly conscious of Biff, turns and looks~~   (*Willy in confusion tries to avoid*
~~up at him, then begins picking up the packages of~~   *Biff's scrutiny and any confronta-*
Willy crawls R on hands and ~~seeds in confusion~~]: (Where) the hell is that seed?   *tion.*)
knees. Biff is SL of Willy. [*Indignantly.*] You can't see nothing out here! They
boxed in the whole goddam neighborhood!

Biff X to Willy. **Biff:** There are people all around (here.) Don't you   (*Biff is embarrassed and doesn't*
realize that?   *allow Willy to avoid him.*)
Willy: I'm busy. Don't bother me.   (*Biff, needing to establish physical*
Biff stands over Willy. **Biff** [*taking the hoe from* **Willy**]: (I'm) saying good-   *contact, removes the object sepa-*
bye to you, Pop. [**Willy** *looks at him, silent, unable*   *rating them. He is firm but not*
to move.] I'm not coming back any more.   *unkind, standing over Willy.*)
Willy: You're not going to see Oliver tomorrow?
Biff: I've got no appointment, Dad.   (*Biff desperately wants to come to*
Willy: He put his arm around you, and you've got   *grips with the past and somehow*
no appointment?   *communicate with his Dad.*)
Biff: Pop, get this now, will you? Everytime I've
left it's been a fight that sent me out of here. Today
I realized something about myself and I tried to ex-
plain it to you and I—I think I'm just not smart
enough to make any sense out of it for you. To hell
Biff tries to raise Willy to his feet. with whose fault it is (or) anything like that. [*He takes*
Willy's *arm.*] Let's just wrap it up, heh? Come on
in, we'll tell Mom. [*He gently tries to pull* **Willy** *to*
left.]
Willy [*frozen, immobile, with guilt in his voice*]:   (*Willy, frozen in the past, can't*
Willy rises but does not move (No,) I don't want to see her.   *move to the inevitable goodbye.*)
with Biff. **Biff:** Come on! [*He pulls again, and* **Willy** *tries to*
pull away.]
Willy X two steps UR and in a **Willy** [*highly nervous*]: No, (no,) I don't want to see   (*Willy has to move away. He can't*
three-quarter back position to au- her.   *face Biff.*)
dience. **Biff** [*tries to look into* **Willy**'s *face, as if to find the*
answer there]: Why don't you want to see her?
Willy [*more harshly now*]: Don't bother me, will
you?
Biff X to Willy. **Biff:** What do you mean, you don't want to (see) her?   (*Biff assumes the guilt, tries to*
You don't want them calling you yellow, do you?   *convince Willy.*)
Biff takes Willy's arm. This isn't your fault; it's me, I'm a bum. (Now) come
Willy XSL into kitchen, faces inside! [**Willy** *strains to get away.*] Did you hear
Linda below table. what I said to (you?)
[**Willy** *pulls away and quickly goes by himself into*   (*Willy finally has to get away—*
the house. **Biff** *follows.*]   *but now finds himself facing*
Linda [*to* **Willy**]: Did you plant, dear?   *Linda.*)
Biff is to L of Willy. (Biff) [*at the door, to* **Linda**]: All right, we had it   (*Biff "It's done—I'm finished*
Biff X below table to UC door. out. (I'm) going and I'm not writing any more.   *with it."*)
Linda ~~going to **Willy** in the kitchen~~: I think that's   (*Linda, still loving both men, re-*
the best way, dear. 'Cause there's no use drawing   *mains the stable force in the*
it out, you'll just never get along.   *house.*)
[**Willy** *doesn't respond.*]
Biff: People ask where I am and what I'm doing,   (*Biff still wants a clean, final*
you don't know, and you don't care. That way it'll   *break with Dad.*)
be off your mind and you can start brightening up
Biff X D to R of Linda. again. (All) right? That clears it, doesn't it? [**Willy** *is*
silent, and **Biff** *goes to him.*] You gonna wish me
luck, scout! [*He extends his hand.*] What do you   (*Biff will try one last time.*)
Willy turns SL with back to Biff. (say?)

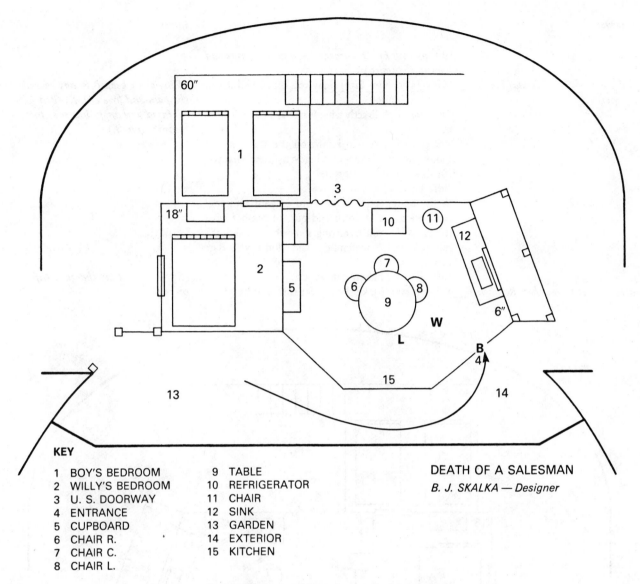

KEY

1	BOY'S BEDROOM	9	TABLE	
2	WILLY'S BEDROOM	10	REFRIGERATOR	
3	U. S. DOORWAY	11	CHAIR	
4	ENTRANCE	12	SINK	
5	CUPBOARD	13	GARDEN	
6	CHAIR R.	14	EXTERIOR	
7	CHAIR C.	15	KITCHEN	
8	CHAIR L.			

DEATH OF A SALESMAN

B. J. SKALKA — Designer

On Biff's line: "All right, we had it out."

External

Internal

Linda: Shake his hand, Willy.
Willy [*turning to her, seething with hurt*]: There's no necessity to mention the pen at all, y'know.
Biff [*gently*]: I've got no appointment, Dad.
Willy [*erupting fiercely*]: He put his arm around . . .?
Biff: Dad, you're never going to see what I am, so what's the use of arguing? If I strike oil I'll send you a check. Meantime forget I'm alive.
Willy [*to* Linda]: Spite, see?
Biff: Shake hands, Dad.
Willy: Not my hand.
Biff: I was hoping not to go this way.
Willy: Well, this is the way you're going. Goodbye.

(Willy isn't listening. "Why is he doing this to me?")

External   *Internal*

[**Biff** *looks at him a moment, then turns sharply and goes to the stairs.*]

Willy X in front of Linda; Linda counters L.

Willy [*stops him with*]: (May) you rot in hell if you leave this house!

Biff [*turning*]: Exactly what is it that you want from me?

Willy: I want you to know, on the train, in the mountains, in the valleys, wherever you go, that you cut down your life for spite!

Biff: No, no.

Willy: Spite, spite, is the word of your undoing! And when you're down and out, remember what did it. When you're rotting somewhere beside the railroad tracks, remember, and don't you dare blame it on me!

Biff: I'm not blaming it on you!

Willy sits at table, chair R, turned

Willy: (I) won't take the rap for this, you hear?

(Willy can't keep it in any more; the pain and love erupt.) (Biff is confused and angry but tries to control himself.)

(Biff—''Don't lay the guilt trip on me!'')

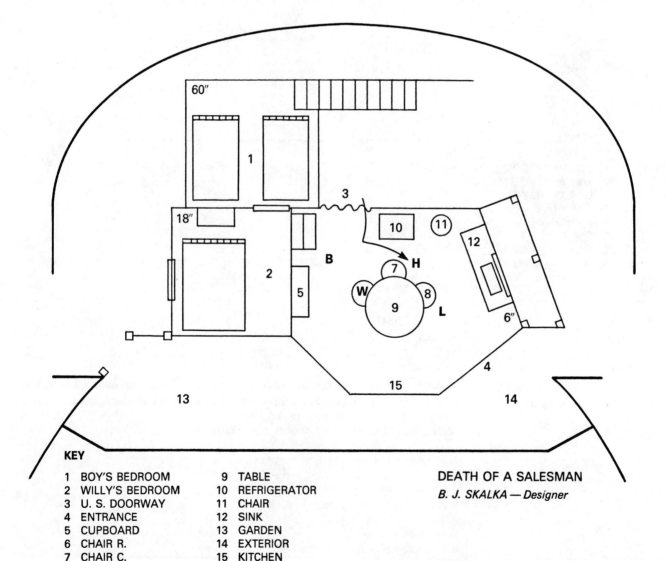

KEY

1	BOY'S BEDROOM	9	TABLE
2	WILLY'S BEDROOM	10	REFRIGERATOR
3	U. S. DOORWAY	11	CHAIR
4	ENTRANCE	12	SINK
5	CUPBOARD	13	GARDEN
6	CHAIR R.	14	EXTERIOR
7	CHAIR C.	15	KITCHEN
8	CHAIR L.		

DEATH OF A SALESMAN

B. J. SKALKA — Designer

Happy's entrance

External		*Internal*
away from Biff. Happy enters UC door and stands L of chair C.	[Happy] ~~comes down the stairs and stands on the bottom step, watching.~~]	*(Willy turns inward, removes himself from the confrontation.)*
	Biff: That's just what I'm telling you!	
	Willy [~~sinking into a chair at the table, with full accusation~~]: You're trying to put a knife in me— don't think I don't know what you're doing!	*(Willy tries to raise Biff's feeling of guilt.)*
Biff X above table.	**Biff:** All right, phony! Then let's lay it on the line. [*He whips the rubber tube out of his pocket and puts it on the table.*]	*(Biff has had it! It's all got to come out now.)*
Happy X to Biff.	**Happy:** You crazy—	
Linda L of table.	**Linda:** Biff! [*She moves to grab the hose, but* **Biff** *holds it down with his hand.*]	
	Biff: Leave it there! Don't move it!	
	Willy [*not looking at it*]: What is that?	*(Willy doesn't dare look or listen; he can't confront anything.)*
	Biff: You know goddam well what that is.	
	Willy [*caged, wanting to escape*]: I never saw that.	
	Biff: You saw it. The mice didn't bring it into the cellar! What is this supposed to do, make a hero out of you? This supposed to make me sorry for you?	
	Willy: Never heard of it.	
	Biff: There'll be no pity for you, you hear it? No pity!	
	Willy [*to* **Linda**]: You hear the spite!	
	Biff: No, you're going to hear the truth—what you are and what I am!	
	Linda: Stop it!	*(Linda is in pain but totally helpless. All her attempts for love and peace have collapsed.)*
	Willy: Spite!	
Happy grabs Biff's L arm.	**Happy** [*coming down toward* **Biff**]. You cut it now!	
	Biff [*to* **Happy**]: The man don't know who we are! The man is gonna know! [*To* **Willy.**] We never told the truth for ten minutes in this house!	*(Biff strips Happy too—another "bull artist.")*
	Happy: We always told the truth!	
	Biff [*turning on him*]: You big blow, are you the assistant buyer? You're one of the two assistants to the assistant, aren't you?	
	Happy: Well, I'm practically—	
	Biff: You're practically full of it! We all are! And I'm through with it. [*To* **Willy.**] Now hear this, Willy, this is me.	
	Willy: I know you!	*(Automatically.)*
	Biff: You know why I had no address for three months? I stole a suit in Kansas City and I was in	*(The truth, take it or leave it.)*
Linda sits chair L.	jail. [*To* **Linda,** *who is sobbing.*] Stop crying. I'm through with it.	
	[**Linda** *turns away from them, her hands covering her face.*]	
	Willy: I suppose that's my fault!	*(Willy hears it, but still doesn't understand.)*
	Biff: I stole myself out of every good job since high school!	
	Willy: And whose fault is that?	
Biff X R to steps and turns.	**Biff:** And I never got anywhere because you blew me so full of hot air I could never stand taking orders from anybody! That's whose fault it is!	*(There's no stopping Biff now.)*
Points to Willy.		
	Willy: I hear that!	*(Still mechanically.)*
	Linda: Don't, Biff!	
	Biff: It's goddam time you heard that! I had to be boss big shot in two weeks, and I'm through with it!	

External

Internal

Willy: Then hang yourself! For spite, hang yourself!

(Willy is hearing the wrong thing. He still doesn't understand.)

Biff takes stage on this speech and ends DR in kitchen.

Biff: No! Nobody's hanging himself, Willy! I ran down eleven flights with a pen in my hand today. And suddenly I stopped, you hear me? And in the middle of that office building, do you hear this? I stopped in the middle of that building and I saw—the sky. I saw the things that I love in this world. The work and the food and time to sit and smoke. And I looked at the pen and said to myself, what the hell am I grabbing this for? Why am I trying to become what I don't want to be? What am I doing in an office, making a contemptuous, begging fool of myself, when all I want is out there, waiting for me the minute I say I know who I am! Why can't I say that, Willy? [*He tries to make* Willy *face him, but* Willy *pulls away and moves to the left.*]

(After all these years Biff will say what has needed to be said—complete confrontation with the truth.)

Willy [*with hatred, threateningly*]: The door of your life is wide open!

Biff: Pop! I'm a dime a dozen, and so are you!

Willy rise and XR toward Biff.

Willy [*turning on him now in an uncontrolled outburst*]: I am not a dime a dozen! I am Willy Loman, and you are Biff Loman!

(Willy confronts Biff; his pride will not permit this assessment of his life.)

Happy XR in between them.

[Biff *starts for* Willy, *but is blocked by* Happy. *In his fury,* Biff *seems on the verge of attacking his father.*]

Biff: I am not a leader of men, Willy, and neither are you. You were never anything but a hard-working drummer who landed in the ash-can like all the rest of them! I'm one dollar an hour, Willy! I tried seven states and couldn't raise it. A buck an hour! Do you gather my meaning? I'm not bringing home any prizes any more, and you're going to stop waiting for me to bring them home!

(Biff begins self-purgation.)

Willy XL to below table.

Willy [*directly to* Biff]: You vengeful, spiteful mutt!

(Willy rejects this and Biff.)

Biff XL to Willy.
Happy counters R.

Biff *breaks from* Happy. Willy, *in fright, starts up the stair.* Biff *grabs him.*]

Biff [*at the peak of his fury*]: Pop, I'm nothing! I'm nothing, Pop. Can't you understand that? There's no spite in it any more. I'm just what I am, that's all.

(Biff is completely drained.)

Biff sinks to knees R of chair R.

[Biff's *fury has spent itself, and he breaks down, sobbing, holding on to* Willy, *who dumbly fumbles for* Biff's *face.*]

Willy sits in chair R holding Biff's head.

Willy [*astonished*]: What're you doing? What're you doing? [*To* Linda.] Why is he crying?

(Willy loves his son but still does not quite understand.)

Biff [*crying, broken*]: Will you let me go, for Christ's sake? Will you take that phony dream and burn it before something happens? [*Struggling to contain himself, he pulls away and moves to the stairs.*] I'll go in the morning. Put him—put him to bed. [*Exhausted,* Biff *moves up the stairs to his room.*]

(The boy is pleading with his Dad.)

Biff X to UC door.

Biff exit UC door.

Willy [*after a long pause, astonished, elevated*]: Isn't that—isn't that remarkable? Biff—he likes me!

(Willy's emotional state undergoes a major change.)

Willy rises.
Linda rises.

Linda: He loves you, Willy!

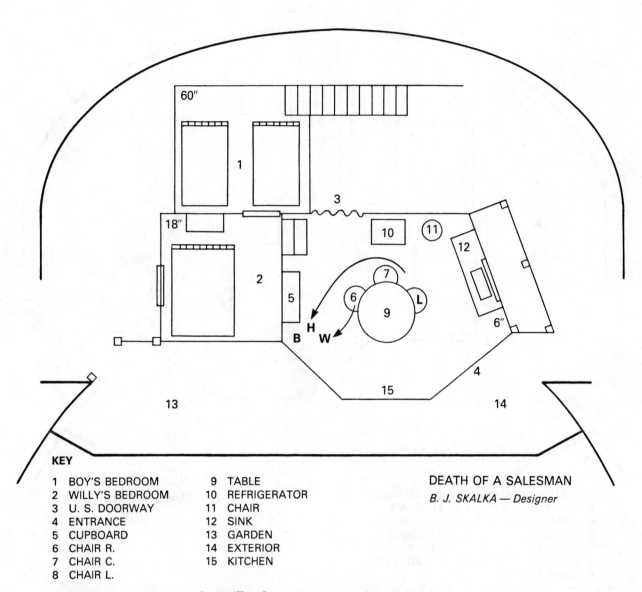

KEY

1	BOY'S BEDROOM	9	TABLE
2	WILLY'S BEDROOM	10	REFRIGERATOR
3	U. S. DOORWAY	11	CHAIR
4	ENTRANCE	12	SINK
5	CUPBOARD	13	GARDEN
6	CHAIR R.	14	EXTERIOR
7	CHAIR C.	15	KITCHEN
8	CHAIR L.		

DEATH OF A SALESMAN

B. J. SKALKA — Designer

On Willy's line: "I am not a dime a dozen!"

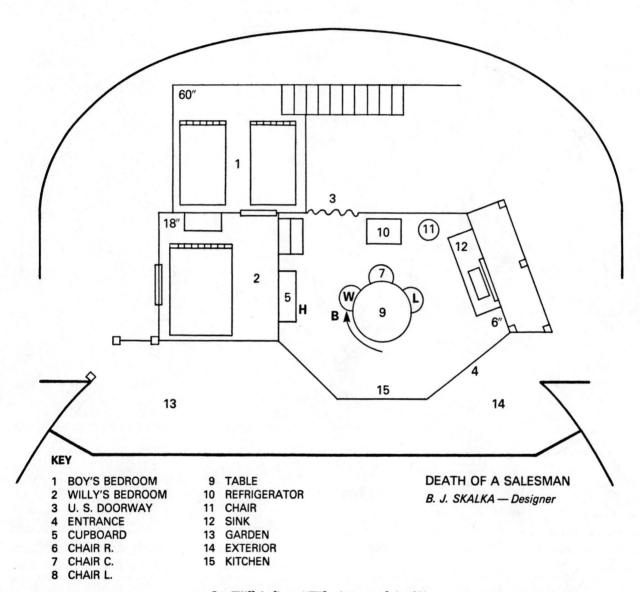

KEY

1	BOY'S BEDROOM	9	TABLE
2	WILLY'S BEDROOM	10	REFRIGERATOR
3	U. S. DOORWAY	11	CHAIR
4	ENTRANCE	12	SINK
5	CUPBOARD	13	GARDEN
6	CHAIR R.	14	EXTERIOR
7	CHAIR C.	15	KITCHEN
8	CHAIR L.		

DEATH OF A SALESMAN
B. J. SKALKA — Designer

On Willy's line: "What're you doing?"

B MODERN REALISTIC SCENES

Scene from
All My Sons by Arthur Miller

From Act II

For 2 women

Characters: **Ann,** a woman in her early twenties.
   Sue, a neighbor in her early thirties.

Setting: Early evening in the backyard of the Keller home in a small midwestern
   city. 1947.

Situation: Ann's father and Joe Keller had been business partners during the Second World War. Their concern sold defective aircraft equipment to the Army Air Force, primarily because Keller was afraid to take the financial loss that holding the equipment back would have entailed. Although both Keller and Ann's father were indicted, Keller was found innocent but Ann's father was sent to prison. Ann had been engaged to Keller's son Larry, an aviator who was killed during the war. Now she intends to marry Larry's brother Chris, who has just returned from the military. Ann is waiting in the Keller backyard for her brother George, who is opposed to the marriage, primarily because he suspects Joe Keller's guilt. As she is waiting, one of Keller's neighbors, Sue, enters.

Script Notations

Sue: Is my husband . . . ?

Ann [*turns, startled*]: Oh!

Sue: I'm terribly sorry.

Ann: It's all right, I . . . I'm a little silly about the dark.

Sue [*looks about*]: It is getting dark.

Ann: Are you looking for your husband?

Sue: As usual. [*Laughs tiredly.*] He spends so much time here, they'll be charging him rent.

Ann: Nobody was dressed so he drove over to the depot to pick up my brother.

Sue: Oh, your brother's in?

Ann: Yeah, they ought to be here any minute now. Will you have a cold drink?

Sue: I will, thanks. [**Ann** *goes to table and pours.*] My husband. Too hot to drive me to beach.—Men are like little boys; for the neighbors they'll always cut the grass.

Ann: People like to do things for the Kellers. Been that way since I can remember.

Sue: It's amazing. I guess your brother's coming to give you away, heh?

Ann [*giving her drink*]: I don't know. I suppose.

Sue: You must be all nerved up.

Ann: It's always a problem getting yourself married, isn't it?

Sue: That depends on your shape, of course. I don't see why you should have had a problem.

Ann: I've had chances—

Sue: I'll bet. It's romantic . . . it's very unusual to me, marrying the brother of your sweetheart.

Ann: I don't know. I think it's mostly that whenever I need somebody to tell me the truth I've always thought of Chris. When he tells you something you know it's so. He relaxes me.

Sue: And he's got money. That's important, you know.

Ann: It wouldn't matter to me.

Sue: You'd be surprised. It makes all the difference. I married an interne. On my salary. And that was bad, because as soon as a woman supports a man he owes her something. You can never owe somebody without resenting them. [**Ann** *laughs.*] That's true, you know.

Ann: Underneath, I think the doctor is very devoted.

Sue: Oh, certainly. But it's bad when a man always sees the bars in front of him. Jim thinks he's in jail all the time.

Ann: Oh . . .

Sue: That's why I've been intending to ask you a small favor, Ann . . . it's something very important to me.

Ann: Certainly, if I can do it.

Sue: You can. When you take up housekeeping, try to find a place away from here.

Ann: Are you fooling?

Sue: I'm very serious. My husband is unhappy with Chris around.

Ann: How is that?

Sue: Jim's a successful doctor. But he's got an idea he'd like to do medical research. Discover things. You see?

Ann: Well, isn't that good?

Sue: Research pays twenty-five dollars a week minus laundering the hair shirt. You've got to give up your life to go into it.

Ann: How does Chris?

Sue [*with growing feeling*]: Chris makes people want to be better than it's possible to be. He does that to people.

Ann: Is that bad?

Sue: My husband has a family, dear. Every time he has a session with Chris he feels as though he's compromising by not giving up everything for research. As though Chris or anybody else isn't compromising. It happens with Jim every couple of years. He meets a man and makes a statue out of him.

Ann: Maybe he's right. I don't mean that Chris is a statue, but . . .

Sue: Now darling, you know he's not right.

Ann: I don't agree with you. Chris . . .

Sue: Let's face it, dear. Chris is working with his father, isn't he? He's taking money out of that business every week in the year.

Ann: What of it?

Sue: You ask me what of it?

Ann: I certainly do. [*She seems about to burst out.*] You oughtn't cast aspersions like that, I'm surprised at you.

Sue: You're surprised at me!

Ann: He'd never take five cents out of that plant if there was anything wrong with it.

Sue: You know that.

Ann: I know it. I resent everything you've said.

Sue [*moving toward her*]: You know what I resent, dear?

Ann: Please, I don't want to argue.

Sue: I resent living next door to the Holy Family. It makes me look like a bum, you understand?

Ann: I can't do anything about that.

Sue: Who is he to ruin a man's life? Everybody knows Joe pulled a fast one to get out of jail.

Ann: That's not true!

Sue: Then why don't you go out and talk to people? Go on, talk to them. There's not a person on the block who doesn't know the truth.

Ann: That's a lie. People come here all the time for cards and . . .

Sue: So what? They give him credit for being smart. I do, too, I've got nothing against Joe. But if Chris wants people to put on the hair shirt let him take off his broadcloth. He's driving my husband crazy with that phony idealism of his, and I'm at the end of my rope on it!

Scene from
And Miss Reardon Drinks a Little by Paul Zindel

From Act III

For 3 women

Characters: **Catherine Reardon,** "drinks a little," assistant principal of a high school.

Anna Reardon, neurotic high school teacher on the brink of "cracking up."

Ceil Adams, their sister who is married and somewhat runs the Board of Education.

Setting: The living room and dining area of the comfortable apartment of Catherine and Anna Reardon. Time is the present.

Situation: These three women represent excellent psychological studies in terms of their past. Deserted by their father at an early age, prevailed upon by a domineering mother only recently deceased, they have lost all previous closeness, especially Ceil in her relationship to the others. Because Anna has committed a scandalous act at school and is at the breaking point, Ceil has arrived to attempt to get Catherine to agree to have Anna committed. This, the final scene in the play, reveals the dramatic impact of Ceil's action as well as the characters' individual reactions to each other and to themselves.

Script Notations

Ceil: (*Rises.*) Anna, go to your room and lie down.

Anna: Go to your own room!

Ceil: (*To* **Catherine**.) Tell her to leave us alone.

Catherine: Now, sis, it is a bit tardy for disciplinary procedures.

Ceil: Catherine . . .

Anna: Oh, Ceil . . . can't you remember all the fun when we were just getting started as teachers? How we'd all come running home at three o'clock and Mama'd have the water boiling and some kind of pie made with Flako pie crust mix? and Mama'd be dying to know what happened in school all day and we'd be dying to tell her—and we'd sit around this same table and almost pass out laughing? We'd tell Mama what was going on in the schools and she wouldn't believe it. She'd say the whole world was going crazy. Remember when I told her about little Gracie Ratinski, that nutty kid with bugs in her hair at Jefferson who used to come into the cafeteria and sing her lunch order out at the top of her lungs? (**Catherine** *begins to laugh.*) GIVE ME A PEANUT BUTTER SANDWICH, TRA LA. GIVE ME A PEANUT BUTTER SANDWICH, TRA LA. Don't you remember that? Don't you?

Catherine: (*Laughing harder, joining* **Anna** *at the table.*) I remember. I remember, all right. And remember how much Mama laughed when I told her about Rose Anadale the principal at P.S. 26 who kept the parakeet in her office . . .

Anna: She used to talk about it on the P.A. system every morning after the Star Spangled Banner . . .

Catherine: (*Howling with* **Anna**.) She'd announce to the whole school, remember—GOOD MORNING, CHILDREN . . . GOOD MORNING, CHILDREN . . . LITTLE POLLY AND I HOPE YOU HAVE A WONDERFUL DAY.

Anna: (*To* **Ceil**.) Don't you miss telling Mama those stories? Don't you miss it?

Ceil: (*To* **Catherine**.) Tell her to leave us alone.

Catherine: Look, Ceil, it's late—you probably have to get up early tomorrow and appoint a committee to study the salient factors of something or other . . .

Ceil: If that's the way you want it. (*She goes for her briefcase.*) I've made arrangements . . .

Catherine: (*Starting to clear the table.*) You don't say. They are floral, aren't they?

Ceil: She's going to a hospital.

Catherine: No kidding. Far away? Tudor or Swiss? Mountains and view of lake?

Ceil: (*Taking legal papers from the briefcase.*) It's only a two hour drive from here.

Catherine: No, don't tell me the best feature. It's state supported.

Ceil: (*Ordering.*) All you have to do is get her packed.

Anna: She's the one who needs a rest, Catherine.

Ceil: (*Moving in with the papers.*) You're going to have to look at these, Catherine.

Catherine: (*Slamming a tray down on the buffet making a deafening noise. Then calmly:*) Don't tell me what I have to do. (*A long silence. Finally:*)

Anna: Ceil, didn't you ever love us? Mama? Any of us?

Ceil: Our lives are not around this table anymore. (*She moves away from the table.*)

Anna: Oh—I must have forgotten. This is all dead now, isn't it? Silent. The voices gone. Even the whispering forgotten: "Straighten up . . . careful your slip isn't showing . . . skirt down . . . knees close together. Be careful if someone sits next to you . . . or across the way . . . beware of your eyes . . . he mustn't think you're looking at him. Even when you're . . . bleeding . . . he'll know . . . he'll try to find a way to force you apart . . . he'll want to hurt you . . . crush you . . . cut into you . . ." (**Anna** *rises—goes towards the bedroom hallway.*) And the sounds—you must have forgotten the sounds in the dark of our rooms . . . the quieting of the wounds by which we could be tracked. (**Anna** *reaches out to touch* **Ceil.**)

Ceil: Get your hands off me. (*Getting away from* **Anna** *and taking a seat at the table.*)

Anna: Tell me, Ceil, when you're in bed—what does Edward manage to do? Does he actually get on top of you—mount you—and ride you like some blubbering old nag? (*In the middle of* **Anna's** *verbal assault,* **Ceil** *reaches for the Fanny Farmer box which falls from her hands. At* **Anna's** *last word she picks up the spilled meat and shoves it into* **Anna's** *face.* **Anna** *falls to her knees, senses the meat, and screams. She exits.* **Catherine** *goes after* **Anna.**)

Ceil: She can wash herself.

Catherine: Get out of my way.

Ceil: How the hell much longer did you think you could go on keeping her here?

Catherine: As long as I want, that's how long.

Ceil: Why? So you won't be alone? After all the filth and wisecracks are scraped off is that what's underneath? How pathetic you are!

Catherine: (*Ringing buffet bell.*) School's over. Everybody's dismissed. (**Ceil** *yanks the bell out of* **Catherine's** *hand.*)

Ceil: Don't you think I need anything?

Catherine: I thought you always took everything you needed?

Ceil: Anything I did you made me do from the years of gnawing at me—you and her and Mama. The whole pack of you. For what? What was it you hated so much?

Catherine: (*Exploding.*) I'll tell you what and I'll tell you when! You see, there was this big hole in the ground with you on one side of it and me on the other—and we were watching them stick a coffin in the ground. But as it was going down I had to shut my eyes because I'll tell you all I could see: I saw you with a lawyer making sure the few bucks of a croaking old lady was transferred to your name. And I was admiring a casket you picked out that wouldn't waste a second getting her corpse back to ashes. And I remember when that imperfect gasping woman was dying how you made certain you didn't have to touch a penny in your bank account. (*She sits at the desk.*)

Ceil: That's not what you hated me for *all* your life! Anything you didn't like you could have done differently. Anything! You're not going to blame me for that or anything about your sick little life. You didn't have to follow me—let me do everything. I didn't bend anybody's arm. You could have lived your own lives you know. You didn't have to feed on me all the time!

Catherine: Get out of here.

Ceil: What is it deep down in your gut you so detest about me? That I haven't gone mad or become an obscene nasty witness? That's what you are, Catherine. (*There is a long pause. Then:*)

Catherine: You know, Ceil—the way you said that—I mean, you're louder and crueller—but there's a part of you that's just like Mama. I think that's the part of you I've always despised. (**Ceil** *gets her coat from the closet and gathers up the papers, the gun and the album.*)

Ceil: I'll call you in the morning.

Catherine: (*Pouring a drink.*) Not in the morning, if you don't mind. You see, Miss Reardon drinks a little and she'll be sleeping off a colossal load.

Ceil: (*Throws album, gloves and papers to the floor.*) Here! Here's everything. I'm not going to let you pin the rap on me or Mama or anybody anymore. Now it's up to you. For once in your life you pick up the pieces however the hell you want. But no matter what you do, let me tell you this—you're not going to drag me down. Not at this stage of the game, my sweet sisters. Not at this stage of the game. (**Ceil** *exits leaving* **Catherine** *sitting at the desk.* **Anna** *enters.*)

Anna: You're worse than all of them. You never do anything to stop the destruction.

Catherine: I got rid of her. What else do you want from me?

Anna: You're godless and you're killing all of us. Everything.

Catherine: Look, I'm warning you. I'm going shopping tomorrow and I'm buying roast beef, frankfurters, liverwurst, knockwurst, brockwurst, and two pounds of Virginia ham. It may be primitive but it sure as hell's going to be delicious. (**Anna** *stops, slowly moves back to her place at the table.*)

Anna: Catherine—sometimes . . . sometimes I see

my reflection in a window . . . or look down at my hand resting in my lap and I see her. Mama. She's inside of me. She frightens me, Catherine. She makes me afraid. I look out the window . . . the telephone poles in the street . . . she makes me see them as dead trees . . . dead crucifixes. I'm losing my mind. I can't stop myself. She's at my throat now, Catherine, she's strangling me. Help me. Oh, God, help me . . . (**Anna** *puts her head on the table. Slowly* **Catherine** *rises, turns off the floor lamp, goes to hall, turns off the foyer light. Only the table area is lighted.*)

Catherine: Everyone's going crazy, Anna, do you know that? The dentist—I went to the new dentist down the street—I went three weeks ago for my first appointment, and then last week, and then yesterday. He wears three wigs, Anna. On the first visit he was wearing a crew-cut wig. Last week he had a medium length wig. And yesterday he had this fuzzy llama-wool wig and he kept saying—"Dear me, oh, dear me—I've got to get a haircut . . ." And next week I know he'll have the crew-cut job on again. (**Catherine** *goes to* **Anna**. *It is the hardest journey she's ever traveled—to reach out and touch* **Anna**. **Anna** *raises her head.*)

Anna: Catherine—what world were we waiting for?

(**Catherine** *and* **Anna** *are alone at the table as:*)

THE CURTAIN FALLS ENDING THE PLAY

Scene from
  Candida by George Bernard Shaw

From Act II

For 1 man, 1 woman

Characters: **Miss Proserpine Garnett,** a brisk little woman, a typist, about 30.
  Eugene Marchbanks, a shy, slight, and sensitive poet of 18.

Setting: The sitting room of a parsonage in London. An afternoon in 1894.

Situation: Eugene Marchbanks, a sensitive and idealistic young man, has been
  brought to a London parsonage by Reverend James Morell, a self-assured
  English cleric. Although Reverend Morell's wife Candida is loyal and devoted
  to her husband, she is attracted by the honest, youthful ardor of Marchbanks,
  who begins to woo her.
     Morell's secretary-typist Proserpine is prim and unattractive, and some
  what jealous of Candida's good looks. Proserpine is also a practical, able young
  woman. Just prior to the beginning of this scene, Marchbanks, hardly the
  ablest of individuals in dealing with mechanical gadgets, has been trying to
  find out how the typewriter works. When Proserpine starts to transcribe Morell's letters from her shorthand, she notes that something is wrong with the
  typewriter.

Script Notations

Proserpine: Bother! Youve been meddling with my typewriter, Mr Marchbanks; and theres not the least use in your trying to look as if you hadnt.

Marchbanks [*timidly*]: I'm very sorry, Miss Garnett. I only tried to make it write. [*Plaintively*] But it wouldnt.

Proserpine: Well, youve altered the spacing.

Marchbanks [*earnestly*]: I assure you I didnt. I didnt indeed. I only turned a little wheel. It gave a sort of click.

Proserpine: Oh, now I understand. [*She restores the spacing, talking volubly all the time*]. I suppose you thought it was a sort of barrel-organ. Nothing to do but turn the handle, and it would write a beautiful love letter for you straight off, eh?

Marchbanks [*seriously*]: I suppose a machine could be made to write love letters. Theyre all the same, arnt they?

Proserpine [*somewhat indignantly: any such discussion, except by way of pleasantry, being outside her code of manners*]: How do I know? Why do you ask me?

Marchbanks: I beg your pardon. I thought clever people—people who can do business and write letters and that sort of thing—always had to have love affairs to keep them from going mad.

Proserpine [*rising, outraged*]: Mr Marchbanks! [*She looks severely at him, and marches majestically to the bookcase*].

Marchbanks [*approaching her humbly*]: I hope I havnt offended you. Perhaps I shouldnt have alluded to your love affairs.

Proserpine [*plucking a blue book from the shelf and turning sharply on him*]: I havnt any love affairs. How dare you say such a thing? The idea! [*She tucks the book under her arm, and is flouncing back to her machine when he addresses her with awakened interest and sympathy*].

Marchbanks: Really! Oh, then you are shy, like me.

Proserpine: Certainly I am not shy. What do you mean?

Marchbanks [*secretly*]: You must be: that is the reason there are so few love affairs in the world. We all go about longing for love: it is the first need of our natures, the first prayer of our hearts; but we dare not utter our longing: we are too shy. [*Very earnestly*] Oh, Miss Garnett, what would you not give to be without fear, without shame—

Proserpine [*scandalized*]: Well, upon my word!

Marchbanks [*with petulant impatience*]: Ah, dont say those stupid things to me: they dont deceive me: what use are they? Why are you afraid to be your real self with me? I am just like you.

Proserpine: Like me! Pray are you flattering me or flattering yourself? I dont feel quite sure which. [*She again tries to get back to her work*].

Marchbanks [*stopping her mysteriously*]: Hush! I

go about in search of love; and I find it in unmeasured stores in the bosoms of others. But when I try to ask for it, this horrible shyness strangles me; and I stand dumb, or worse than dumb, saying meaningless things: foolish lies. And I see the affection I am longing for given to dogs and cats and pet birds, because they come and ask for it. [*Almost whispering*] It must be asked for: it is like a ghost: it cannot speak unless it is first spoken to. [*At his usual pitch, but with deep melancholy*] All the love in the world is longing to speak; only it dare not, because it is shy! shy! shy! That is the world's tragedy. [*With a deep sigh he sits in the visitors' chair and buries his face in his hands*].

Proserpine [*amazed, but keeping her wits about her: her point of honor in encounters with strange young men*]: Wicked people get over that shyness occasionally, dont they?

Marchbanks [*scrambling up almost fiercely*]: Wicked people means people who have no love: therefore they have no shame. They have the power to ask love because they dont need it: they have the power to offer it because they have none to give. [*He collapses into his seat, and adds, mournfully*] But we, who have love, and long to mingle it with the love of others: we cannot utter a word. [*Timidly*] You find that, dont you?

Proserpine: Look here, if you dont stop talking like this, I'll leave the room, Mr Marchbanks: I really will. It's not proper.

She resumes her seat at the typewriter, opening the blue book and preparing to copy a passage from it.

Marchbanks [*hopelessly*]: Nothing thats worth saying is proper. [*He rises, and wanders about the room in his lost way*]. I cant understand you, Miss Garnett. What am I to talk about?

Proserpine [*snubbing him*]: Talk about indifferent things. Talk about the weather.

Marchbanks: Would you talk about indifferent things if a child were by, crying bitterly with hunger?

Proserpine: I suppose not.

Marchbanks: Well: *I* cant talk about indifferent things with my heart crying out bitterly in its hunger.

Proserpine: Then hold your tongue.

Marchbanks: Yes: that is what it always comes to. We hold our tongues. Does that stop the cry of your heart? for it does cry: doesnt it? It must, if you have a heart.

Proserpine [*suddenly rising with her hand pressed on her heart*]: Oh, it's no use trying to work while you talk like that. [*She leaves her little table and sits on the sofa. Her feelings are keenly stirred*]. It's no business of yours whether my heart cries or not; but I have a mind to tell you, for all that.

Marchbanks: You neednt. I know already that it must.

Proserpine: But mind! if you ever say I said so, I'll deny it.

Marchbanks [*compassionately*]: Yes, I know. And so you havnt the courage to tell him?

Proserpine [*bouncing up*]: Him! Who?

Marchbanks: Whoever he is. The man you love. It might be anybody. The curate, Mr Mill, perhaps.

Proserpine [*with disdain*]: Mr Mill!!! A fine man to break my heart about, indeed! I'd rather have you than Mr Mill.

Marchbanks [*recoiling*]: No, really: I'm very sorry; but you mustnt think of that. I—

Proserpine [*testily, going to the fire-place and standing at it with her back to him*]: Oh, dont be frightened: it's not you. It's not any one particular person.

Marchbanks: I know. You feel that you could love anybody that offered—

Proserpine [*turning, exasperated*]: Anybody that offered! No, I do not. What do you take me for?

Marchbanks [*discouraged*]: No use. You wont make me real answers: only those things that everybody says. [*He strays to the sofa and sits down disconsolately*].

Proserpine [*nettled at what she takes to be a disparagement of her manners by an aristocrat*]: Oh well, if you want original conversation, youd better go and talk to yourself.

Marchbanks: That is what all poets do: they talk to themselves out loud; and the world overhears them. But it's horribly lonely not to hear someone else talk sometimes.

Proserpine: Wait until Mr Morell comes. He'll talk to you. [**Marchbanks** *shudders*]. Oh, you neednt make wry faces over him: he can talk better than you. [*With temper*] He'd talk your little head off. [*She is going back angrily to her place, when he, suddenly enlightened, springs up and stops her*].

Marchbanks: Ah! I understand now.

Proserpine [*reddening*]: What do you understand?

Marchbanks: Your secret. Tell me: is it really and truly possible for a woman to love him?

Proserpine [*as if this were beyond all bounds*]: Well!!

Marchbanks [*passionately*]: No: answer me. I want to know: I must know. I cant understand it. I can see nothing in him but words, pious resolutions, what people call goodness. You cant love that.

Proserpine [*attempting to snub him by an air of cool propriety*]: I simply dont know what youre talking about. I dont understand you.

Marchbanks [*vehemently*]: You do. You lie.

Proserpine: Oh!

Marchbanks: You do understand; and you know. [*Determined to have an answer*] Is it possible for a woman to love him?

Proserpine [*looking him straight in the face*]: Yes.

Scene from
Come Back, Little Sheba by William Inge

From Act I, Scene 2

For 1 man, 1 woman

Characters: **Marie,** a college student boarding in the Delaney house.
Turk, Marie's boyfriend; a college jock.

Setting: The living room of the Delaneys' shabby home in a midwestern city. The late 1940s.

Situation: Doc Delaney, a chiropractor, has drowned his disappointments in drink, although he is currently a member of Alcoholics Anonymous and working with other alcoholics. He resents having been trapped in marriage as a young man to Lola, who has become slovenly and frumpy. In his young boarder, Marie, a young and precious girl, he sees the daughter he might have had if Lola had not been forced to abort their child soon after marriage.

As Doc leaves, Turk, Marie's boyfriend, recognizes Doc's hostility to him but at the moment is primarily concerned with furthering his developing affair with Marie. Turk knows he is attractive to women and is not shy about discussing his physical prowess and body.

Script Notations

Turk: He hates my guts. (*Goes to front door*)

Marie: Oh, he does not. (*Follows* **Turk**, *blocks his exit in door.*)

Turk: Yes, he does. If you ask me, he's jealous.

Marie: Jealous?

Turk: I've always thought he had a crush on you.

Marie: Now, Turk, don't be silly. Doc is nice to me. It's just in a few little things he does, like fixing my breakfast, but he's nice to everyone.

Turk: He ever make a pass?

Marie: No. He'd never get fresh.

Turk: He better not.

Marie: Turk, don't be ridiculous. Doc's such a nice, quiet man; if he gets any fun out of being nice to me, why not?

Turk: He's got a wife of his own, hasn't he? Why doesn't he make a few passes at her?

Marie: Things like that are none of our business.

Turk: O.K. How about a snuggle, lovely?

Marie: (*A little prim and businesslike*) No more for tonight, Turk.

Turk: Why's tonight different from any other night?

Marie: I think we should make it a rule, every once in a while, just to sit and talk. (*Starts to sit on couch, but goes to chair.*)

Turk: (*Restless, sits on couch*) O.K. What'll we talk about?

Marie: Well . . . there's lotsa things.

Turk: O.K. Start in.

Marie: A person doesn't start a conversation that way.

Turk: Start it any way you want to.

Marie: Two people should have something to talk about, like politics or psychology or religion.

Turk: How 'bout sex?

Marie: Turk!

Turk: (*Chases her around couch*) Have you read the Kinsey Report, Miss Buckholder?

Marie: I should say not.

Turk: How old were you when you had your first affair, Miss Buckholder? And did you ever have relations with your grandfather?

Marie: Turk, stop it.

Turk: You wanted to talk about something; I was only trying to please. Let's have a kiss.

Marie: Not tonight.

Turk: Who you savin' it up for?

Marie: Don't talk that way.

Turk: (*Gets up, yawns*) Well, thanks, Miss Buckholder, for a nice evening. It's been a most enjoyable talk.

Marie: (*Anxious*) Turk, where are you going?

Turk: I guess I'm a man of action, Baby.

Marie: Turk, don't go.

Turk: Why not? I'm not doin' any good here.

Marie: Don't go.

Turk: (*Returns and she touches him. They sit on couch*) Now why didn't you think of this before? C'mon, let's get to work.

Marie: Oh, Turk, this is all we ever do.

Turk: Are you complaining?

Marie: (*Weakly*) No.

Turk: Then what do you want to put on such a front for?

Marie: It's not a front.

Turk: What else is it? (*Mimicking*) Oh, no, Turk. Not tonight, Turk. I want to talk about philosophy, Turk. (*Himself again*) When all the time you know that if I went outa here without givin' you a good lovin' up you'd be sore as hell . . . Wouldn't you?

Marie: (*She has to admit to herself it's true; she chuckles*) Oh . . . Turk . . .

Turk: It's true, isn't it?

Marie: Maybe.

Turk: How about tonight, lovely; going to be lonesome?

Marie: Turk, you're in training.

Turk: What of it? I can throw that old javelin any old time, *any* old time. C'mon, Baby, we've got by with it before, haven't we?

Marie: I'm not so sure.

Turk: What do you mean?

Marie: Sometimes I think Mrs. Delaney knows.

Turk: Well, bring her along. I'll take care of her, too, if it'll keep her quiet.

Marie: (*A pretense of being shocked*) Turk!

Turk: What makes you think so?

Marie: Women just sense those things. She asks so many questions.

Turk: She ever *say* anything?

Marie: No.

Turk: Now *you're* imagining things.

Marie: Maybe.

Turk: Well, stop it.

Marie: O.K.

Turk: (*Follows* **Marie**) Honey, I know I talk awful rough around you at times; I never was a very gentlemanly bastard, but you really don't mind it . . . do you? (*She only smiles mischievously*) Anyway, you know I'm nuts about you.

Marie: (*Smug*) Are you? (*Now they engage in a little rough-house, he cuffing her like an affectionate bear, she responding with "Stop it," "Turk, that hurt," etc. And she slaps him playfully. Then they laugh together at their own pretense. . . . *)

Turk: Now, Miss Buckholder, what is your opinion of the psychodynamic pressure of living in the atomic age?

Marie: (*Playfully*) Turk, don't make fun of me.

Turk: Tonight?

Marie: (*Her eyes dance as she puts him off just a little longer*) Well.

Turk: Tonight will never come again. (*This is true. She smiles.*) O.K.?

Marie: Tonight will never come again. . . . (*They embrace and start to dance*) Let's go out somewhere first and have a few beers. We can't come back till they're asleep.

Turk: O.K. (*They dance slowly out the door.*)

Scene from
  Death of a Salesman by Arthur Miller

From Act I

For 2 men

Characters: **Biff Loman,** 34, the older son of Willy.
            Happy Loman, 32, the younger son.

Setting: The kitchen and bedroom of a small, middle-class frame house in Brooklyn
        in the late 1940s.

Situation: Willy Loman, a salesman, is old and exhausted and looks to his sons for
        some hope, especially to Biff. In this excerpt, one of the early scenes in this
        powerful drama, we are introduced to the characters of Biff and Happy.
             (Note: For a more complete analysis of this play, see the Actor and
        Director Sample Exercises.)

Script Notations

Happy: [*getting out of bed*] He's going to get his license taken away if he keeps that up. I'm getting nervous about him, y'know, Biff?

Biff: His eyes are going.

Happy: No, I've driven with him. He sees all right. He just doesn't keep his mind on it. I drove into the city with him last week. He stops at a green light and then it turns red and he goes. [*He laughs.*]

Biff: Maybe he's color-blind.

Happy: Pop? Why he's got the finest eye for color in the business. You know that.

Biff: [*sitting down on his bed*] I'm going to sleep.

Happy: You're not still sour on Dad, are you, Biff?

Biff: He's all right, I guess. . . .You smoking?

Happy: [*holding out a pack of cigarettes*] Want one?

Biff: [*taking a cigarette*] I can never sleep when I smell it. . .

Happy: [*with deep sentiment*] Funny, Biff, y'know? Us sleeping in here again? The old beds. [*He pats his bed affectionately.*] All the talk that went across those two beds, huh? Our whole lives.

Biff: Yeah. Lotta dreams and plans.

Happy: [*with a deep and masculine laugh*] About five hundred women would like to know what was said in this room.

[*They share a soft laugh.*]

Biff: Remember that big Betsy something—what the hell was her name—over on Bushwick Avenue?

Happy: [*combing his hair*] With the collie dog!

Biff: That's the one. I got you in there, remember?

Happy: Yeah, that was my first time—I think. Boy, there was a pig! [*They laugh, almost crudely.*] You taught me everything I know about women. Don't forget that.

Biff: I bet you forgot how bashful you used to be. Especially with girls.

Happy: Oh, I still am, Biff.

Biff: Oh, go on.

Happy: I just control it, that's all. I think I got less bashful and you got more so. What happened, Biff? Where's the old humor, the old confidence? [*He shakes Biff's knee. Biff gets up and moves restlessly about the room.*] What's the matter?

Biff: Why does Dad mock me all the time?

Happy: He's not mocking you, he—

Biff: Everything I say there's a twist of mockery on his face. I can't get near him.

Happy: He just wants you to make good, that's all. I wanted to talk to you about Dad for a long time, Biff. Something's—happening to him. He—talks to himself.

Biff: I noticed that this morning. But he always mumbled.

Happy: But not so noticeable. It got so embarrassing I sent him to Florida. And you know something? Most of the time he's talking to you.

Biff: What's he say about me?

Happy: I can't make it out.

Biff: What's he say about me?

Happy: I think the fact that you're not settled, that you're still kind of up in the air . . .

Biff: There's one or two other things depressing him, Happy.

Happy: What do you mean?

Biff: Never mind. Just don't lay it all to me.

Happy: But I think if you just got started—I mean—is there any future for you out there?

Biff: I tell ya, Hap, I don't know what the future is. I don't know—what I'm supposed to want.

Happy: What do you mean?

Biff: Well, I spent six or seven years after high school trying to work myself up. Shipping clerk, salesman, business of one kind or another. And it's a measly manner of existence. To get on that subway on the hot mornings in summer. To devote your whole life to keeping stock, or making phone calls, or selling or buying. To suffer fifty weeks of the year for the sake of a two-week vacation, when all you really desire is to be outdoors, with your shirt off. And always to have to get ahead of the next fella. And still—that's how you build a future.

Happy: Well, you really enjoy it on a farm? Are you content out there?

Biff: [*with rising agitation*] Hap, I've had twenty or thirty different kinds of jobs since I left home before the war, and it always turns out the same. I just realized it lately. In Nebraska when I herded cattle, and the Dakotas, and Arizona, and now in Texas. It's why I came home now, I guess, because I realized it. This farm I work on, it's spring there now, see? And they've got about fifteen new colts. There's nothing more inspiring or—beautiful than the sight of a mare and a new colt. And it's cool there now, see? Texas is cool now, and it's spring. And whenever spring comes to where I am, I suddenly get the feeling, my God, I'm not gettin' anywhere! What the hell am I doing, playing around with horses, twenty-eight dollars a week! I'm thirty-four years old, I oughta be makin' my future. That's when I come running home. And now, I get here, and I don't know what to do with myself. [*after a pause*] I've always made a point of not wasting my life, and everytime I come back here I know that all I've done is to waste my life.

Happy: You're a poet, you know that, Biff? You're a—you're an idealist!

Biff: No, I'm mixed up very bad. Maybe I oughta get married. Maybe I oughta get stuck into something. Maybe that's my trouble. I'm like a boy. I'm not married, I'm not in business, I just—I'm like a boy. Are you content, Hap? You're a success, aren't you? Are you content?

Happy: Hell, no!

Biff: Why? You're making money, aren't you?

Happy: [*moving about with energy, expressiveness*] All I can do now is wait for the merchandise manager to die. And suppose I get to be merchandise manager? He's a good friend of mine, and he just built a terrific estate on Long Island. And he lived there about two months and sold it, and now he's building another one. He can't enjoy it once it's finished. And I know that's just what I would do. I don't know what the hell I'm workin' for. Sometimes I sit in my apartment—all alone. And I think of the rent I'm paying. And it's crazy. But then, it's what I always wanted. My own apartment, a car, and plenty of women. And still, goddammit, I'm lonely.

Biff: [*with enthusiasm*] Listen, why don't you come out West with me?

Happy: You and I, heh?

Biff: Sure, maybe we could buy a ranch. Raise cattle, use our muscles. Men built like we are should be working out in the open.

Happy: [*avidly*] The Loman Brothers, heh?

Biff: [*with vast affection*] Sure, we'd be known all over the counties!

Happy: [*enthralled*] That's what I dream about, Biff. Sometimes I want to just rip my clothes off in the middle of the store and outbox that goddam merchandise manager. I mean I can outbox, outrun, and outlift anybody in that store, and I have to take orders from those common, petty sons-of-bitches till I can't stand it any more.

Biff: I'm tellin' you, kid, if you were with me I'd be happy out there.

Happy: [*enthused*] See, Biff, everybody around me is so false that I'm constantly lowering my ideals . . .

Biff: Baby, together we'd stand up for one another, we'd have someone to trust.

Happy: If I were around you—

Biff: Hap, the trouble is we weren't brought up to grub for money. I don't know how to do it.

Happy: Neither can I!

Biff: Then let's go!

Happy: The only thing is—what can you make out there?

Biff: But look at your friend. Builds an estate and then hasn't the peace of mind to live in it.

Happy: Yeah, but when he walks into the store the waves part in front of him. That's fifty-two thousand dollars a year coming through the revolving door, and I got more in my pinky finger than he's got in his head.

Biff: Yeah, but you just said—

Happy: I gotta show some of those pompous, self-important executives over there that Hap Loman can make the grade. I want to walk into the store the way he walks in. Then I'll go with you, Biff. We'll be together yet, I swear. But take those two we had tonight. Now weren't they gorgeous creatures?

Biff: Yeah, yeah, most gorgeous I've had in years.

Happy: I get that any time I want, Biff. Whenever I feel disgusted. The only trouble is, it gets like bowling or something. I just keep knockin' them over and it doesn't mean anything. You still run around a lot?

Biff: Naa. I'd like to find a girl—steady, somebody with substance.

Happy: That's what I long for.

Biff: Go on! You'd never come home.

Happy: I would! Somebody with character, with resistance! Like Mom, y'know? You're gonna call me a bastard when I tell you this. That girl Charlotte I was with tonight is engaged to be married in five weeks. [*He tries on his new hat.*]

Biff: No kiddin'!

Happy: Sure, the guy's in line for the vice-presidency of the store. I don't know what gets into me, maybe I just have an overdeveloped sense of competition or something, but I went and ruined her, and furthermore I can't get rid of her. And he's the third executive I've done that to. Isn't that a crummy characteristic? And to top it all, I go to their weddings! [*indignantly, but laughing*] Like I'm not supposed to take bribes. Manufacturers offer me a hundred-dollar bill now and then to throw an order their way. You know how honest I am, but it's like this girl, see. I hate myself for it. Because I don't want the girl, and, still, I take it and—I love it!

Biff: Let's go to sleep.

Happy: I guess we didn't settle anything, heh?

Biff: I just got one idea that I think I'm going to try.

Happy: What's that?

Biff: Remember Bill Oliver?

Happy: Sure, Oliver is very big now. You want to work for him again?

Biff: No, but when I quit he said something to me. He put his arm on my shoulder, and he said, "Biff, if you ever need anything, come to me."

Happy: I remember that. That sounds good.

Biff: I think I'll go to see him. If I could get ten thousand or even seven or eight thousand dollars I could buy a beautiful ranch.

Happy: I bet he'd back you. 'Cause he thought highly of you, Biff. I mean, they all do. You're well liked, Biff. That's why I say to come back here, and we both have the apartment. And I'm tellin' you, Biff, any babe you want . . .

Biff: No, with a ranch I could do the work I like and still be something. I just wonder though. I wonder if Oliver still thinks I stole that carton of basketballs.

Happy: Oh, he probably forgot that long ago. It's almost ten years. You're too sensitive. Anyway, he didn't really fire you.

Biff: Well, I think he was going to. I think that's why I quit. I was never sure whether he knew or not. I know he thought the world of me, though. I was the only one he'd let lock up the place.

Scene from
A Doll's House by Henrik Ibsen

From Act III

For 1 man, 1 woman

Characters: **Torvald Helmer,** manager of a bank.
Nora, his wife.

Setting: The home of Torvald Helmer in the late nineteenth century.

Situation: During her marriage to Torvald, Nora has been treated by her husband like a delicate doll, incapable of thinking or doing anything significant. In reality, she saved her husband's life at one point by borrowing money, forging her father's signature to a bond, and then slowly repaying the debt. Her forgery is discovered, however, and eventually revealed to an irate Torvald. When he finds out that the forgery will remain a secret and the bond will be returned, he seems to be happy (only because he is saved from dishonor), and he proceeds to forgive Nora. This excerpt, the final scene in the play, reveals her reaction to his attitudes toward her.

Script Notations

Nora: There is another task I must undertake first. I must try and educate myself—you are not the man to help me in that. I must do that for myself. And that is why I am going to leave you now.

Helmer: (*springing up*). What do you say?

Nora: I must stand quite alone, if I am to understand myself and everything about me. It is for that reason that I cannot remain with you any longer.

Helmer: Nora! Nora!

Nora: I am going away from here now, at once. I am sure Christine will take me in for the night——

Helmer: You are out of your mind! I won't allow it! I forbid you!

Nora: It is no use forbidding me anything any longer. I will take with me what belongs to myself. I will take nothing from you, either now or later.

Helmer: What sort of madness is this!

Nora: To-morrow I shall go home—I mean, to my old home. It will be easiest for me to find something to do there.

Helmer: You blind, foolish woman!

Nora: I must try and get some sense, Torvald.

Helmer: To desert your home, your husband and your children! And you don't consider what people will say!

Nora: I cannot consider that at all. I only know that it is necessary for me.

Helmer: It's shocking. This is how you would neglect your most sacred duties.

Nora: What do you consider my most sacred duties?

Helmer: Do I need to tell you that? Are they not your duties to your husband and your children?

Nora: I have other duties just as sacred.

Helmer: That you have not. What duties could those be?

Nora: Duties to myself.

Helmer: Before all else, you are a wife and a mother.

Nora: I don't believe that any longer. I believe that before all else I am a reasonable human being, just as you are—or, at all events, that I must try and become one. I know quite well, Torvald, that most people would think you right, and that views of that kind are to be found in books; but I can no longer content myself with what most people say, or with what is found in books. I must think over things for myself and get to understand them.

Helmer: Can you not understand your place in your own home? Have you not a reliable guide in such matters as that?—have you no religion?

Nora: I am afraid, Torvald, I do not exactly know what religion is.

Helmer: What are you saying?

Nora: I know nothing but what the clergyman said

when I went to be confirmed. He told us that religion was this, and that, and the other. When I am away from all this, and am alone, I will look into that matter too. I will see if what the clergyman said is true, or at all events if it is true for me.

Helmer: This is unheard of in a girl of your age! But if religion cannot lead you aright, let me try and awaken your conscience. I suppose you have some moral sense? Or—answer me—am I to think you have none?

Nora: I assure you, Torvald, that is not an easy question to answer. I really don't know. The thing perplexes me altogether. I only know that you and I look at it in quite a different light. I am learning, too, that the law is quite another thing from what I supposed; but I find it impossible to convince myself that the law is right. According to it a woman has no right to spare her old dying father, or to save her husband's life. I can't believe that.

Helmer: You talk like a child. You don't understand the conditions of the world in which you live.

Nora: No, I don't. But now I am going to try. I am going to see if I can make out who is right, the world or I.

Helmer: You are ill, Nora; you are delirious; I almost think you are out of your mind.

Nora: I have never felt my mind so clear and certain as to-night.

Helmer: And is it with a clear and certain mind that you forsake your husband and your children?

Nora: Yes, it is.

Helmer: Then there is only one possible explanation.

Nora: What is that?

Helmer: You do not love me any more.

Nora: No, that is just it.

Helmer: Nora!—and you can say that?

Nora: It gives me great pain, Torvald, for you have always been so kind to me, but I cannot help it. I do not love you any more.

Helmer: (*regaining his composure*). Is that a clear and certain conviction too?

Nora: Yes, absolutely clear and certain. That is the reason why I will not stay here any longer.

Helmer: And can you tell me what I have done to forfeit your love?

Nora: Yes, indeed I can. It was to-night, when the wonderful thing did not happen; then I saw you were not the man I had thought you.

Helmer: Explain yourself better—I don't understand you.

Nora: I have waited so patiently for eight years; for goodness knows, I knew very well that wonderful things don't happen every day. Then this horrible misfortune came upon me; and then I felt quite certain that the wonderful thing was going to happen at last. When Krogstad's letter was lying out there, never for a moment did I imagine that you would consent to accept this man's conditions. I was so absolutely certain that you would say to him: Publish the thing to the whole world. And when that was done——

Helmer: Yes, what then?—when I had exposed my wife to shame and disgrace?

Nora: When that was done, I was so absolutely certain, you would come forward and take everything upon yourself, and say: I am the guilty one.

Helmer: Nora——!

Nora: You mean that I would never have accepted such a sacrifice on your part? No, of course not. But what would my assurances have been worth against yours? That was the wonderful thing which I hoped for and feared; and it was to prevent that, that I wanted to kill myself.

Helmer: I would gladly work night and day for you, Nora—bear sorrow and want for your sake. But no man would sacrifice his honour for the one he loves.

Nora: It is a thing hundreds of thousands of women have done.

Helmer: Oh, you think and talk like a heedless child.

Nora: Maybe. But you neither think nor talk like the man I could bind myself to. As soon as your fear was over—and it was not fear for what threatened me, but for what might happen to you—when the whole thing was past, as far as you were concerned it was exactly as if nothing at all had happened. Exactly as before, I was your little skylark, your doll, which you would in future treat with doubly gentle care, because it was so brittle and fragile. (*Getting up.*) Torvald—it was then it dawned upon me that for eight years I had been living here with a strange man, and had borne him three children——. Oh, I can't bear to think of it! I could tear myself into little bits!

Helmer: (*sadly*). I see, I see. An abyss has opened between us—there is no denying it. But, Nora, would it not be possible to fill it up?

Nora: As I am now, I am no wife for you.

Helmer: I have it in me to become a different man.

Nora: Perhaps—if your doll is taken away from you.

Helmer: But to part!—to part from you! No, no, Nora, I can't understand that idea.

Nora: (*going out to the right*). That makes it all the more certain that it must be done.

[*She comes back with her cloak and hat and a small bag which she puts on a chair by the table.*]

Helmer: Nora, Nora, not now! Wait till to-morrow.

Nora: (*putting on her cloak*). I cannot spend the night in a strange man's room.

Helmer: But can't we live here like brother and sister——?

Nora: (*putting on her hat*). You know very well that

would not last long. (*Puts the shawl round her.*) Good-bye, Torvald. I won't see the little ones. I know they are in better hands than mine. As I am now, I can be of no use to them.

Helmer: But some day, Nora—some day?

Nora: How can I tell? I have no idea what is going to become of me.

Helmer: But you are my wife, whatever becomes of you.

Nora: Listen, Torvald. I have heard that when a wife deserts her husband's house, as I am doing now, he is legally freed from all obligations towards her. In any case I set you free from all your obligations. You are not to feel yourself bound in the slightest way, any more than I shall. There must be perfect freedom on both sides. See here is your ring back. Give me mine.

Helmer: That too?

Nora: That too.

Helmer: Here it is.

Nora: That's right. Now it is all over. I have put the keys here. The maids know all about everything in the house—better than I do. To-morrow, after I have left here Christine will come here and pack up my own things that I brought with me from home. I will have them sent after me.

Helmer: All over! All over!—Nora, shall you never think of me again?

Nora: I know I shall often think of you and the children and this house.

Helmer: May I write to you, Nora?

Nora: No—never. You must not do that.

Helmer: But at least let me send you——

Nora: Nothing—nothing——

Helmer: Let me help you if you are in want.

Nora: No. I can receive nothing from a stranger.

Helmer: Nora—can I never be anything more than a stranger to you?

Nora: (*taking her bag*). Ah, Torvald, the most wonderful thing of all would have to happen.

Helmer: Tell me what that would be!

Nora: Both you and I would have to be so changed that——. Oh, Torvald, I don't believe any longer in wonderful things happening.

Helmer: But I will believe in it. Tell me? So changed that——?

Nora: That our life together would be a real wedlock. Good-bye.

              [*She goes out through the hall.*]

Helmer: (*sinks down on a chair at the door and buries his face in his hands*). Nora! Nora! (*Looks round, and rises.*) Empty. She is gone. (*A hope flashes across his mind.*) The most wonderful thing of all——?

[*The sound of a door shutting is heard from below.*]

Scene from
   The Gingerbread Lady by Neil Simon

From Act I

For 2 women

Characters: **Evy Meara,** 43.
   Polly Meara, 17, her daughter.

Setting: Evy's third-floor apartment in a brownstone in New York's West Seventies
   on a late afternoon in mid-November.

Situation: Evy, a popular singer who has allowed booze and sex to ruin her life,
   has just been released from a sanitarium where she has taken a ten-week cure
   and lost considerable weight. On the day of her return to her apartment, after
   several friends have left she feels alone and tries to telephone her daughter,
   Polly. During the call Polly appears in the doorway.

Script Notations

Evy: (*Then* **Evy** *speaks into the phone*)—never mind, I just heard from her.

(*She hangs up and stares at* **Polly**)

Polly: I don't want to get your hopes up, but I have reason to believe I'm your daughter!

Evy: No, you're not. *My* daughter would have called first . . . (*No longer able to contain herself*) . . . You rotten kid, you want to give me a heart attack? (*They rush to each other, arms around each other in a huge, warm embrace.* **Evy** *squeezes her tightly*) Oh, God, Polly, Polly . . .

Polly: I was hoping I'd get here before you. But I was late getting out of school. Of all damn days . . .

(*They break the embrace.* **Evy** *wipes her eyes*)

Evy: Okay, I'm crying. You satisfied? You just destroyed a helpless old woman . . . Well, why the hell aren't you crying?

Polly: I'm too happy. I can't believe it. My God, look at you.

Evy: What do you think?

Polly: You're gorgeous. Skinniest mother I ever had. I can wear your clothes now.

Evy: What size dress do you wear?

Polly: Five.

Evy: Tough, kid, I wear a four. (*Wipes teary eyes again*) Damn, I knew this would happen. You weren't supposed to know I was home. I needed three days before I could face you.

Polly: I called the hospital this morning. You didn't think I could wait, did you?

Evy: Neither could I. Oh God, give me another hug, I can't stand it. (*They embrace*) All right, if we're going to get physical, let's close the door. There's enough talk about me in this building.

(**Evy** *closes the door.* **Polly** *goes to get the suitcase from in front of the door*)

Polly: I'll get that.

(*She picks it up*)

Evy: Have you had dinner yet?

Polly: I haven't even had lunch. I was too nervous.

Evy: I just loaded up for the winter. We'll have a food festival. Come on, take your coat off, let me look at you. Hey, what'd you do with your hair?

Polly: Nothing.

Evy: I know. It's been three months. When you gonna do something?

Polly: Don't bug me about the way I look. I'm not that secure yet.

(*She heads for the bedroom with the suitcase*)

Evy: I should have your problems. Where you going with that?

Polly: In the bedroom.

Evy: What is it?

Polly: (*Looks at it*) Looks like a suitcase.

Evy: Thanks, I was wondering. What's in the suitcase?

Polly: (*Shrugs*) Dresses, shoes, books, things like that.

Evy: Why do you have things like that in your suitcase?

Polly: Well, otherwise they fall on the floor.

Evy: All right, no one likes a smart-ass for a daughter. What's going on here?

Polly: Nothing's going on. Can't I stay?

Evy: Tonight? You know you can.

Polly: Okay. I'm staying tonight.

(*She starts for the bedroom again*)

Evy: With all that? You must be some heavy sleeper.

Polly: Okay, *two* nights. Let's not haggle.

Evy: Hey, hey, just a minute. Put the suitcase down. (**Polly** *looks at her, then puts it down*) . . . Now look at me.

Polly: I'm looking.

Evy: And I know what you're thinking. Oh, no, you don't.

Polly: Why not?

Evy: Because I don't need any roommates, thank you . . . If you had a beard, it would be different.

Polly: I don't want to be your roommate, I just want to live with you.

Evy: You lonely? I'll send you to camp. You have a home, what are you bothering me for?

Polly: You can't throw me out, I'm your flesh and blood.

Evy: I just got rid of my flesh, I'm not sentimental.

Polly: I've already decided I'm moving in. You have nothing to say about it.

Evy: In the first place, idiot, you're not allowed to live here. It's not up to you or me.

Polly: And in the second place?

Evy: I don't need a second place. The first one wiped us out. You live where your father tells you to live.

Polly: Exactly. Where do I put the suitcase?

Evy: Are you telling me *your* father gave you permission to move in here with me?

Polly: Right.

Evy: *Your* father?

Polly: That's the one.

Evy: A tall man, grayish hair, wears blue suits, spits a little when he talks?

Polly: Would you like to speak to him yourself?

Evy: Not sober, I don't. What does your stepmother think about this? What's her name, Lucretia?

Polly: Felicia.

Evy: Felicia, some name. He must spit pretty good when he says that. Did she ever get that clicking in her teeth fixed?

Polly: Nope. Still clicking.

Evy: That's a nice way to live, with a spitter and a clicker. Thank God he didn't get custody of me too.

Polly: That's why I'm begging you to take me in. I can't do my homework with all that noise.

Evy: God's truth, Polly? He really said yes?

Polly: He likes me. He wouldn't kid around with my life.

Evy: Why don't I believe it?

Polly: We've been talking about it for months. He knows how hard you've been trying. He spoke to your doctor, he knows you're all right . . . And he thinks you need me now.

Evy: *Now* I need you? Where does he think I've been the last seven years, Guatemala?

Polly: He knows where you've been.

Evy: And what about you? Is this what you really want?

Polly: I've been packed for three years. Every June I put in bigger sizes.

Evy: You wanna hear something? My whole body is shaking. I'm scared stiff. I wouldn't know the first thing about taking care of you.

Polly: I'm seventeen years old. How hard could it be?

Evy: I'll level with you—it's not the best thing I do. I was feeling very motherly one time, I bought a couple of turtles, two for eighty-five cents, Irving and Sam. I fed them once—in the morning they were floating on their backs. I don't think I could go through that again.

Polly: I'm a terrific swimmer.

Evy: Jesus, the one thing I hoped I wouldn't have is a dumb daughter. What kind of influence would I be on you? I talk filthy. I have always talked filthy. I'm a congenital filthy talker.

Polly: Son of a bitch.

Evy: I don't think that's funny.

Polly: Well, I just got here, give me a chance.

Evy: What the hell is the big attraction? I thought we were doing fine with visiting days.

Polly: When I was nine years old, do you remember what you gave me for Christmas?

Evy: An empty bottle of Dewar's White Label? I don't know, I can't remember yesterday.

Polly: Don't you remember the gingerbread house with the little gingerbread lady in the window?

Evy: If you say so.

Polly: I always kept it to remind me of you. Of course, today I have the biggest box of crumbs in the neighborhood. Come on, be a sport. Buy me another one this Christmas.

Evy: I don't know if I could afford it.

Polly: What are you afraid of?

Evy: Of leaving you with the crumbs again . . . You know what I'm like.

Polly: I've seen you drunk. Mostly I hated it but once or twice you sure were cute.

Evy: You only saw dress rehearsals. I was very careful around you. A mother doesn't like to get too pissed around her own daughter. Am I supposed to say things like that in front of you? Pissed?

Polly: If you can do it, you can say it.

Evy: There are other things I can't tell you . . . Ah, Christ, I might as well tell you. You knew about Lou Tanner.

Polly: I met him here a few times.

Evy: Did you know we lived here together for eight months?

Polly: I didn't think he got off a bus in those pajamas.

Evy: Jesus, at least have the decency to be shocked.

Polly: There's a sixteen-year-old girl who just left school because she's pregnant. You're forty-three. If you're not allowed, who is?

Evy: How'd I suddenly end up with the Mother of the Year Award?

Polly: I don't want to judge you, Evy. I just want to live with you.

Scene from
   Harvey by Mary Chase

From Act I, Scene 2

For 1 man, 1 woman

Characters: **Elwood P. Dowd,** about 47, dreamy yet dignified.
        Betty Chumley, about 55, good-natured, bustling wife of Dr. Chumley, head of the sanitarium.

Setting: The reception room of Chumley's Rest, somewhere in the Far West. The time may be the present.

Situation: Elwood is a charming, likeable alcoholic whose constant companion is a six-foot-tall imaginary (?) rabbit named Harvey. They are constantly embarrassing family and friends, and finally Elwood's sister, Veta Louise, is convinced she must have Elwood committed to Chumley's Rest. Mistakenly, she is temporarily incarcerated while Elwood is released. As he prepares to leave, he looks around for his friend, Harvey, and meets Mrs. Chumley in the reception room.

Script Notations

Elwood: (*Removing his hat and bowing.*) Good evening. (*Puts hat on desk. Walks over to her.*)

Betty: I am Mrs. Chumley. Doctor Chumley's wife.

Elwood: I'm happy to know that. Dowd is my name. Elwood P. Let me give you one of my cards. (*Gives her one.*) If you should want to call me—call me at this one. Don't call me at that one, because that's—(*Points at card.*) the old one. (*Starts one step. Looking.*)

Betty: Thank you. Is there something I can do for you?

Elwood: (*Turns to her.*) What did you have in mind?

Betty: You seem to be looking for someone.

Elwood: (*Walking.*) Yes, I am. I'm looking for Harvey. I went off without him.

Betty: Harvey? Is he a patient here?

Elwood: (*Turns.*) Oh, no. Nothing like that. (*Cross to door down* L.)

Betty: Does he work here?

Elwood: (*Looking out down* L. *door.*) Oh no. He is what you might call my best friend. He is also a pooka. He came out here with me and Veta this afternoon.

Betty: Where was he when you last saw him?

Elwood: (*Behind chair* L. *of desk.*) In that chair there—with his hat and coat on the table.

Betty: There doesn't seem to be any hat and coat around here now. Perhaps he left?

Elwood: Apparently. I don't see him anywhere. (*Looks in* **Sanderson's** *office.*)

Betty: What was that word you just said—pooka?

Elwood: (*Crosses* C. *He is looking in hallway* C.) Yes—that's it.

Betty: Is that something new? (*Looks in hallway.*)

Elwood: (*Coming down.*) Oh, no. As I understand it. That's something very old.

Betty: Oh, really? I had never happened to hear it before.

Elwood: I'm not too surprised at that. I hadn't myself, until I met him. I do hope you get an opportunity to meet him. I'm sure he would be quite taken with you. (*Down* C. *on a line with* **Betty.**)

Betty: Oh, really? Well, that's very nice of you to say so, I'm sure.

Elwood: Not at all. If Harvey happens to take a liking to people he expresses himself quite definitely. If he's not particularly interested, he sits there like an empty chair or an empty space on the floor. Harvey takes his time making his mind up about people. Choosey, you see. (*Crosses above table to door* R.)

Betty: That's not such a bad way to be in this day and age.

Elwood: Harvey is fond of my sister, Veta. That's

because he is fond of me, and Veta and I come from the same family. Now you'd think that feeling would be mutual, wouldn't you? (*Looks in office* R. *Crosses to chair* R. *of table.*) But Veta doesn't seem to care for Harvey. Don't you think that's rather too bad, Mrs. Chumley?

Betty: Oh, I don't know, Mr. Dowd. I gave up a long time ago expecting my family to like my friends. It's useless.

Elwood: But we must keep on trying. (*Sits chair* R. *of table.*)

Betty: Well, there's no harm in trying, I suppose.

Elwood: Because if Harvey has said to me once he has said a million times—"Mr. Dowd, I would do anything for you." Mrs. Chumley—

Betty: Yes—

Elwood: Did you know that Mrs. McElhinney's Aunt Rose is going to drop in on her unexpectedly tonight from Cleveland?

Betty: Why, no I didn't—

Elwood: Neither does she. That puts you both in the same boat, doesn't it?

Betty: Well, I don't know anybody named—Mrs.—

Elwood: Mrs. McElhinney? Lives next door to us. She is a wonderful woman. Harvey told me about her Aunt Rose. That's an interesting little news item, and you are perfectly free to pass it around.

Betty: Well, I ——

Elwood: Would you care to come downtown with me now, my dear? I would be glad to buy you a drink.

Betty: Thank you very much, but I am waiting for Dr. Chumley and if he came down and found me gone he would be liable to raise—he would be irritated!

Elwood: We wouldn't want that, would we? Some other time, maybe? (*He rises.*)

Betty: I'll tell you what I'll do, however.

Elwood: What will you do, however? I'm interested.

Betty: If your friend comes in while I'm here I'd be glad to give him a message for you.

Elwood: (*Gratefully.*) Would you do that? I'd certainly appreciate that. (*Goes up* C. *to top of desk for his hat.*)

Betty: No trouble at all. I'll write it down on the back of this. (*Holds up card. Takes pencil from purse.*) What would you like me to tell him if he comes in while I'm still here?

Elwood: Ask him to meet me downtown—if he has no other plans.

Betty: (*Writing.*) Meet Mr. Dowd downtown. Any particular place downtown?

Elwood: He knows where. Harvey knows this town like a book.

Betty: (*Writing.*) Harvey—you know where. Harvey what?

Elwood: Just Harvey.

Betty: (*Rises—crosses to desk.*) I'll tell you what.

Elwood: What?

Betty: (*Swings chair* R. *of desk in position.*) Doctor and I are going right downtown—to 12th and Montview. Dr. McClure is having a cocktail party.

Elwood: (*At* L. *of desk; he writes that down on pad on desk.*) A cocktail party at 12th and Montview.

Betty: We're driving there in a few minutes. We could give your friend a lift into town.

Elwood: I hate to impose on you—but I would certainly appreciate that.

Betty: No trouble at all. Dr. McClure is having this party for his sister from Wichita.

Elwood: I didn't know Dr. McClure had a sister in Wichita.

Betty: Oh, you *know* Dr. McClure?

Elwood: No.

Betty: (*Puts* **Elwood's** *card down on desk.*) But— (*Sits chair* R. *of desk.*)

Elwood: You're quite sure you haven't time to come into town with me and have a drink?

Betty: I really couldn't—but thank you just the same.

Elwood: Some other time, perhaps?

Betty: Thank you.

Elwood: It's been very pleasant to meet you, and I hope to see you again.

Betty: Yes, so do I.

Elwood: Goodnight, my dear. (*Tips hat—bows—goes to door, turns.*) You can't miss Harvey. He's very tall—(*Shows with hands.*) Like that—(*Exits down* L.)

Scene from
    Inherit the Wind by Jerome Lawrence and Robert E. Lee

From Act I

For 2 men, 1 woman

Characters: **Rachel,** 22, a minister's daughter.
                Bert Cates, a high school teacher.
                Mr. Meeker, the bailiff.

Setting: The courtroom of the small town of Hillsboro in Tennessee. A July morn-
             ing in 1922.

Situation: Based on the famous Scopes "monkey trial" which raised the question
               of a teacher's right to teach the theory of evolution, the play is a thinly dis-
               guised treatment of the event, which pitted Clarence Darrow for the defense
               against the three-time presidential candidate William Jennings Bryan for the
               prosecution.
                   Bert Cates, like the real-life Scopes, has tested a state law that has for-
               bidden the teaching of evolution in the public schools. In jail awaiting trial,
               Cates is visited by the girl who loves him. She has been pressured by her
               father, a minister who is opposed to Cates's position, and she is upset by the
               fact that William Harrison Brady (Bryan) has come to prosecute Cates.

Script Notations

Rachel: Mr. Meeker . . . ?

(*After a pause, a door at stage right opens.* **Mr. Meeker,** *the bailiff, enters. There is no collar on his shirt; his hair is tousled, and there is shaving soap on his face, which he is wiping off with a towel as he enters.*)

Meeker: (*A little irritably*) Who is it? (*Surprised*) Why, hello, Rachel. 'Scuse the way I look. (*He wipes the soap out of his ear. Then he notices her suitcase.*) Not goin' away, are you? Excitement's just startin'.

Rachel: (*Earnestly*) Mr. Meeker, don't let my father know I came here.

Meeker: (*Shrugs*) The Reverend don't tell me his business. Don't know why I should tell him mine.

Rachel: I want to see Bert Cates. Is he all right?

Meeker: Don't know why he shouldn't be. I always figured the safest place in the world is a jail.

Rachel: Can I go down and see him?

Meeker: Ain't a very proper place for a minister's daughter.

Rachel: I only want to see him for a minute.

Meeker: Sit down, Rachel. I'll bring him up. You can talk to him right here in the courtroom. (**Rachel** *sits in one of the stiff wooden chairs.* **Meeker** *starts out, then pauses*) Long as I've been bailiff here, we've never had nothin' but drunks, vagrants, couple of chicken thieves. (*A little dreamily*) Our best catch was that fella from Minnesota that chopped up his wife; we had to extradite him. (*Shakes his head*) Seems kinda queer havin' a school-teacher in our jail. (*Shrugs*) Might improve the writin' on the walls.

(**Meeker** *goes out. Nervously,* **Rachel** *looks around at the cold, official furnishings of the courtroom.* **Meeker** *returns to the courtroom, followed by* **Bert Cates. Cates** *is a pale, thin young man of twenty-four. He is quiet, shy, well-mannered, not particularly good-looking.* **Rachel** *and* **Cates** *face each other expressionlessly, without speaking.* **Meeker** *pauses in the doorway.*)

Meeker: I'll leave you two alone to talk. Don't run off, Bert. (**Meeker** *goes out.* **Rachel** *and* **Cates** *look at each other.*)

Rachel: Hello, Bert.

Cates: Rache, I told you not to come here.

Rachel: I couldn't help it. Nobody saw me. Mr. Meeker won't tell. (*Troubled*) I keep thinking of you, locked up here—

Cates: (*Trying to cheer her up*) You know something funny? The food's better than the boarding house. And you'd better not tell anybody how cool it is down there, or we'll have a crime wave every summer.

Rachel: I stopped by your place and picked up some

of your things. A clean shirt, your best tie, some handkerchiefs.

Cates: Thanks.

Rachel: (*Rushing to him*) Bert, why don't you tell 'em it was all a joke? Tell 'em you didn't mean to break a law, and you won't do it again!

Cates: I suppose everybody's all steamed up about Brady coming.

Rachel: He's coming in on a special train out of Chattanooga. Pa's going to the station to meet him. Everybody is!

Cates: Strike up the band.

Rachel: Bert, it's still not too late. Why can't you admit you're wrong? If the biggest man in the country—next to the President, maybe—if Matthew Harrison Brady comes here to tell the whole world how wrong you are—

Cates: You still think I did wrong?

Rachel: Why did you do it?

Cates: You know why I did it. I had the book in my hand, Hunter's *Civic Biology.* I opened it up, and read my sophomore science class Chapter 17, Darwin's *Origin of Species.* (**Rachel** *starts to protest*) All it says is that man wasn't just stuck here like a geranium in a flower pot; that living comes from a *long* miracle, it didn't just happen in seven days.

Rachel: There's a law against it.

Cates: I know that.

Rachel: Everybody says what you did is bad.

Cates: It isn't as simple as that. Good or bad, black or white, night or day. Do you know, at the top of the world the twilight is six months long?

Rachel: But we don't live at the top of the world. We live in Hillsboro, and when the sun goes down, it's dark. And why do you try to make it different? (**Rachel** *gets the shirt, tie, and handkerchiefs from the suitcase.*) Here.

Cates: Thanks, Rache.

Rachel: Why can't you be on the right side of things?

Cates: Your father's side. (**Rachel** *starts to leave.* **Cates** *runs after her.*) Rache—love me!

(*They embrace.* **Meeker** *enters with a long-handled broom.*)

Meeker: (*Clears his throat*) I gotta sweep.

(**Rachel** *breaks away and hurries off.*)

Cates: (*Calling*) Thanks for the shirt!

(**Meeker,** *who has been sweeping impassively now stops and leans on the broom.*)

Meeker: Imagine. Matthew Harrison Brady, comin' here. I voted for him for President. Twice. In nineteen hundred, and again in oh-eight. Wasn't old enough to vote for him the first time he ran. But my pa did. (*Turns proudly to* **Cates**) I *seen* him once. At a Chautauqua meeting in Chattanooga. (*Impressed, remembering*) The tent-poles shook! (**Cates** *moves nervously*) Who's gonna be your lawyer, son?

Cates: I don't know yet. I wrote to that newspaper in Baltimore. They're sending somebody.

Meeker: (*Resumes sweeping*) He better be loud.

Cates: (*Picking up the shirt*) You want me to go back down?

Meeker: No need. You can stay up here if you want.

Cates: (*Going toward the jail*) I'm supposed to be in jail; I'd better be in jail!

Scene from
   Last of the Red Hot Lovers by Neil Simon

From Act III

For 1 man, 1 woman

Characters: **Barney Cashman,** 47, a successful seafood-restaurant owner.
   Jeanette Fisher, 39, his wife's best friend, a "gloomy, depressed"
person.

Setting: Barney's mother's apartment in Manhattan on a late afternoon in September.

Situation: Barney has been married for twenty-three years and has been faithful to his wife. He is basically a loving, gentle, serious soul who has decided to become a "red hot lover" at the age of forty-seven. In each of the two previous acts he has failed in trying to seduce two quite different females in his mother's apartment. In this act he has invited his wife's best friend into the same lair. One should know that he will fail this time as well and end by calling his wife and inviting her to the apartment.

Script Notations

Jeanette: Why am I here, Barney?

Barney: What was that?

Jeanette: Why am I here? I've known you and Thelma for twelve years. She's been a good friend to me. I wouldn't hurt her for the world. You and Mel are closer than brothers. So why am I here?

Barney: Why? Because I *asked* you here, that's why. I'm very fond of you. Look, why don't you put your pocketbook down, Jeanette, and relax, and I'll go inside and get us a drink, okay?

(*He starts for the kitchen*)

Jeanette: I don't find you physically attractive. You knew that, didn't you?

(*That stops him*)

Barney: No! No, I didn't know that . . . It doesn't surprise me . . . I mean it's not mandatory . . .

Jeanette: I think you're sweet . . . I think you're basically a good person. I do not think you're physically attractive.

Barney: (*Cheerfully*) Listen, you can't win 'em all.

Jeanette: I can be honest with you, Barney, can't I? I think we've known each other long enough for that, haven't we?

Barney: (*The good sport*) Hell, yes.

Jeanette: So I can just come out and say it, can't I? I do not find you physically attractive.

Barney: (*Smiling*) Fine, fine. Listen, I think we've covered that ground pretty good, Jeanette. So why don't I go get the drinks and you put down your pocketbook and relax and then—

Jeanette: Don't misunderstand me. It's not the weight. The weight thing doesn't bother me. I have never been repelled by obesity.

Barney: I'm glad to hear that, Jeanette. Actually I was a skinny kid. I blew up in the army. I was a mess sergeant in Fort Totten for about two years and I would constantly—

Jeanette: I am attracted to you emotionally, intellectually—

Barney: Isn't that funny? I always felt that you and I had a certain rapport—

Jeanette: But not physically.

Barney: (*Nods*) Not physically. We established that a number of times. Would you excuse me one second, Jeanette. I want to get the champagne.

(*He starts again*)

Jeanette: Barney, do you know I haven't slept with Mel in eight months?

Barney: (*That stops him again*) No, I didn't. Eight months, my God. I knew Mel had a bad back but I had no idea—

Jeanette: *Have not* slept with him in eight months.

Barney: Well, listen, Jeanette, that's none of my business, really. That's between you and Mel . . .

Jeanette: He's slept with me. I haven't slept with him.

Barney: (*Looks at her, puzzled*) How does that work out?

Jeanette: I don't particularly enjoy sex, Barney.

Barney: Is that right? Ever?

Jeanette: It was important to me once. Nothing is very important to me any more.

Barney: You're just tense, Jeanette. You're going through a dry period right now. Eight months, my God, no wonder . . .

Jeanette: Has Mel indicated in any way there was any trouble between us?

Barney: None. Mel is not a talker.

Jeanette: I know you see him all the time.

Barney: I play handball with him on Saturday mornings. We never discuss personal problems. He serves, I hit it back.

Jeanette: He didn't seem upset?

Barney: No. Can I take your pocketbook, Jeanette?

Jeanette: *You* wouldn't talk, would you, Barney?

Barney: Me, Jeanette? I'm surprised that you would even think—

Jeanette: Then I don't have to worry about my name ever coming up in a cocktail party—

Barney: May God strike me dead! May I never live to see my oldest girl married, if I ever mentioned even casually—

Jeanette: Swear!

Barney: I just swore. May I become totally paralyzed from the hips down—

Jeanette: It was not easy for me to come here today.

Barney: May my hands get crippled with arthritis. I'm surprised that you would even think . . .

Jeanette: I'm not very good at this sort of thing, Barney.

Barney: Who *is*, Jeanette?

Jeanette: I don't even know what I'm supposed to do.

Barney: I'd put my pocketbook down first if I were you . . .

Jeanette: (*She gets up*) My only concern is that whatever happens between us will never go beyond these four walls.

(*She crosses to the window*)

Barney: May my restaurant be destroyed by fire, Jeanette. You'll never have to worry as long as you live. I told you that the other night.

Jeanette: Did Mel ever mention being involved with another woman?

Barney: No.

Jeanette: Would you tell me if he did?

Barney: Yes. Yes, I would tell you.

Jeanette: You would?

Barney: Yes.

Jeanette: Why would you tell me?

Barney: I don't know why. You asked me if I would; I'm trying to be polite, that's all.

Jeanette: I see.

Barney: Can I take your pocketbook, Jeanette?

Jeanette: What do you think about all this, Barney?

Barney: About all what?

Jeanette: About all this that's going on.

Barney: *Nothing's* going on, Jeanette. I can't even get your pocketbook.

Jeanette: You're not appalled by the times we live in, by all the promiscuity you find everywhere?

Barney: I don't find it anywhere. I *hear* a lot about it, I haven't found any. You want to sit down a few minutes? You're here, you might as well sit.

Jeanette: Let me ask you a question, Barney. Do you have any guilt about asking me here today?

Barney: Do I have any guilt?

Jeanette: Don't repeat the question, just answer it.

Barney: What? Do I have any guilt? . . . No, I do not.

Jeanette: In other words, you don't care who you hurt?

Barney: I'm not hurting anyone.

Jeanette: Really? You want to think about that answer?

Barney: Not necessarily . . . Why probe deeply into everything?

Jeanette: Exactly. That's the attitude we live with today. Don't think about it. Well, I'm not going to think about it, Barney. I'm going to become like everyone else in the world. That's why I'm here today.

(*She opens her purse, takes out a pillbox and puts a pill in her mouth*)

Barney: Somehow I think we've gotten off on a tangent, Jeanette . . . What are you doing? What's that?

Jeanette: Digilene. It's for depression.

Barney: Don't you want any water?

Jeanette: I couldn't wait.

Barney: Until I brought the water? You're *that* depressed?

Jeanette: Isn't that how we cope with our problems today, Barney? With pills, drugs . . . Do you know how many people in this country take pills because they cannot cope with emotional problems? Do you know the number in this country? It was in *Look* magazine.

Barney: I didn't get a haircut this week, I missed the new *Look*.

Jeanette: Sixty million.

Barney: That many?

Jeanette: Do you know the alternative to taking pills?

Barney: Was this in the same issue?

Jeanette: Melancholia. Do you know what that is? Melancholia?

Barney: Brooding, isn't it? Heavy brooding?

Jeanette: I'll tell you what melancholia is, Barney, because I've had it for the last eight months. It's total and complete despair. It's waking up each morning of your life not wanting anything, not hoping, not caring, not needing. You don't pray for happiness because you don't believe it exists, and you don't wish for death because if you don't exist, then death is meaningless. All that's left is a quiet, endless, bottomless, relentless, eternal, infinite gloom. That's melancholia.

(*There is a long, awkward pause as* **Barney** *thinks about how to retrieve the afternoon*)

Scene from
  The Miracle Worker by William Gibson

From Act II

For 2 women

Characters: **Annie Sullivan,** 20, teacher/governess of Helen Keller.
  Helen Keller as a young girl, deaf, blind, and mute.

Setting: The Kellers' family room in Tuscumbia, Alabama, in the 1880s.

Situation: This biographical dramatization reveals the attempt and eventual success
  of a previously blind Irish woman, Annie, to teach and put in touch with the
  world an undisciplined, spoiled, temperamental, almost animalistic young
  girl, Helen, who has been deaf, blind, and mute since infancy.
    As this scene begins, Annie has just told the Keller family to leave the
  room and locked the door after them; she now returns to pursue a battle of
  wills.

Script Notations

Annie meanwhile has begun by slapping both keys down on a shelf out of Helen's *reach; she returns to the table, upstage.* Helen's *kicking has subsided, and when from the floor her hand finds* Annie's *chair empty she pauses.* Annie *clears the table of* Kate's, James's, *and* Keller's *plates; she gets back to her own across the table just in time to slide it deftly away from* Helen's *pouncing hand. She lifts the hand and moves it to* Helen's *plate, and after an instant's exploration,* Helen *sits again on the floor and drums her heels.* Annie *comes around the table and resumes her chair. When* Helen *feels her skirt again, she ceases kicking, waits for whatever is to come, renews some kicking, waits again.* Annie *retrieving her plate takes up a forkful of food, stops it halfway to her mouth, gazes at it devoid of appetite, and half-lowers it; but after a look at* Helen *she sighs, dips the forkful toward* Helen *in a for-your-sake toast, and puts it in her own mouth to chew, not without an effort.*

Helen now gets hold of the chair leg, and half-succeeds in pulling the chair out from under her. Annie *bangs it down with her rear, heavily, and sits with all her weight.* Helen's *next attempt to topple it is unavailing, so her fingers dive in a pinch at* Annie's *flank.* Annie *in the middle of her mouthful almost loses it with startle, and she slaps down her fork to round on* Helen. *The child comes up with curiosity to feel what* Annie *is doing, so* Annie *resumes eating, letting* Helen's *hand follow the movement of her fork to her mouth; whereupon* Helen *at once reaches into* Annie's *plate.* Annie *firmly removes her hand to her own plate.* Helen *in reply pinches* Annie's *thigh, a good mean pinchful that makes* Annie *jump.* Annie *sets the fork down, and sits with her mouth tight.* Helen *digs another pinch into her thigh, and this time* Annie *slaps her hand smartly away;* Helen *retaliates with a roundhouse fist that catches* Annie *on the ear, and* Annie's *hand leaps at once in a forceful slap across* Helen's *cheek;* Helen *is the startled one now.* Annie's *hand in compunction falters to her own face, but when* Helen *hits at her again,* Annie *deliberately slaps her again.* Helen *lifts her fist irresolute for another roundhouse,* Annie *lifts her hand resolute for another slap, and they freeze in this posture, while* Helen *mulls it over. She thinks better of it, drops her fist, and giving* Annie *a wide berth, gropes around to her* Mother's *chair, to find it empty; she blunders her way along the table, upstage, and encountering the empty chairs and missing plates, she looks bewildered; she gropes back to her* Mother's *chair, again touches her cheek and indicates the chair, and waits for the world to answer.*

Annie *now reaches over to spell into her hand, but* **Helen** *yanks it away; she gropes to the front door, tries the knob, and finds the door locked, with no key. She gropes to the rear door, and finds it locked, with no key. She commences to bang on it.* **Annie** *rises, crosses, takes her wrists, draws her resisting back to the table, seats her, and releases her hands upon her plate; as* **Annie** *herself begins to sit,* **Helen** *writhes out of her chair, runs to the front door, and tugs and kicks at it.* **Annie** *rises again, crosses, draws her by one wrist back to the table, seats her, and sits;* **Helen** *escapes back to the door, knocking over her* **Mother's** *chair en route.* **Annie** *rises again in pursuit, and this time lifts* **Helen** *bodily from behind and bears her kicking to her chair. She deposits her, and once more turns to sit.* **Helen** *scrambles out, but as she passes* **Annie** *catches her up again from behind and deposits her in the chair;* **Helen** *scrambles out on the other side, for the rear door, but* **Annie** *at her heels catches her up and deposits her again in the chair. She stands behind it.* **Helen** *scrambles out to her right, and the instant her feet hit the floor* **Annie** *lifts and deposits her back; she scrambles out to her left, and is at once lifted and deposited back. She tries right again and is deposited back, and tries left again and is deposited back, and now feints* **Annie** *to the right but is off to her left, and is promptly deposited back. She sits a moment, and then starts straight over the tabletop, dishware notwithstanding;* **Annie** *hauls her in and deposits her back, with her plate spilling in her lap, and she melts to the floor and crawls under the table, laborious among its legs and chairs; but* **Annie** *is swift around the table and waiting on the other side when she surfaces, immediately bearing her aloft;* **Helen** *clutches at* **James's** *chair for anchorage, but it comes with her, and halfway back she abandons it to the floor.* **Annie** *deposits her in her chair, and waits.* **Helen** *sits tensed motionless. Then she tentatively puts out her left foot and hand,* **Annie** *interposes her own hand, and at the contact* **Helen** *jerks hers in. She tries her right foot,* **Annie** *blocks it with her own, and* **Helen** *jerks hers in. Finally, leaning back, she slumps down in her chair, in a sullen biding.*

Annie *backs off a step, and watches;* **Helen** *offers no move.* **Annie** *takes a deep breath. Both of them and the room are in considerable disorder, two chairs down and the table a mess, but* **Annie** *makes no effort to tidy it; she only sits on her own chair, and lets her energy refill. Then she takes up knife and fork, and resolutely addresses her food.* **Helen's** *hand comes out to explore, and seeing it* **Annie** *sits without moving; the child's hand goes over her hand and fork, pauses—* **Annie** *still does not move—and withdraws. Presently it moves for her own plate,* *slaps about for it, and stops, thwarted. At this,* **Annie** *again rises, recovers* **Helen's** *plate from the floor and a handful of scattered food from the deranged tablecloth, drops it on the plate, and pushes the plate into contact with* **Helen's** *fist. Neither of them now moves for a pregnant moment—until* **Helen** *suddenly takes a grab of food and wolfs it down.* **Annie** *permits herself the humor of a minor bow and warming of her hands together; she wanders off a step or two, watching.* **Helen** *cleans up the plate.*

After a glower of indecision, she holds the empty plate out for more. **Annie** *accepts it, and crossing to the removed plates, spoons food from them onto it; she stands debating the spoon, tapping it a few times on* **Helen's** *plate; and when she returns with the plate she brings the spoon, too. She puts the spoon first into* **Helen's** *hand, then sets the plate down.* **Helen** *discarding the spoon reaches with her hand, and* **Annie** *stops it by the wrist; she replaces the spoon in it.* **Helen** *impatiently discards it again, and again* **Annie** *stops her hand, to replace the spoon in it. This time* **Helen** *throws the spoon on the floor.* **Annie** *after considering it lifts* **Helen** *bodily out of the chair, and in a wrestling match on the floor closes her fingers upon the spoon, and returns her with it to the chair.* **Helen** *again throws the spoon on the floor.* **Annie** *lifts her out of the chair again; but in the struggle over the spoon* **Helen** *with* **Annie** *on her back sends her sliding over her head;* **Helen** *flees back to her chair and scrambles into it. When* **Annie** *comes after her she clutches it for dear life;* **Annie** *pries one hand loose, then the other, then the first again, then the other again, and then lifts* **Helen** *by the waist, chair and all, and shakes the chair loose.* **Helen** *wrestles to get free, but* **Annie** *pins her to the floor, closes her fingers upon the spoon, and lifts her kicking under one arm; with her other hand she gets the chair in place again, and plunks* **Helen** *back on it. When she releases her hand,* **Helen** *throws the spoon at her.*

Annie *now removes the plate of food.* **Helen** *grabbing finds it missing, and commences to bang with her fists on the table.* **Annie** *collects a fistful of spoons and descends with them and the plate on* **Helen;** *she lets her smell the plate, at which* **Helen** *ceases banging, and* **Annie** *puts the plate down and a spoon in* **Helen's** *hand.* **Helen** *throws it on the floor.* **Annie** *puts another spoon in her hand.* **Helen** *throws it on the floor.* **Annie** *puts another spoon in her hand.* **Helen** *throws it on the floor. When* **Annie** *comes to her last spoon she sits next to* **Helen,** *and gripping the spoon in* **Helen's** *hand compels her to take food in it up to her mouth.* **Helen** *sits with lips shut.* **Annie** *waits a solid moment, then lowers* **Helen's** *hand. She tries again;* **Helen's** *lips* *remain shut. Annie waits, lowers Helen's hand. She tries again; this time Helen suddenly opens her mouth and accepts the food. Annie lowers the spoon with a sigh of relief, and Helen spews the mouthful out at her face. Annie sits a moment with eyes closed, then takes the pitcher and dashes its water into Helen's face, who gasps astonished. Annie with Helen's hand takes up another spoonful, and shoves it into her open mouth. Helen swallows involuntarily, and while she is catching her breath Annie forces her palm open, throws four swift letters into it, then another four, and bows toward her with devastating pleasantness.)*

Annie: Good girl.

(Annie lifts Helen's hand to feel her face nodding; Helen grabs a fistful of her hair, and yanks. The pain brings Annie to her knees, and Helen pummels her; they roll under the table, and the lights commence to dim out on them.)

Scene from
    The Odd Couple by Neil Simon

From Act II, Scene 2

For 2 men

Characters: **Oscar Madison,** 43, a carefree sports writer for the New York Post.
             Felix Ungar, 44, his meticulous friend.

Setting: Oscar's apartment on Riverside Drive in New York City, about 8:00 P.M.
on a warm summer night.

Situation: Oscar, who has been divorced, offers to let his friend, Felix, only recently
separated from his wife, live with him in Oscar's apartment. They are extreme
opposites. Felix is meticulous, well-groomed, uptight. Oscar is carefree, a slob,
outgoing. Prior to this scene, Oscar has met in the elevator two British sisters,
one a widow, the other a divorcee, who live in the same apartment building.
To help Felix readjust to his new life, Oscar has invited the two sisters to dine
with them, and Felix has volunteered to cook the dinner. This will be Felix's
first venture with the opposite sex since his separation.

Script Notations

Oscar: (*Calls out in a playful mood*) I'm home, dear! (*He goes into his bedroom, taking off his shirt, and comes skipping out shaving with a cordless razor, with a clean shirt and a tie over his arm. He is joyfully singing as he admires the table*) Beautiful! Just beautiful! (*He sniffs, obviously catching the aroma from the kitchen*) Oh, yeah. Something wonderful is going on in that kitchen. (*He rubs his hands gleefully*) No, sir. There's no doubt about it. I'm the luckiest man on earth. (*He puts the razor into his pocket and begins to put on the shirt.* **Felix** *enters slowly from the kitchen. He's wearing a small dish towel as an apron. He has a ladle in one hand. He looks silently and glumly at* **Oscar**, *crosses to the armchair and sits*) I got the wine. (*He takes the bottle out of the bag and puts it on the table*) Batard Montrachet. Six and a quarter. You don't mind, do you, pussycat? We'll walk to work this week. (**Felix** *sits glumly and silently*) Hey, no kidding, Felix, you did a great job. One little suggestion? Let's come down a little with the lights (*He switches off the wall brackets*)—and up very softly with the music. (*He crosses to the stereo set in the bookcase and picks up some record albums*) What do you think goes better with London broil, Mancini or Sinatra? (**Felix** *just stares ahead*) Felix? What's the matter? (*He puts the albums down*) Something's wrong. I can tell by your conversation. (*He goes into the bathroom, gets a bottle of after-shave lotion and comes out putting it on*) All right, Felix, what is it?

Felix: (*Without looking at him*) What is it? Let's start with what time do you think it is?

Oscar: What time? I don't know. Seven thirty?

Felix: Seven thirty? Try eight o'clock.

Oscar: (*Puts the lotion down on the small table*) All right, so it's eight o'clock. So?
(*He begins to fix his tie*)

Felix: So? You said you'd be home at seven.

Oscar: Is that what I said?

Felix: (*Nods*) That's what you said. "I will be home at seven" is what you said.

Oscar: Okay, I said I'd be home at seven. And it's eight. So what's the problem?

Felix: If you knew you were going to be late, why didn't you call me?

Oscar: (*Pauses while making the knot in his tie*) I couldn't call you. I was busy.

Felix: Too busy to pick up a phone? Where were you?

Oscar: I was in the office, working.

Felix: Working? Ha!

Oscar: Yes. Working!

Felix: I called your office at seven o'clock. You were gone.

Oscar: (*Tucking in his shirt*) It took me an hour to get home. I couldn't get a cab.

Felix: Since when do they have cabs in Hannigan's Bar?

Oscar: Wait a minute. I want to get this down on a tape recorder, because no one'll believe me. You mean now I have to call you if I'm coming home late for dinner?

Felix: (*Crosses to* **Oscar**) Not *any* dinner. Just the ones I've been slaving over since two o'clock this afternoon—to help save *you* money to pay your wife's alimony.

Oscar: (*Controlling himself*) Felix, this is no time to have a domestic quarrel. We have two girls coming down any minute.

Felix: You mean you told them to be here at eight o'clock?

Oscar: (*Takes his jacket and crosses to the couch, then sits and takes some dip from the coffee table*) I don't remember what I said. Seven thirty, eight o'clock. What difference does it make?

Felix: (*Follows* **Oscar**) I'll tell you what difference. You told me they were coming at seven thirty. You were going to be here at seven to help me with the hors d'oeuvres. At seven thirty they arrive and we have cocktails. At eight o'clock we have dinner. It is now eight o'clock. *My London broil is finished!* If we don't eat now the whole damned thing'll be *dried out!*

Oscar: Oh, God, help me.

Felix: Never mind helping *you*. Tell Him to save the meat. Because we got nine dollars and thirty-four cents worth drying up in there right now.

Oscar: Can't you keep it warm?

Felix: (*Pacing*) What do you think I am, the Magic Chef? I'm lucky I got it to come out at eight o'clock. What am I going to do?

Oscar: I don't know. Keep pouring gravy on it.

Felix: What gravy?

Oscar: Don't you have any gravy?

Felix: (*Storms over to* **Oscar**) Where the hell am I going to get gravy at eight o'clock?

Oscar: (*Getting up*) I thought it comes when you cook the meat.

Felix: (*Follows him*) When you *cook the meat?* You don't know the first thing you're talking about. You have to make gravy. It doesn't come!

Oscar: You asked my advice, I'm giving it to you. (*He puts on his jacket*)

Felix: Advice? (*He waves the ladle in his face*) You didn't know where the kitchen was till I came here and showed you.

Oscar: You wanna talk to me, put down the spoon.

Felix: (*Exploding in rage, again waving the ladle in his face*) Spoon? You dumb ignoramus. It's a ladle. You don't even know it's a ladle.

Oscar: All right, Felix, get a hold of yourself.

Felix: (*Pulls himself together and sits on the love seat*) You think it's so easy? Go on. The kitchen's all yours. Go make a London broil for four people who come a half hour late.

Oscar: (*To no one in particular*) Listen to me. I'm arguing with him over gravy.

(*The bell rings*)

Felix: (*Jumps up*) Well, they're here. Our dinner guests. I'll get a saw and cut the meat.

(*He starts for the kitchen*)

Oscar: (*Stopping him*) Stay where you are!

Felix: I'm not taking the blame for this dinner.

Oscar: Who's blaming you? Who even *cares* about the dinner?

Felix: (*Moves to* **Oscar**) I care. I take *pride* in what I do. And you're going to explain to them exactly what happened.

Oscar: All right, you can take a Polaroid picture of me coming in at eight o'clock! Now take off that stupid apron because I'm opening the door.

(*He rips the towel off* **Felix** *and goes to the door*)

Felix: (*Takes his jacket from a dining chair and puts it on*) I just want to get one thing clear. This is the last time I ever cook for you. Because people like you don't even appreciate a decent meal. That's why they have TV dinners.

Oscar: You through?

Felix: I'm through!

Oscar: Then smile. (**Oscar** *smiles and opens the door.*)

Scene from
Of Mice and Men by John Steinbeck

From Act III, Scene 1

For 1 man, 1 woman

Characters: **Lennie.**
Curley's wife.

Setting: One end of a great barn in an agricultural valley in Southern California. Midafternoon on Sunday. The 1930s.

Situation: Lennie, an enormously powerful but simple-minded itinerant farm worker, and George, his friend, have taken jobs on a farm in the Salinas Valley in California. Lennie's great strength has gotten him into trouble in the past, and George has had to take care of his friend much as one takes care of a child. Both Lennie and George have been planning to save enough money to buy a small farm. It is Lennie's dream that he will be permitted to take care of the rabbits.

The owner's son Curley is a bully, who picks on the men and jealously guards his slatternly wife. Once Curley began to beat Lennie, but the powerful giant, instead of striking back, seized Curley's hand and crushed it. Curley's wife, lonely and bored on the farm, is attracted to Lennie. In this scene she comes upon him in the barn, where he has been petting a newborn puppy that had been given to him. Lennie is so strong that he has accidentally killed the puppy. Lennie is afraid of the woman's advances, knowing that George will be angry with him if he gets into trouble again.

Script Notations

[**Lennie,** *alone, uncovers the pup. Lies down in the hay and sinks deep in it. Puts the pup on his arm and strokes it.* **Curley's wife** *enters secretly. A little mound of hay conceals* **Lennie** *from her. In her hand she carries a small suitcase, very cheap. She crosses the barn and buries the case in the hay. Stands up and looks to see whether it can be seen.* **Lennie** *watching her quietly tries to cover the pup with hay. She sees the movement.*]

Curley's wife: What—what you doin' here?

Lennie: (*sullenly*) Jus' settin' here.

Curley's wife: You seen what I done.

Lennie: Yeah! you brang a valise.

Curley's wife: (*comes near to him*) You won't tell—will you?

Lennie: (*still sullen*) I ain't gonna have nothing to do with you. George tole me. I ain't to talk to you or nothing. (*covers the pup a little more*)

Curley's wife: George give you all your orders?

Lennie: Not talk nor nothing.

Curley's wife: You won't tell about that suitcase? I ain't gonna stay here no more. Tonight I'm gonna get out. Come here an' get my stuff an' get out. I ain't gonna be run over no more. I'm gonna go in pitchers. (*sees* **Lennie's** *hand stroking the pup under the hay*) What you got there?

Lennie: Nuthing. I ain't gonna talk to you. George says I ain't.

Curley's wife: Listen. The guys got a horseshoe tenement out there. It's on'y four o'clock. Them guys ain't gonna leave that tenement. They got money bet. You don't need to be scared to talk to me.

Lennie: (*weakening a little*) I ain't supposed to.

Curley's wife: (*watching his buried hand*) What you got under there?

Lennie: (*His woe comes back to him.*) Jus' my pup. Jus' my little ol' pup. (*sweeps the hay aside*)

Curley's wife: Why! He's dead.

Lennie: (*explaining sadly*) He was so little. I was jus' playin' with him—an' he made like he's gonna bite me—an' I made like I'm gonna smack him—an'—I done it. An' then he was dead.

Curley's wife: (*consoling*) Don't you worry none. He was just a mutt. The whole country is full of mutts.

Lennie: It ain't that so much. George gonna be mad. Maybe he won't let me—what he said I could tend.

Curley's wife: (*sits down in the hay beside him, speaks soothingly*) Don't you worry. Them guys got money bet on that horseshoe tenement. They ain't gonna leave it. And tomorra I'll be gone. I ain't gonna let them run over me.

[*In the following scene it is apparent that neither is listening to the other and yet as it goes on, as a happy tone increases, it can be seen that they are growing closer together.*]

Lennie: We gonna have a little place an' raspberry bushes.

Curley's wife: I ain't meant to live like this. I come from Salinas. Well, a show come through an' I talked to a guy that was in it. He says I could go with the show. My ol' lady wouldn't let me, 'cause I was on'y fifteen. I wouldn't be no place like this if I had went with that show, you bet.

Lennie: Gonna take a sack an' fill it up with alfalfa an'—

Curley's wife: (*hurrying on*) 'Nother time I met a guy an' he was in pitchers. Went out to the Riverside Dance Palace with him. He said he was gonna put me in pitchers. Says I was a natural. Soon's he got back to Hollywood he was gonna write me about it. (*looks impressively at* **Lennie**) I never got that letter. I think my ol' lady stole it. Well, I wasn't gonna stay no place where they stole your letters. So I married Curley. Met *him* out to the Riverside Dance Palace too.

Lennie: I hope George ain't gonna be mad about this pup.

Curley's wife: I ain't tol' this to nobody before. Maybe I oughtn' to. I don't like Curley. He ain't a nice fella. I might a stayed with him but last night him an' his ol' man both lit into me. I don't have to stay here. (*moves closer and speaks confidentially*) Don't tell nobody till I get clear away. I'll go in the night an' thumb a ride to Hollywood.

Lennie: We gonna get out a here purty soon. This ain't no nice place.

Curley's wife: (*ecstatically*) Gonna get in the movies an' have nice clothes—all them nice clothes like they wear. An' I'll set in them big hotels and they'll take pitchers of me. When they have them openings I'll go an' talk in the radio . . . an' it won't cost me nothing 'cause I'm in the pitcher. (*puts her hand on* **Lennie's** *arm for a moment*) All them nice clothes like they wear . . . because this guy says I'm a natural.

Lennie: We gonna go way . . . far away from here.

Curley's wife: 'Course, when I run away from Curley, my ol' lady won't never speak to me no more. She'll think I ain't decent. That's what she'll say. (*defiantly*) Well, we really ain't decent, no matter how much my ol' lady tries to hide it. My ol' man was a drunk. They put him away. There! Now I told.

Lennie: George an' me was to the Sacramento Fair. One time I fell in the river an' George pulled me out an' saved me, an' then we went to the Fair. They got all kinds of stuff there. We seen long-hair rabbits.

Curley's wife: My ol' man was a signpainter when he worked. He used to get drunk an' paint crazy pitchers an' waste paint. One night when I was a little kid, him an' my ol' lady had an awful fight. They was always fightin'. In the middle of the night he come into my room, and he says, "I can't stand this no more. Let's you an' me go away." I guess he was drunk. (*Her voice takes on a curious wondering tenderness.*) I remember in the night— walkin' down the road, and the trees was black. I was pretty sleepy. He picked me up, an' he carried me on his back. He says, "We gonna live together. We gonna live together because you're my own little girl, an' not no stranger. No arguin' and fightin'," he says, "because you're my little daughter." (*Her voice becomes soft.*) He says, "Why you'll bake little cakes for me, and I'll paint pretty pitchers all over the wall." (*sadly*) In the morning they caught us . . . an' they put him away. (*pause*) I wish we'd a' went.

Lennie: Maybe if I took this here pup an' throwed him away George wouldn't never know.

Curley's wife: They locked him up for a drunk, and in a little while he died.

Lennie: Then maybe I could tend the rabbits without no trouble.

Curley's wife: Don't you think of nothing but rabbits? (*sound of a horseshoe on metal*) Somebody made a ringer.

Lennie: (*patiently*) We gonna have a house and a garden, an' a place for alfalfa. And I take a sack and get it full of alfalfa, and then I take it to the rabbits.

Curley's wife: What makes you so nuts about rabbits?

Lennie: (*moves closer to her*) I like to pet nice things. Once at a fair I seen some of them long-hair rabbits. And they was nice, you bet. (*despairingly*) I'd even pet mice, but not when I could get nothin' better.

Curley's wife: (*giggles*) I think you're nuts.

Lennie: (*earnestly*) No, I ain't. George says I ain't. I like to pet nice things with my fingers. Soft things.

Curley's wife: Well, who don't? Everybody likes that. I like to feel silk and velvet. You like to feel velvet?

Lennie: (*chuckling with pleasure*) You bet, by God. And I had some too. A lady give me some. And that lady was—my Aunt Clara. She give it right to me. . . . (*measuring with his hands*) 'Bout this big a piece. I wish I had that velvet right now. (*He frowns.*) I lost it. I ain't seen it for a long time.

Curley's wife: (*laughing*) You're nuts. But you're a kinda nice fella. Jus' like a big baby. A person can see kinda what you mean. When I'm doin' my hair sometimes I jus' set there and stroke it, because it's so soft. (*runs her fingers over the top of her head*) Some people got kinda coarse hair. You take Curley, his hair's just like wire. But mine is soft and fine. Here, feel. Right here. (*takes **Lennie's** hand*

and puts it on her head) Feel there and see how soft it is. (**Lennie's** *fingers fall to stroking her hair.*) Don't you muss it up.

Lennie: Oh, that's nice. (*strokes harder*) Oh, that's nice.

Curley's wife: Look out now, you'll muss it. (*angrily*) You stop it now, you'll mess it all up. (*She jerks her head sideways and* **Lennie's** *fingers close on her hair and hang on. In a panic*) Let go. (*She screams.*) You let go. (*She screams again. His other hand closes over her mouth and nose.*)

Lennie: (*begging*) Oh, please don't do that. George'll be mad. (*She struggles violently to be free. A soft screaming comes from under* **Lennie's** *hand. Crying with fright*) Oh, please don't do none of that. George gonna say I done a bad thing. (*He raises his hand from her mouth and a hoarse cry escapes. Angrily*) Now don't. I don't want you to yell. You gonna get me in trouble just like George says you will. Now don't you do that. (*She struggles more.*) Don't you go yellin'. (*He shakes her violently. Her neck snaps sideways and she lies still. Looks down at her and cautiously removes his hand from her mouth*) I don't wanta hurt you. But George will be mad if you yell. (*When she doesn't answer he bends closely over her. He lifts her arm and lets it drop. For a moment he seems bewildered.*) I done a bad thing. I done another bad thing. (*He paws up the hay until it partly covers her. The sound of the horseshoe game comes from the outside. And for the first time* **Lennie** *seems conscious of it. He crouches down and listens.*) Oh, I done a real bad thing. I shouldn't a did that. George will be mad. And . . . he said . . . and hide in the brush till he comes. That's what he said. (*He picks up the puppy from beside the girl.*) I'll throw him away. It's bad enough like it is.

[*He puts the pup under his coat, creeps to the barn wall and peers out between the cracks and then he creeps around to the end of the manger and disappears.*]

Scene from
   Street Scene by Elmer Rice

From Act I

For 1 man, 1 woman

Characters: **Samuel Kaplan,** 21, slender, with dark unruly hair and a sensitive, mobile face.
   Rose Moran, 20, a pretty girl, cheaply but rather tastefully dressed.

Setting: The exterior of a "walk-up" apartment house in a mean quarter of New York in the late 1920s.

Situation: In this stage portrayal of numerous types of people who are poor and seem to be trapped in a tenement environment, there are some optimistic, poetic moments. One of them is this scene, which directly follows a scene in which Sam has unsuccessfully attempted to defend Rose against a bully who tried to pick her up. (Rose's mother, referred to in the scene, has been having an affair with Steven Sankey, the milkman, and most of the neighbors are aware of it. During the scene an occupant, Mrs. Buchanan, screams during childbirth and Sam and Rose react.)

Script Notations

Rose (~~turning and going to him~~): It's all right, Sam. Never mind.

Sam (*sobbing*): I'll kill him! I'll kill him!

(*He throws himself on the stoop and, burying his head in his arms, sobs hysterically.* **Rose** *sits beside him and puts her arm about him.*)

Rose: It's all right, Sam. Everything's all right. Why should you pay any attention to a big tough like that? (**Sam** *does not answer.* **Rose** *caresses his hair and he grows calmer.*) He's nothing but a loafer, you know that. What do you care what he says?

Sam (*without raising his head*): I'm a coward.

Rose: Why no, you're not, Sam.

Sam: Yes, I am. I'm a coward.

Rose: Why, he's not worth your little finger, Sam. You wait and see. Ten years from now, he'll still be driving a taxi and you—why, you'll be so far above him, you won't even remember he's alive.

Sam: I'll never be anything.

Rose: Why, don't talk like that, Sam. A boy with your brains and ability. Graduating from college with honors and all that! Why, if I were half as smart as you, I'd be just so proud of myself!

Sam: What's the good of having brains, if nobody ever looks at you—if nobody knows you exist?

Rose (*gently*): I know you exist, Sam.

Sam: It wouldn't take much to make you forget me.

Rose: I'm not so sure about that. Why do you say that, Sam?

Sam: Because I know. It's different with you. You have beauty—people look at you—you have a place in the world—

Rose: I don't know. It's not always so easy, being a girl—I often wish I were a man. It seems to me that when you're a man, it's so much easier to sort of—be yourself, to kind of be the way you feel. But when you're a girl, it's different. It doesn't seem to matter what you are, or what you're thinking or feeling—all that men seem to care about is just the one thing. And when you're sort of trying to find out just where you're at, it makes it hard. Do you see what I mean? (*Hesitantly.*) Sam, there's something I want to ask you——

(*She stops.*)

Sam (*turning to her*): What is it, Rose?

Rose: I wouldn't dream of asking anybody but you. (*With a great effort.*) Sam, do you think it's true—what they're saying about my mother?

(**Sam** *averts his head, without answering.*)

Rose (*wretchedly*): I guess it is, isn't it?

Sam (*agitatedly*): They were talking here, before—I couldn't stand it any more! (*He clasps his head and, springing to his feet, goes to the right of the stoop.*) Oh, God, why do we go on living in this sewer?

Rose (*appealingly*): What can I do, Sam? (*Sam makes a helpless gesture.*) You see, my father means well enough, and all that, but he's always been sort of strict and—I don't know—sort of making you freeze up, when you really wanted to be nice and loving. That's the whole trouble, I guess; my mother never had anybody to really love her. She's sort of gay and happy-like—you know, she likes having a good time and all that. But my father is different. Only—the way things are now—everybody talking and making remarks, all the neighbors spying and whispering—it sort of makes me feel—— (*She shudders.*) I don't know——!

Sam (*coming over to her again*): I wish I could help you, Rose.

Rose: You do help me, Sam—just by being nice and sympathetic and talking things over with me. There's so few people you can really talk to, do you know what I mean? Sometimes, I get the feeling that I'm all alone in the world and that——

.   .   .

Rose (*springing to her feet*): Oh, just listen to her!

Sam: Oh, God!

Rose: The poor thing! She must be having terrible pains.

Sam: That's all there is in life—nothing but pain. From before we're born, until we die! Everywhere you look, oppression and cruelty! If it doesn't come from Nature, it comes from humanity—humanity trampling on itself and tearing at its own throat. The whole world is nothing but a blood-stained arena, filled with misery and suffering. It's too high a price to pay for life—life isn't worth it!

(*He seats himself despairingly on the stoop.*)

Rose (*putting her hand on his shoulder*): Oh, I don't know, Sam. I feel blue and discouraged sometimes, too. And I get a sort of feeling of, oh, what's the use. Like last night. I hardly slept all night, on account of the heat and on account of thinking about—well, all sorts of things. And this morning, when I got up, I felt so miserable. Well, all of a sudden, I decided I'd walk to the office. And when I got to the Park, everything looked so green and fresh, that I got a kind of feeling of, well, maybe it's not so bad, after all. And then, what do you think?—all of a sudden, I saw a big lilac-bush, with some flowers still on it. It made me think about the poem you said for me—remember?—the one about the lilacs.

Sam (*quoting*):

"When lilacs last in the dooryard bloom'd
And the great star early droop'd in the western sky
     in the night,
I mourn'd and yet shall mourn, with ever-returning
     Spring.''

(*He repeats the last line.*)

I mourn'd and yet shall mourn, with ever-returning
   Spring? Yes!
Rose: No, not that part. I mean the part about the
farmhouse. Say it for me, Sam. (*She sits at his feet.*)
Sam: "In the door-yard, fronting an old farm-
   house, near the white-washed palings,
Stands the lilac-bush, tall-growing, with heart-
   shaped leaves of rich green,
With many a pointed blossom, rising delicate, with
   the perfume strong I love,
With every leaf a miracle—and from this bush in
   the door-yard,
With delicate-color'd blossoms and heart-shaped
   leaves of rich green,
A sprig with its flower I break."
Rose (*eagerly*): Yes, that's it! That's just what I felt
like doing—breaking off a little bunch of the flowers. But then I thought, maybe a policeman or
somebody would see me, and then I'd get into trouble; so I didn't.

Scene from
  Uncle Vanya by Anton Chekhov

From Act II

For 2 women

Characters: **Yelena Andreyevna,** 27, young wife of a retired professor.
  Sofya Alexandrovna (Sonya), the professor's daughter by his first wife.

Setting: The dining room in the professor's house. A night in the late nineteenth century in Russia.

Situation: In this beautifully developed character study of people who seemingly are isolated on a Russian country estate, it is necessary to understand certain intricately developed relationships in order to approach the following scene. Yelena, a lovely young woman, is married to an elderly, ill professor but is strongly attracted to a doctor named Astrov. Her stepdaughter, Sonya, is very much in love with the same man. Also, to complicate matters, Uncle Vanya, Sonya's uncle, is passionately fond of Yelena. Immediately prior to this scene, Sonya has subtly attempted to explore Dr. Astrov's true feelings.

Script Notations

Sonya (*alone*): He has said nothing to me. . . . His soul and his heart are still shut away from me, but why do I feel so happy? (*Laughs with happiness.*) I said to him, you are refined, noble, you have such a soft voice. . . . Was it inappropriate? His voice trembles and caresses one . . . I still feel it vibrating in the air. And when I spoke to him of a younger sister, he did not understand. . . . (*Wringing her hands*) Oh, how awful it is that I am not beautiful! How awful it is! And I know I am not, I know it, I know it! . . . Last Sunday, as people were coming out of church, I heard them talking about me, and one woman said: "She is a sweet generous nature, but what a pity she is so plain. . . . Plain. . . ."

(*Enter* Yelena Andreyevna.)

Yelena (*opens the window*): The storm is over. What delicious air! (*a pause*) Where is the doctor?

Sonya: He is gone (*a pause*).

Yelena: Sophie!

Sonya: What is it?

Yelena: How long are you going to be sulky with me? We have done each other no harm. Why should we be enemies? Let us make it up. . . .

Sonya: I wanted to myself . . . (*embraces her*). Don't let us be cross any more.

Yelena: That's right. (*Both are agitated.*)

Sonya: Has father gone to bed?

Yelena: No, he is sitting in the drawing-room. . . . We don't speak to each other for weeks, and goodness knows why. . . . (*Seeing that the sideboard is open*) How is this?

Sonya: Mihail Lvovitch has been having some supper.

Yelena: And there is wine too. . . . Let us drink to our friendship.

Sonya: Yes, let us.

Yelena: Out of the same glass . . . (*fills it*). It's better so. So now we are friends?

Sonya: Friends. (*They drink and kiss each other.*) I have been wanting to make it up for ever so long, but somehow I felt ashamed . . . (*cries*).

Yelena: Why are you crying?

Sonya: It's nothing.

Yelena: Come, there, there . . . (*weeps*). I am a queer creature, I am crying too . . . (*a pause*). You are angry with me because you think I married your father from interested motives. . . . If that will make you believe me, I will swear it—I married him for love. I was attracted by him as a learned, celebrated man. It was not real love, it was all made up; but I fancied at the time that it was real. It's not my fault. And ever since our marriage you have been punishing me with your clever, suspicious eyes.

Sonya: Come, peace! peace! Let us forget.

Yelena: You mustn't look like that—it doesn't suit you. You must believe in everyone—there is no living if you don't (*a pause*).

Sonya: Tell me honestly, as a friend . . . are you happy?

Yelena: No.

Sonya: I knew that. One more question. Tell me frankly, wouldn't you have liked your husband to be young?

Yelena: What a child you are still! Of course I should! (*Laughs*) Well, ask something else, ask away.
. . .

Sonya: Do you like the doctor?

Yelena: Yes, very much.

Sonya (*laughs*): Do I look silly . . . yes? He has gone away, but I still hear his voice and his footsteps, and when I look at the dark window I can see his face. Do let me tell you. . . . But I can't speak so loud; I feel ashamed. Come into my room, we can talk there. You must think me silly? Own up. . . . Tell me something about him.

Yelena: What am I to tell you?

Sonya: He is clever. . . . He understands everything, he can do anything. . . . He doctors people, and plants forests too. . . .

Yelena: It is not a question of forests and medicine. . . . My dear, you must understand he has a spark of genius! And you know what that means? Boldness, freedom of mind, width of outlook. . . . He plants a tree and is already seeing what will follow from it in a thousand years, already he has visions of the happiness of humanity. Such people are rare, one must love them. . . . He drinks, he is sometimes a little coarse—but what does that matter? A talented man cannot keep spotless in Russia. Only think what sort of life that doctor has! Impassable mud on the roads, frosts, snowstorms, the immense distances, the coarse savage peasants, poverty and disease all around him—it is hard for one who is working and struggling day after day in such surroundings to keep spotless and sober till he is forty (*kisses her*). I wish you happiness with all my heart; you deserve it . . . (*gets up*). But I am a tiresome, secondary character. . . . In music and in my husband's house, and in all the love affairs, everywhere in fact, I have always played a secondary part. As a matter of fact, if you come to think of it, Sonya, I am very, very unhappy! (*Walks up and down the stage in agitation.*) There is no happiness in this world for me, none! Why do you laugh?

Sonya (*laughs, hiding her face*): I am so happy . . . so happy!

Yelena: I have a longing for music. I should like to play something.

Sonya: Do play something! (*Embraces her.*) I can't sleep. . . . Play something!

Yelena: In a minute. Your father is not asleep. Music irritates him when he is ill. Go and ask his leave. If he doesn't object, I'll play. Go!

Sonya: Very well (*goes out*).

MODERN NONREALISTIC SCENES

Scene from
  The Adding Machine by Elmer Rice

From Scene 2

For 1 man, 1 woman

Characters: **Mr. Zero,** a middle-aged clerk.
             Daisy, another clerk, also middle-aged.

Setting: An office in a department store. In the middle of the room are two tall desks and two tall stools.

Situation: This play, a major work of the 1920s, relates the story of the last days of Mr. Zero, a poor cypher caught in the wheels of an impersonal business machine. Filled with petty hates, jealousies, and fears, Mr. Zero continues to act in his job and personal relationships with detached and unimaginative regularity.

In this scene he is seated at his desk in the department store, putting figures in his ledger as he has done for twenty-five years. Opposite him is Daisy, a frustrated spinster. Each character rhythmically continues the endless process, as their personal thoughts become interwoven with their work routine.

Script Notations

Daisy: [*Reading aloud*] Three ninety-eight. Forty-two cents. A dollar fifty. A dollar fifty. A dollar twenty-five. Two dollars. Thirty-nine cents. Twenty-seven fifty.

Zero: [*Petulantly*] Speed it up a little, cancha?

Daisy: What's the rush? To-morrer's another day.

Zero: Aw, you make me sick.

Daisy: An' you make me sicker.

Zero: Go on. Go on. We're losin' time.

Daisy: Then quit bein' so bossy.

[*She reads*] Three dollars. Two sixty-nine. Eighty-one fifty. Forty dollars. Eight seventy-five. Who do you think you are, anyhow?

Zero: Never mind who I think I am. You tend to your work.

Daisy: Aw, don't be givin' me so many orders. Sixty cents. Twenty-four cents. Seventy-five cents. A dollar fifty. Two fifty. One fifty. One fifty. Two fifty. I don't have to take it from you and what's more I won't.

Zero: Aw, quit talkin'.

Daisy: I'll talk all I want. Three dollars. Fifty cents. Fifty cents. Seven dollars. Fifty cents. Two fifty. Three fifty. Fifty cents. One fifty. Fifty cents. [*She goes bending over the slips and transferring them from one pile to another.* **Zero** *bends over his desk, busily entering the figures.*]

Zero: [*Without looking up*] You make me sick. Always shootin' off your face about somethin'. Talk, talk, talk. Just like all the other women. Women make me sick.

Daisy: [*Busily fingering the slips*] Who do you think you are, anyhow? Bossin' me around. I don't have to take it from you, and what's more I won't. [*They both attend closely to their work, neither looking up.*]

Zero: Women make me sick. They're all alike. The judge gave her six months. I wonder what they do in the work-house. Peel potatoes. I'll bet she's sore at me. Maybe she'll try to kill me when she gets out. I better be careful. Hello, Girl Slays Betrayer. Jealous Wife Slays Rival. You can't tell what a woman's liable to do. I better be careful.

Daisy: I'm gettin' sick of it. Always pickin' on me about somethin'. Never a decent word out of you. Not even the time o' day.

Zero: I guess she wouldn't have the nerve at that. Maybe she don't even know it's me. They didn't even put my name in the paper, the big bums. Maybe she's been in the work-house before. A bum like that. She didn't have nothin' on that one time—nothin' but a shirt. [*He glances up quickly, then bends over again*] You make me sick. I'm sick of lookin' at your face.

Daisy: Gee, ain't that whistle ever goin' to blow?

You didn't used to be like that. Not even good mornin' or good evenin'. I ain't done nothin' to you. It's the young girls. Goin' around without corsets.

Zero: Your face is gettin' all yeller. Why don't you put some paint on it? She was puttin' on paint that time. On her cheeks and on her lips. And that blue stuff on her eyes. Just sittin' there in a shimmy puttin' on the paint. An' walkin' around the room with her legs all bare.

Daisy: I wish I was dead.

Zero: I was a goddam fool to let the wife get on to me. She oughta get six months at that. The dirty bum. Livin' in a house with respectable people. She'd be livin' there yet, if the wife hadn't o' got on to me. Damn her!

Daisy: I wish I was dead.

Zero: Maybe another one'll move in. Gee, that would be great. But the wife's got her eye on me now.

Daisy: I'm scared to do it, though.

Zero: You oughta move into that room. It's cheaper than where you're livin' now. I better tell you about it. I don't mean to be always pickin' on you.

Daisy: Gas. The smell of it makes me sick.

[**Zero** *looks up and clears his throat.*]

Daisy: [*Looking up, startled*] Whadja say?

Zero: I didn't say nothin'.

Daisy: I thought you did.

Zero: You thought wrong.

[*They bend over their work again.*]

Daisy: A dollar sixty. A dollar fifty. Two ninety. One sixty-two.

Zero: Why the hell should I tell you? Fat chance of you forgettin' to pull down the shade!

Daisy: If I asked for carbolic they might get on to me.

Zero: Your hair's gettin' gray. You don't wear them shirt waists any more with the low collars. When you'd bend down to pick somethin' up——

Daisy: I wish I knew what to ask for. Girl Takes Mercury After All-Night Party. Woman In Ten-Story Death Leap.

Zero: I wonder where'll she go when she gets out. Gee, I'd like to make a date with her. Why didn't I go over there the night my wife went to Brooklyn? She never woulda found out.

Daisy: I seen Pauline Frederick do it once. Where could I get a pistol though?

Zero: I guess I didn't have the nerve.

Daisy: I'll bet you'd be sorry then that you been so mean to me. How do I know, though? Maybe you wouldn't.

Zero: Nerve! I got as much nerve as anybody. I'm on the level, that's all. I'm a married man and I'm on the level.

Daisy: Anyhow, why ain't I got a right to live? I'm

as good as anybody else. I'm too refined, I guess. That's the whole trouble.

Zero: The time the wife had pneumonia I thought she was goin' to pass out. But she didn't. The doctor's bill was eighty-seven dollars. [*Looking up*] Hey, wait a minute! Didn't you say eighty-seven dollars?

Daisy: [*Looking up*] What?

Zero: Was the last you said eighty-seven dollars?

Daisy: [*Consulting the slip*] Forty-two fifty.

Zero: Well, I made a mistake. Wait a minute. [*He busies himself with an eraser*] All right. Shoot.

Daisy: Six dollars. Three fifteen. Two twenty-five. Sixty-five cents. A dollar twenty. You talk to me as if I was dirt.

Zero: I wonder if I could kill the wife without anybody findin' out. In bed some night. With a pillow.

Daisy: I used to think you was stuck on me.

Zero: I'd get found out, though. They always have ways.

Daisy: We used to be so nice and friendly together when I first came here. You used to talk to me then.

Zero: Maybe she'll die soon. I noticed she was coughin' this mornin'.

Daisy: You used to tell me all kinds o' things. You were goin' to show them all. Just the same, you're still sittin' here.

Zero: Then I could do what I damn please. Oh, boy!

Daisy: Maybe it ain't all your fault neither. Maybe if you'd had the right kind o' wife—somebody with a lot of common-sense, somebody refined—me!

Zero: At that, I guess I'd get tired of bummin' around. A feller wants some place to hang his hat.

Daisy: I wish she would die.

Zero: And when you start goin' with women you're liable to get into trouble. And lose your job maybe.

Daisy: Maybe you'd marry me.

Zero: Gee, I wish I'd gone over there that night.

Daisy: Then I could quit workin'.

Zero: Lots o' women would be glad to get me.

Daisy: You could look a long time before you'd find a sensible, refined girl like me.

Zero: Yes, sir, they could look a long time before they'd find a steady meal-ticket like me.

Daisy: I guess I'd be too old to have any kids. They say it ain't safe after thirty-five.

Zero: Maybe I'd marry you. You might be all right, at that.

Daisy: I wonder—if you don't want kids— whether—if there's any way——

Zero: [*Looking up*] Hey! Hey! Can't you slow up? What do you think I am—a machine?

Daisy: [*Looking up*] Say, what do you want, anyhow? First it's too slow an' then it's too fast. I guess you don't know what you want.

Zero: Well, never mind about that. Just you slow up.

Daisy: I'm getting' sick o' this. I'm goin' to ask to be transferred.

Zero: Go ahead. You can't make me mad.

Daisy: Aw, keep quiet. [*She reads*] Two forty-five. A dollar twenty. A dollar fifty. Ninety cents. Sixty-three cents.

Zero: Marry you! I guess not! You'd be as bad as the one I got.

Daisy: You wouldn't care if I did ask. I got a good mind to ask.

Zero: I was a fool to get married.

Daisy: Then I'd never see you at all.

Zero: What chance has a guy got with a woman tied around his neck?

Daisy: That time at the store picnic—the year your wife couldn't come—you were nice to me then.

Zero: Twenty-five years holdin' down the same job!

Daisy: We were together all day—just sittin' around under the trees.

Zero: I wonder if the boss remembers about it bein' twenty-five years.

Daisy: And comin' home that night—you sat next to me in the big delivery wagon.

Zero: I got a hunch there's a big raise comin' to me.

Daisy: I wonder what it feels like to be really kissed. Men—dirty pigs! They want the bold ones.

Zero: If he don't come across I'm goin' right up to the front office and tell him where he gets off.

Daisy: I wish I was dead.

Scene from
   Anne of a Thousand Days by Maxwell Anderson

From Act I, Scene 3

For 1 man, 1 woman

Characters: **Henry VIII,** King of England.
   Anne Boleyn, a young girl, later Henry's mistress and wife.

Setting: Exterior of Hever Castle, England, during Tudor times (sixteenth century).

Situation: As Anne Boleyn, wife of Henry VIII, awaits execution in the tower, both she and Henry think back to their early relationship, when she was his mistress, and to the brief period when she was his wife (the thousand days) when she gave birth to Elizabeth (who would later become Queen of England).

   In this sequence we see Henry and Anne at the beginning of their relationship. Henry has been making passionate advances to Anne, who has coolly repulsed them, suggesting that she cannot kiss him because she has been drinking medicine for a cold and offering similar lame excuses. Henry is not to be put off, however. After dismissing Anne's family and Cardinal Wolsey, he is finally alone with her.

Script Notations

Henry: You would never credit how fast my heart beats, nor how hard it is to draw breath. A king is not fortunate in these matters, Nan. I come to you as frightened as a 'prentice who takes his first nosegay to a wench—but whether you like me or not— whether any woman likes me or not—I shall never know. I shall never be sure I have the truth—because I am the King, and love is paid to me like taxes.—Do me this favor, Nan. Look on me not as a monarch who commands and may demand, but as the doubting, hoping, tremulous man I am— wishing to be loved for myself.

Anne: If you were a common man, doubtful of yourself, and tremulous, would you have sent an ambassador to warn me and make sure of me?

Henry: Did I send an ambassador?

Anne: Wolsey speaks for you, I believe.

Henry: Has he spoken clumsily?

Anne: No, very deftly. He made it plain that what the King wanted he would have.

Henry: Then he was clumsy. I swear to you, Nan, only this very cruel thing has happened to me: I have fallen in love. I tried to argue myself out of it, but seeing you day by day here, and trying not to see you, not to think about you, I have tangled myself deeper day by day, till now I can't keep it to myself. I must tell you. And ask your pity.—The truth is I dared not speak to you first myself. I was afraid.

Anne: You were afraid?

Henry: Yes.

Anne: Of what?

Henry: That you wouldn't care for me.

Anne: Then perhaps you will understand the very cruel thing that has happened to me: I have fallen in love.—And not with you.

Henry: By God!

Anne: You were complaining a moment ago that such remarks were not made to kings.

Henry: By God, I got it full in the face that time!— Who is it? Northumberland?

Anne: Would I be wise to tell you?

Henry: Never mind. I know. I've been told but I didn't believe it. How far has it gone?

Anne: We mean to be married.

Henry: Yes?

Anne: But not as my sister's married. He would not be a complaisant husband—and I would not be an accessible wife.

Henry: All wives are accessible—any husband can be placated.

Anne: Not all.

Henry: Yes, all! But I don't want you that way! Damn my soul and yours—I've heard tales of this. I've told lies about it, but I never thought to feel

the blade in my own vitals! I don't want you that
way! I want you to myself!

Anne: What can I do?

Henry: Give up this young wattle-and-daub—
give him up, I tell you,
and this kingdom shall turn around you, bishops
and
peers—
and whatever you've wanted, for anyone,
a knighthood,
an estate, a great income rolling in forever,
titles and places, you shall dispose of them
just as you please!

Anne: And be thrown out in the end
like a dirty rag.—I haven't seen Mary disposing
of revenues.

Henry: She asked for nothing. Look, Anne,
I'm here desperate. I can't bargain with you.
Ask for what you want.

Anne: To be free. To be free
to marry where I love.

(**Henry** *pauses.*)

Henry: No.

Anne: I too can say no!
I've seen you too close
and known you too long. I've heard what your
courtiers say,
and then I've seen what you are. You're spoiled
and vengeful,
and malicious and bloody. The poetry they praise
so much is sour, and the music you write's worse.
You dance like a hobbledehoy; you make love
as you eat—with a good deal of noise and no sub-
tlety.
It was my doubtful pleasure once to sleep in
Mary's room—
or to lie awake when you thought me asleep, and
observe
the royal porpoise at play—

Henry: This is not safe.

Anne: Yes, I've been told it's not safe for any of
us
to say no to our squire Harry. This put-on, kindly
hail-fellow-well-met of yours. My father's house
will be pulled down—and Northumberland's,
too, they tell me.
Well, pull them down. You are what I said.

Henry: I had no wish to come here. I came
because I must, and couldn't help myself.
Well—I'm well out of it. Let it end here tonight.
I thank you for your anger,
and for raising anger in me. There's no better way
to make an end.—Wolsey! Where's the fat sad-
dle-bags?

Anne: You will not—touch—Northumberland?

Henry: I'll try not.
Vengeful as I am, I'll try not.

(*He calls.*)
Wolsey!
(*He goes out* C. *arch.*)
Where's this vicar of hell?
(**Anne** *falls* C. *stage in a dead faint.*)

BLACKOUT

Scene from
  J.B. by Archibald MacLeish

From Scene Eleven

For 1 man, 1 woman

Characters: **J.B.,** a successful businessman.
               Sarah, his wife.

Setting: "A corner inside an enormous circus tent where a side show of some kind has been set up."

Situation: In this contemporary verse drama which in some ways parallels the Book of Job, J.B. and his wife face a series of modern catastrophes in their lives which should cause them to "curse God." Overseen throughout these unjustified events by two circus peddlers who assume the roles of God and the Devil, the couple become destitute and lost from one another, but J.B. still refuses to curse God. This, the final scene in the play, reunites J.B. and Sarah as they reaffirm their faith in God and determine to begin life anew.

Script Notations

A light comes from the canvas door. It increases as though day were beginning somewhere. **Nickles has gone.**

J.B.:   Who is it?

He crosses toward the door walking with his old ease. Stops.

                              Is there someone there?

There is no answer. He goes on. Reaches the door.

             Sarah!

The light increases. She is sitting on the sill, a broken twig in her hand.

Sarah: Look, Job: the forsythia,
            The first few leaves . . .

                              not leaves though . . .

                                   petals . .

J.B.: *roughly* Get up!

Sarah: Where shall I go?

J.B.:   Where you went!
            Wherever!

She does not answer.

More gently.   Where?

Sarah: Among the ashes.
            All there is now of the town is ashes.
            Mountains of ashes. Shattered glass.
            Glittering cliffs of glass all shattered
            Steeper than a cat could climb
            If there were cats still . . .
                              And the pigeons—
            They wheel and settle and whirl off
            Wheeling and almost settling . . .
                              And the silence—
            There is no sound there now—no
                 wind sound—
            Nothing that could sound the
                 wind—
            Could make it sing—no door—no
                 doorway . . .

            Only this.

She looks at the twig in her hands.

> Among the ashes!
> I found it growing in the ashes,
> Gold as though it did not know . . .

Her voice rises hysterically.

> I broke the branch to strip the leaves off—
> Petals again! . . .

She cradles it in her arms.

> But they so clung to it!

J.B.:   Curse God and die, you said to me.

Sarah: Yes.

She looks up at him for the first time, then down again.

> You wanted justice, didn't you?

> There isn't any. There's the world . . .

She begins to rock on the doorsill, the little branch in her arms.

> Cry for justice and the stars
> Will stare until your eyes sting. Weep,
> Enormous winds will thrash the water.
> Cry in sleep for your lost children,
> Snow will fall . . .
>   snow will fall . . .

J.B.:   Why did you leave me alone?

Sarah: I loved you.
> I couldn't help you any more.
> You wanted justice and there was none—
> Only love.

J.B.:   He does not love. He
> Is.

Sarah: But we do. That's the wonder.

J.B.:   Yet you left me.

Sarah: Yes, I left you.
> I thought there was a way away . . .

> Water under bridges opens
> Closing and the companion stars
> Still float there afterwards. I thought the
>   door
> Opened into closing water.

J.B.:   Sarah!

He drops on his knees beside her in the doorway, his arms around her.

Sarah: Oh, I never could!
I never could! Even the forsythia . . .

She is half laughing, half crying.

Even the forsythia beside the
Stair could stop me.

They cling to each other. Then she rises, drawing him up, peering at the darkness inside the door.

J.B.:   It's too dark to see.

She turns, pulls his head down between her hands and kisses him.

Sarah: Then blow on the coal of the heart,
        my darling.

J.B.:   The coal of the heart . . .

Sarah: It's all the light now.

Sarah *comes forward into the dim room,* **J.B.** *behind her. She lifts a fallen chair, sets it straight.*

Blow on the coal of the heart.
The candles in churches are out.
The lights have gone out in the sky.
Blow on the coal of the heart
And we'll see by and by . . .

J.B. *has joined her, lifting and straightening the chairs.*

We'll see where we are
The wit won't burn and the wet soul
        smoulders.
Blow on the coal of the heart and
        we'll know . . .
We'll know . . .

The light increases, plain white daylight from the door, as they work.

CURTAIN

Scene from
   The Lesson by Eugene Ionesco, translated by Donald M. Allen

For 1 man, 1 woman

Characters: **The Professor,** 50 to 60.
                The Young Pupil, 18, a girl.

Setting: The office of the old professor, which also serves as a dining room.

Situation: In this cyclical play, thirty-nine other young pupils have preceded the present one, and each has been destroyed by the professor. This scene presents the initial stages of ''the lesson'' as given by the professor. At this point, the student is ''lively, gay, dynamic, a fresh smile on her lips,'' while the professor is ''very timid, very proper, very much the teacher.'' During the course of the play, the pupil becomes ''progressively sad and morose and aphasic,'' while the professor becomes ''more and more sure of himself, more and more nervous, aggressive, dominating, until he is able to do as he pleases with the Pupil.'' Obviously, one of the major ideas dealt with in the play is the difficulty of communication.

Script Notations

Professor: You know how to count? How far can you count up to?

Pupil: I can count to . . . to infinity.

Professor: That's not possible, miss.

Pupil: Well then, let's say to sixteen.

Professor: That is enough. One must know one's limits. Count then, if you will, please.

Pupil: One . . . two . . . and after two, comes three . . . then four . . .

Professor: Stop there, miss. Which number is larger? Three or four?

Pupil: Uh . . . three or four? Which is the larger? The larger of three or four? In what sense larger?

Professor: Some numbers are smaller and others are larger. In the larger numbers there are more units than in the small . . .

Pupil: Than in the small numbers?

Professor: Unless the small ones have smaller units. If they are very small, then there might be more units in the small numbers than in the large . . . if it is a question of other units . . .

Pupil: In that case, the small numbers can be larger than the large numbers?

Professor: Let's not go into that. That would take us much too far. You must realize simply that more than numbers are involved here . . . there are also magnitudes, totals, there are groups, there are heaps, heaps of such things as plums, trucks, geese, prune pits, etc. To facilitate our work, let's merely suppose that we have only equal numbers, then the bigger numbers will be those that have the most units.

Pupil: The one that has the most is the biggest? Ah, I understand, Professor, you are identifying quality with quantity.

Professor: That is too theoretical, miss, too theoretical. You needn't concern yourself with that. Let us take an example and reason from a definite case. Let's leave the general conclusions for later. We have the number four and the number three, and each has always the same number of units. Which number will be larger, the smaller or the larger?

Pupil: Excuse me, Professor . . . What do you mean by the larger number? Is it the one that is not so small as the other?

Professor: That's it, miss, perfect. You have understood me very well.

Pupil: Then, it is four.

Professor: What is four—larger or smaller than three?

Pupil: Smaller . . . no, larger.

Professor: Excellent answer. How many units are there between three and four? . . . Or between four and three, if you prefer?

Pupil: There aren't any units, Professor, between three and four. Four comes immediately after three; there is nothing at all between three and four!

Professor: I haven't made myself very well understood. No doubt, it is my fault. I've not been sufficiently clear.

Pupil: No, Professor, it's my fault.

Professor: Look here. Here are three matches. And here is another one, that makes four. Now watch carefully—we have four matches. I take one away, now how many are left?

[*We don't see the matches, nor any of the objects that are mentioned. The* **Professor** *gets up from the table, writes on the imaginary blackboard with an imaginary piece of chalk, etc.*]

Pupil: Five. If three and one make four, four and one make five.

Professor: That's not it. That's not it at all. You always have a tendency to add. But one must be able to subtract too. It's not enough to integrate, you must also disintegrate. That's the way life is. That's philosophy. That's science. That's progress, civilization.

Pupil: Yes, Professor.

Professor: Let's return to our matches. I have four of them. You see, there are really four. I take one away, and there remain only . . .

Pupil: I don't know, Professor.

Professor: Come now, think. It's not easy, I admit. Nevertheless, you've had enough training to make the intellectual effort required to arrive at an understanding. So?

Pupil: I can't get it, Professor. I don't know, Professor.

Professor: Let us take a simpler example. If you had two noses, and I pulled one of them off . . . how many would you have left?

Pupil: None.

Professor: What do you mean, none?

Pupil: Yes, it's because you haven't pulled off any, that's why I have one now. If you had pulled it off, I wouldn't have it anymore.

Professor: You've not understood my example. Suppose that you have only one ear.

Pupil: Yes, and then?

Professor: If I gave you another one, how many would you have then?

Pupil: Two.

Professor: Good. And if I gave you still another ear. How many would you have then?

Pupil: Three ears.

Professor: Now, I take one away . . . and there remain . . . how many ears?

Pupil: Two.

Professor: Good. I take away still another one, how many do you have left?

Pupil: Two.

Professor: No. You have two, I take one away, I eat one up, then how many do you have left?
Pupil: Two.
Professor: I eat one of them . . . one.
Pupil: Two.
Professor: One.
Pupil: Two.
Professor: One!
Pupil: Two!
Professor: One!!!
Pupil: Two!!!
Professor: One!!!
Pupil: Two!!!
Professor: One!!!
Pupil: Two!!!
Professor: No. No. That's not right. The example is not . . . it's not convincing. Listen to me.
Pupil: Yes, Professor.
Professor: You've got . . . you've got . . . you've got . . .
Pupil: Ten fingers!
Professor: If you wish. Perfect. Good. You have then ten fingers.
Pupil: Yes, Professor.
Professor: How many would you have if you had only five of them?
Pupil: Ten, Professor.
Professor: That's not right!
Pupil: But it is, Professor.
Professor: I tell you it's not!
Pupil: You just told me that I had ten . . .
Professor: I also said, immediately afterwards, that you had five!
Pupil: I don't have five, I've got ten!
Professor: Let's try another approach . . . for purposes of subtraction let's limit ourselves to the numbers from one to five . . . Wait now, miss, you'll soon see. I'm going to make you understand.
[*The* **Professor** *begins to write on the imaginary blackboard. He moves it closer to the* **Pupil**, *who turns around in order to see it.*]
Professor: Look here, miss . . . [*He pretends to draw a stick on the blackboard and the number 1 below the stick; then two sticks and the number 2 below, then three sticks and the number 3 below, then four sticks with the number four below.*] You see . . .
Pupil: Yes, Professor.
Professor: These are sticks, miss, sticks. This is one stick, these are two sticks, and three sticks, then four sticks, then five sticks. One stick, two sticks, three sticks, four and five sticks, these are numbers. When we count the sticks, each stick is a unit, miss . . . What have I just said?
Pupil: "A unit, miss! What have I just said?"
Professor: Or a figure! Or a number! One, two, three, four, five, these are the elements of numeration, miss.

Pupil: [*hesitant*] Yes, Professor. The elements, figures, which are sticks, units and numbers . . .

Professor: At the same time . . . that's to say, in short—the whole of arithmetic is there.

Pupil: Yes, Professor. Good, Professor. Thanks, Professor.

Professor: Now, count, if you will please, using these elements . . . add and subtract . . .

Pupil: [*as though trying to impress them on her memory*] Sticks are really figures and numbers are units?

Professor: Hmm . . . so to speak. And then?

Pupil: One could subtract two units from three units, but can one subtract two twos from three threes? And two figures from four numbers? And three numbers from one unit?

Professor: No, miss.

Pupil: Why, Professor?

Professor: Because, miss.

Pupil: Because why, Professor? Since one is the same as the other?

Professor: That's the way it is, miss. It can't be explained. This is only comprehensible through internal mathematical reasoning. Either you have it or you don't.

Pupil: So much the worse for me.

Scene from
   The Madwoman of Chaillot by Jean Giraudoux, adapted by Maurice Valency

From Act II

For 3 women

Characters: **Countess Aurelia,** the Madwoman of Chaillot.
   Mme. Constance, the Madwoman of Passy.
   Mme. Gabrielle, the Madwoman of St. Sulpice.

Setting: The Countess's cellar—21 Rue de Chaillot, Paris. The time is next year, but the characters' costuming is of the 1880s.

Situation: At a cafe in Paris some entrepreneurs make plans for obtaining oil by tearing up parts of Paris. The Madwoman of Chaillot, who very well may be more sane than most people, hears of the plot and proceeds to make her own plans for getting rid of the greedy capitalists in the world. In this scene set in her quarters, she has a tea party and attempts to explain the situation to two of her guests, other "mad" (?) women of Paris. (During the scene the brief appearance of Irma and related lines may be deleted.)

Script Notations

Constance: Aurelia! Here we are! Don't tell us they've found your boa?

Gabrielle: You don't mean Adolphe Bertaut has proposed at last! I knew he would.

Countess: How are you, Constance? (*She shouts.*) How are you, Gabrielle? Thank you both so much for coming.

Gabrielle: You needn't shout today, my dear. It's Wednesday. Wednesdays, I hear perfectly.

Constance: It's Thursday. (*To an imaginary dog who has stopped on landing* L.) Come along, Dickie. Come along. And stop barking. What a racket you're making! Come on, darling—we've come to see the longest boa and the handsomest man in Paris. Come on. (*Crossing to* R. *chair.*)

Countess: Constance, it's not a question of my boa today. Nor of Adolphe. It's a question of the future of the human race.

Constance: You think it has a future?

Countess: Don't make silly jokes. Sit down and listen to me. (**Constance** *and* **Gabrielle** *sit.*) We have got to make a decision today, which may alter the fate of the world.

Constance: Couldn't we do it tomorrow? I want to wash my slippers. Now, Dickie, please!

Countess: We haven't a moment to waste. Where is Josephine? Well, we'd better have our tea, and as soon as Josephine comes——

Gabrielle: Josephine is sitting on her bench by the palace waiting for President Wilson to come out. She says she's sorry, but she must see him today.

Constance: Dickie!

Countess: What a pity she had to see him today! She has a first-class brain. (*She gets tea things from a side table, pours tea, and serves cake and honey.*)

Constance: Well, go ahead, dear. We're listening. (*To* **Dickie.**) What is it, Dickie? You want to sit in Aunt Aurelia's lap? All right, darling. Go on. Jump, Dickie.

Countess: Constance, we love you dearly, as you know. And we love Dickie, too. But this is too serious a matter. So let's stop being childish for once.

Constance: And what does that mean, if you please?

Countess: It means Dickie. You know perfectly well that we love him and fuss over him just as if he were still alive. He's a sacred memory and we wouldn't hurt his feelings for the world. But please don't plump him in my lap when I'm settling the future of mankind. His basket is in the corner—he knows where it is, and he can just go and sit in it. (*Tea to* **Constance.**)

Constance: So you're against Dickie, too!

Countess: I'm not in the least bit against Dickie. I adore Dickie. But you know as well as I that Dickie is only a convention with us. It's a beautiful convention. But that doesn't mean it has to bark all the time. Besides, it's you that spoil him. The time you went to visit your niece and left him with me, we got along marvellously together. When you're not there, he's a model dog—he doesn't bark, he doesn't tear things, he doesn't even eat. But with you around him, one really can't pay attention to anything else. I'm not going to take Dickie in my lap at a solemn moment like this—no, not for anything in the world—and that's that!

Gabrielle: (*Very sweetly.*) Constance, dear, I don't mind taking him in my lap. He loves to sit in my lap, don't you, darling?

Constance: Kindly stop putting on angelic airs, Gabrielle. I know you very well. You're much too sweet to be sincere. There's plenty of times that I make believe that Dickie is here, when really I've left him home, and you cuddle and pet him just the same.

Gabrielle: I adore animals.

Constance: If you adore animals, you shouldn't pet them when they're not there. It's a form of hypocrisy.

Countess: Now, Constance, Gabrielle has as much right as you——

Constance: Gabrielle has no right to do what she does. Do you know what she does? She invites people to come to tea with us. People whom we know nothing about, people—who exist only in her imagination.

Countess: You think that's not an existence?

Gabrielle: I don't invite them at all. They come by themselves. What can I do?

Constance: You might introduce us.

Countess: If you think they're imaginary, what do you want to meet them for?

Constance: Of course they're imaginary. But who likes to have imaginary people staring at one? Especially strangers.

Gabrielle: Oh, they're really very nice——

Constance: Tell me one thing, Gabrielle.—Are they here now?

Countess: Am I to be allowed to speak? Or is this going to be the same as the argument about inoculating Josephine's cat, when we didn't get to the subject at all?

Constance: Never! Never! Never! I'll never give my consent to that. (*To* **Dickie**.) I'd never do a thing like that to you, Dickie sweet—— (*She begins to weep softly.*)

Countess: Good Heavens! Now she's in tears. What an impossible creature! Everything will be spoiled because of her. All right, all right, Constance, stop crying. I'll take him in my lap.

Constance: (*Rises.*) No. He won't go now.—Oh, how can you be so cruel? Don't you suppose I know about Dickie? Don't you think I'd rather have him here alive and woolly and frisking around the way he used to? You have your Adolphe. Gabrielle has her birds. But I have only Dickie. Do you think I'd be so silly about him if it wasn't that it's only by pretending that he's here all the time that I get him to come sometimes, really? Next time I won't bring him! (*Sits.*)

Countess: (*Rises, crossing* L.) Now let's not get excited over nothing at all! Come here, Dickie. Irma is going to take you for a walk. Irma! (*Rings bell.* **Irma** *appears.*)

Constance: (*Crossing* L. *to below* **Countess.**) No. He doesn't want to go. Besides, I didn't bring him today. So there! (*Back to her chair* R.)

Countess: Irma, make sure the door is locked. (**Irma** *nods and exits.*)

Constance: What do you mean? Why locked? Who's coming?

Countess: (*Crosses to iron chair* C.) You'd know by now, if you'd let me get a word in. A horrible thing has happened.—This very morning, exactly at noon——

Constance: Oh, how exciting!

Countess: Be quiet!—this morning, exactly at noon, thanks to a young man, who drowned himself in the Seine—. Oh yes, while I think of it—do you know a mazurka called *La Belle Polonaise?*

Constance: Yes, Aurelia.

Countess: Could you sing it now, this very minute?

Constance: Yes, Aurelia.

Countess: All of it?

Constance: Yes, Aurelia. But who's interrupting now, Aurelia?

Countess: You're right. Well, this morning exactly at noon, I discovered a terrible plot. There is a group of men who want to destroy the whole city.

Constance: Is that all?

Gabrielle: But I don't understand, Aurelia. Why should men want to destroy the city? It was they themselves who put it up.

Countess: There are people in the world who want to destroy everything. They have the fever of destruction. Even when they pretend that they're building, it's only in order to destroy. When they put up a new building, they quietly knock down two old ones. They build cities in order to destroy the countryside.—They destroy space with telephones, and time with airplanes. Humanity is now dedicated to a task of universal demolition! I speak, of course, primarily of the male sex——

Gabrielle: (*Shocked.*) Oh——!

Constance: Aurelia! Must you talk sex in front of Gabrielle?

Countess: After all, there are two sexes.

Constance: Gabrielle is a virgin!

Countess: Oh, she can't be that innocent. She keeps canaries.

Scene from
Mary of Scotland by Maxwell Anderson

From Act I, Scene 3

For 1 man, 1 woman

Characters: **Mary Stuart,** Queen of Scotland.
Lord Bothwell, a Scottish noble.

Setting: A great hall in Mary Stuart's apartment at Holyrood House, Edinburgh.
The mid-sixteenth century.

Situation: Anderson's modern verse play tells the story of the Catholic Queen Mary
Stuart, who was finally killed by Elizabeth I of England because of the danger
she posed as a claimant to the English throne.

Mary has returned to Scotland after the death of her husband, Francis
II of France. Because many Catholics consider Mary to be the rightful Queen
of England, Elizabeth has begun plotting against her. Elizabeth does not wish
Mary to marry the forceful and quick-witted Bothwell, for fear of the popular
support she might be able to raise. Although Mary has strong feelings for
Bothwell, she has become the dupe of Elizabeth and her counselors and does
not realize that a liaison with Bothwell is, in fact, her best political choice.
Before this scene begins she has decided to marry Lord Darnley.

Script Notations

Mary: My Lord, I have heard from England.

Bothwell: (L. *of throne*) Mary, my queen, what you heard

I could have guessed. She's your demon. She bodes you ill.

Mary: I believe it now.

Bothwell: And moreover, between the two,

This cormorant brother of yours, and that English harpy,

They'll have the heart out of you, and share it. Trust

Not one word they say to you, trust not even the anger

Their words rouse in you. They calculate effects.

Mary: My anger?

Where is Lord Morton?

Bothwell: Lord Morton is not well.

(*He is very serious*)

A sudden indisposition.

Mary: You've fought with him!

Bothwell: A mere puncture. What men think

I cannot punish, nor what they say elsewhere, but when

I hear them, by Christ, they'll learn manners.

Mary: I forbade it.

Bothwell: Forbade it? My dear, not God nor the angels

Forbid me when I'm angry.

Mary: I say I forbade it.

It's I who's responsible for my kingdom—not you—

You were bound to keep the peace!

Bothwell: (*A step up on throne platform*) When my lady's slandered?

I'll teach them to hold their peace where you're concerned

Or find their sweet peace in heaven.

Mary: Would God I'd been born

Deep somewhere in the Highlands, and there met you—

A maid in your path, and you but a Highland bowman

Who needed me.

Bothwell: Why, if you love me, Marie,

You're my maid and I your soldier.

Mary: (*Rising and crossing* L.) And it won't be.

Bothwell: Aye, it will be.

Mary: (*Walking up and down* L.) For, hear me, my Lord of Bothwell.

I too have a will—a will as strong as your own,

And enemies of my own, and my long revenges

To carry through. I will have my way in time

Though it burn my heart out and yours. The gods set us tasks,

My Lord, what we must do.

Bothwell: (R. *of* **Mary**) Let me understand you.
   The gods, supposing there are such, have thrown
      us together
   Somewhat, of late.
Mary: Look, Bothwell. I am a sovereign,
   And you obey no one. Were I married to you I'd
      be
   Your woman to sleep with. You'd be king here
      in Edinburgh,
   And I have no mind to your ruling.
Bothwell: (*Taking a step toward* **Mary**) They'll beat
   you alone.
   Together we could cope them. And you're mine,
   You're mine only, as I'm yours.
Mary: Love you I may—
   Love you I have—but not now, and no more. It's
      for me
   To rule, not you. I'll deliver up no land
   To such a hot-head. If you'd been born to the
      blood
   I'd say, aye, take it, the heavens had a meaning
      in this,
   But the royal blood's in me.—It's to me they turn
   To keep the peace, patch up old quarrels, bring
      home
   Old exiles, make a truce to anarchy. Escape it I
      cannot.
   Delegate it I cannot. The blame's my own
   For whatever's done in my name.—I will have no
      master.
(**Bothwell** *is silent when she pauses.* **Mary** *crosses
to* C. **Bothwell** *goes up* L.)
   Nay, I am jealous of this my Stuart blood.
   Jealous of what it has meant in Scotland, jealous
   Of what it may mean. They've attacked that
      blood, and I'm angry.
   They'll meet more anger than they know.
Bothwell: And who
   Has angered you? Not I?
Mary: Elizabeth.
Bothwell: I thought so.
   She's afraid, if I'm half a prophet,
   That you'll marry me.
Mary: (*Crossing* R.) Her fears run the other way.
   She's afraid I'll marry a Catholic and threaten her
      throne!
   She threatens disinheritance! Offers me Leicester!
   Her leavings!
Bothwell: (*Coming down* C.) Yes, by God, that's a
   cold potato.
Mary: And means to choose another heir for her
      throne!
   I may never sit on it, but the Stuart line
   Shall not suffer by me!
Bothwell: Will you tell me what that means?
Mary: I mean if I have a son he'll govern England.
Bothwell: And so he might, if he were mine, too.

Mary: Nay, might—
  But it must be!
  She dares to threaten my heritage!
Bothwell: Does that mean Lord Darnley?
(*She is silent.* **Bothwell** *crosses* R. *to* **Mary.**)
  Aye, lady, will you stoop so low to choose
  A weapon? This is not worthy of the girl
  I've known. Am I to be ousted by a papejay
  Who drinks in the morning and cannot carry his
      drink?
  An end of mouldy string? You take too much
  On yourself of the future. Think of us, and the
      hours
  Close on us here we might have together. Leave
      something
  To the Gods in heaven! They look after lovers!
Mary: (*With back to* **Bothwell**) Oh, what's a little
      love, a trick of the eyes,
  A liking, to be set beside the name
  You'll have forever, or your son will have?
Bothwell: Well, it's been nibbling at you this long
      while,
  And now it's got you, the blight of Charle-
      magne—
  The itch to conquer.
Mary: (*Facing* **Bothwell**) I have an itch to conquer?
Bothwell: It goes deep, too, that itch. It eats out
      the brain.
Mary: Well, and my love for you, how worthy is
      that?
  It's my body wants you. Something I've fought
      against
  Comes out in me when you're near. You've not
      held it sacred.
  You've taken others. I've known. And then come
      wooing.
  It would happen again.
Bothwell: It's a man's way. I've loved you
  None the less.
Mary: You don't offer enough, Lord Bothwell,
  You're not true in it, and I'm not true to myself
  In what I feel for you.
Bothwell: I'm no lute-player,
  To languish and write sonnets when my lady
  Says me nay. Faith, I've lived rough on the bor-
      der,
  And cut some throats I don't forgive myself
  Too easily, when I look back, but I tell you
  If I give my pledge to you it's an honest pledge,
  And I'll keep it. Yes, and when the tug begins
  Around your throne, you'll be lost without me.
      Try
  No threats toward England.—It will tax a hardy
      man
  All his time to hold what you have.
Mary: We differ there, too.
  What I have I'll defend for myself.

Bothwell: If you marry this Darnley
   I take away my hand.
Mary: Before God, he believes
   He's held me up so far, and I'd fall without him!
   (*Crossing to* C.)
Bothwell: I believe it, and it's true; Darnley, sweet
      Christ!
   No miracle could make him a king! He's a punk,
   And he'll rule like a punk!
Mary: We shall see, Lord Bothwell.
Bothwell: Will you whore yourself for the English
   crown?
Mary: I have chosen.
Bothwell: Well, I'm sped. My suit's cold. But, dod,
      lady—Darnley—
   He sticks in my craw—I can't go him. You'll find
      few that can.
   Think twice about that. Let him not cross my way,
   Or he'll lose his plumes like Morton!
Mary: Will you learn, Lord Bothwell,
   That this is not your palace, but mine? Or must
      you
   Be taught that lesson?
Bothwell: There's been a bond between us
   We'll find it hard to forget.
Mary: You may. Not I.
   I've set my face where I'm going.

Scene from
   Medea, freely adapted from the *Medea* of Euripides by Robinson Jeffers

For 1 man, 1 woman

Characters: **Medea,** daughter of the king of Colchis, ex-wife of Jason, possessing
   supernatural powers.

   Jason, now married to Creon's daughter, thus successor to the throne
   of Corinth.

Setting: Corinth, before the palace of Medea in ancient Greece.

Situation: (In addition to the text, the major changes in this modern poetic adap-
   tation are the reduction of the chorus to three women, the strengthening of
   Medea's role in comparison to Jason's, and the placing of psychological emphasis on Medea's character.)

   In quest of the Golden Fleece, Jason went to Colchis where he and
   Medea fell passionately in love. Through her supernatural powers, she aided
   him, slaying her own brother and others, and fled with him to Corinth where
   they received sanctuary and had two sons. The king of Corinth, Creon, without heir, offered Jason his daughter in marriage in return for Jason's becoming
   his successor. Because Jason accepts, Medea's passion, rage, and sorcery lead
   her to seek revenge. In this, the final scene in the play, she has just killed
   their two sons in order to punish Jason. The scene may be performed without
   actually using bodies for the children.

   (Note: It should be an interesting challenge to deal with two quite different versions of what is essentially the same scene. Please see original version
   by Euripedes in Section D.)

Script Notations

Medea: What feeble night-bird overcome by misfortunes beats at my door? Can this be that great adventurer,

The famous lord of the seas and delight of women, the heir of rich Corinth—this crying drunkard

On the dark doorstep? —Yet you've not had enough. You have come to drink the last bitter drops.

I'll pour them for you.

Jason: What's that stain on your hand?

Medea: The wine I was pouring for you spilled on my hand.

Dear were the little grapes that were crushed to make it; dear were the vineyards.

Jason: I came to kill you, Medea,

Like a caught beast, like a crawling viper. Give me my sons, that I may save them from Creon's men,

I'll go quietly away.

Medea: Hush, they are sleeping. Perhaps I will let you look at them: you cannot have them.

But the hour is late, you ought to go home to that high-born bride; the night has fallen, surely she longs for you.

Surely her flesh is not crusted black, nor her mouth a horror.

[Jason *kneels on the steps, painfully groping for his sword.*]

She is very young,

But surely she will be fruitful.—Your sword you want?

There it is. Not that step, the next lower. No, the next higher.

Jason: [*Finds it and stands erect*] I'll kill you first and then find my sons.

Medea: You must be careful, Jason. Do you see the two fire-snakes

That guard this door? [*Indicating the two lamps*] Here and here: one on each side: two serpents.

Their throats are swollen with poison,

Their eyes are burning coals and their tongues are fire. They are coiled ready to strike: if you come near them,

They'll make you what Creon is. But stand there very quietly, I'll let you

Look at your sons. [*She speaks to someone in the house, behind the left door-jamb.*]

Bring them across the doorway that he may see them.

[*She stands back, and two serving-women pass within the doorway from left to right, bearing the slain children on a litter between them. It stands a moment in the gape of the door, and passes.*]

Jason: [*Dropping the sword, flinging his hands to his temples*] I knew it already.

I knew it before I saw it. No wild beast could have done it.

Medea: I have done it; because I loathed you more Than I loved them. Mine is the triumph.

Jason: Your triumph. No iron-fleshed demon of those whom your father worships

In that blood-crusted temple— Did you feel nothing, no pity, are you pure evil? I should have killed you

The day I saw you.

Medea: I tore my own heart and laughed: I was tearing yours.

Jason: Will you laugh while I strangle you?

Medea: I would still laugh. —Beware my door-holders, Jason! these eager serpents. —I'd still be joyful

To know that every bone of your life is broken; you are left hopeless, friendless, mateless, childless,

Avoided by gods and men, unclean with awful excess of grief—childless—

Jason: [*Exhausted*] It is no matter now

Who lives, or who dies.

Medea: Go down to your ship Argo and weep beside it, that rotting hulk on the harbor-beach

Drawn dry astrand, never to be launched again— even the weeds and barnacles on the warped keel

Are dead and stink:—that's your last companion—

And only hope: for some time one of the rotting timbers

Will fall on your head and kill you—meanwhile sit there and mourn, remembering the infinite evil, and the good

That has turned evil.

Jason: Exult in evil, gloat your fill, have your glory.

Medea: My heart's blood bought it.

Jason: Enjoy it then.

Only give me my boys: the little pitiful violated bodies: that I may bury them

In some kind place.

Medea: To you? —You would betray even the little bodies: coin them for silver,

Sell them for power. No.

Jason: [*Kneeling*] Let me touch their dear flesh, let me touch their hair!

Medea: No. They are mine.

They are going with me: the chariot is in the gate. You had love and betrayed it; now of all men

You are utterly the most miserable. As I of women. But I, a woman, a foreigner, alone

Against you and the might of Corinth—have met you throat for throat, evil for evil. Now I go forth

Under the cold eyes of the weakness-despising
stars:—not me they scorn.
[*She goes out of sight behind the right door-jamb,
following the dead children. Jason stumbles up the
steps to follow her, and falls between the two flick-
ering lamps. The door remains open, the light in
the house is partially extinguished. A music of mixed
triumph and lamentation is heard to pass from the
house, and diminish into the distance beyond it.*]

Scene from
*Oh Dad, Poor Dad, Momma's Hung You in the Closet and I'm Feelin' So
Sad* by Arthur L. Kopit

From Scene 2

For 1 man, 1 woman

Characters: **Jonathan Rosepettle,** 17. However, he dresses as a 10-year-old.
Rosalie, 19, a sensuous girl. She dresses in sweet pink.

Setting: A hotel room in Havana, Cuba.

Situation: Kopit tells the story of Jonathan, who has been traveling with his strange
mother who has developed the unusual habit of hanging her dead husband's
body in the closet wherever they may be traveling. His mother keeps a col-
lection of man-eating plants and carnivorous fish as well. Jonathan is an emotional child and finds himself in something of a quandary when Rosalie, a
seductive young girl, sets her mind on bringing Jonathan to manhood.

Script Notations

Rosalie: But if you've been here two weeks, why haven't I seen you?

Jonathan: I've . . . I've been in my room.

Rosalie: All the time?

Jonathan: Yes. . . . All the time.

Rosalie: Well, you must get out sometimes. I mean, sometimes you simply must get out. You just couldn't stay inside all the time . . . could you?

Jonathan: Yyyyyes.

Rosalie: You never get out at all? I mean, never at all?

Jonathan: Some-sometimes I do go out on the porch. M-Ma-Mother has some . . . Venus'-flytraps which she bra-brought back from the rain forests of Va-Va-Va-Venezuela. They're va-very rrrrrare and need a . . . a lot of sunshine. Well sir, she ka-keeps them on the porch and I . . . I feed them. Twice a day, too.

Rosalie: Oh.

Jonathan: Ma-Ma-Mother says everyone must have a vocation in life. [*With a slight nervous laugh.*] I ga-guess that's . . . my job.

Rosalie: I don't think I've ever met anyone before who's fed . . . uh . . . Venus'-flytraps.

Jonathan: Ma-Ma-Mother says I'm va-very good at it. That's what she . . . says. I'm va-very good at it. I . . . don't know . . . if . . . I am, but . . . that's . . . what she says so I . . . guess I am.

Rosalie: Well, uh, what . . . what do you . . . feed them? You see, I've never met anyone before who's fed Venus'-flytraps so . . . that's why I don't know what . . . you're supposed to feed them.

Jonathan: [*Happy that she asked*]. Oh, I fa-feed them . . . l-l-lots of things. Ga-ga-green peas, chicken feathers, rubber bands. They're . . . not very fussy. They're . . . nice, that way. Ma-Ma-Mother says it it it ga-gives me a feeling of a-co-co-complishment. Iffffff you would . . . like to see them I . . . could show them to you. It's . . . almost fa-feeding time. It is, and . . . and I could show them to you.

Rosalie: No. That's all right. [Jonathan *looks away, hurt.*] Well, how about later?

Jonathan: Do-do-do you ra-really wwwwwant to see them?

Rosalie: Yes. Yes I really think I would like to see them . . . later. If you'll show them to me then, I'd really like that. [Jonathan *looks at her and smiles. There is an awkward silence while he stares at her thankfully.*] I still don't understand why you never go out. How can you just sit in——?

Jonathan: Sometimes, when I'm on the porch . . . I do other things.

Rosalie: *What?*

Jonathan: Sa-sa-sometimes, when I'm . . . on the

porch, you know, when I'm on the porch? Ssssssssome-times I . . . do *other things*, too.

Rosalie: What sort of things? [**Jonathan** *giggles.*] What sort of things do you do?

Jonathan: Other things.

Rosalie: [*Coyly*]. What do you mean, "Other things"?

Jonathan: Other things besides feeding my mother's plants. Other things besides that. That's what I mean. Other things besides that.

Rosalie: What kind of things . . . *in particular?*

Jonathan: Oh, watching.

Rosalie: Watching?

Jonathan: Yes. Like . . . watching.

Rosalie: Watching what? [*He giggles.*] *Watching what!?*

Jonathan: You. [*Short pause. She inches closer to him on the couch.*]

Rosalie: What do you mean . . . watching me?

Jonathan: I . . . watch you from the porch. That's what I mean. I watch you from the porch. I watch you a lot, too. Every day. It's . . . it's the truth. I . . . I swear it . . . is. I watch you ev-ry day. Do you believe me?

Rosalie: Of course I believe you, Albert. Why—

Jonathan: Jonathan!

Rosalie: What?

Jonathan: Jonathan. Ca-ca-call me Ja-Jonathan. That's my na-na-na——

Rosalie: But your mother said your name was—

Jonathan: Nooooo! Call . . . me Jonathan. Pa-pa-please?

Rosalie: All right . . . Jonathan.

Jonathan: [*Excitedly*]. You *do* believe me! You rrrrreally do believe me. I-I-I can tell!

Rosalie: Of course I believe you. Why shouldn't —?

Jonathan: You want me to tell you how I watch you? You want me to tell you? I'll bet you'll na-never guess.

Rosalie: How?

Jonathan: *Guess.*

Rosalie: [*Ponders*]. Through a telescope?

Jonathan: How did you guess?

Rosalie: I . . . I don't know. I was just joking. I didn't really think that was—

Jonathan: I'll bet everyone watches you through a telescope. I'll bet everyone you go out with watches you through a telescope. That's what I'll bet.

Rosalie: No. Not at all.

Jonathan: Well, that's how I watch you. Through a telescope.

Rosalie: I never would have guessed that—

Jonathan: I thought you were . . . ga-going to say I . . . I watch you with . . . with love in my eyes or some . . . thing like that. I didn't think you were going to guess that I . . . watch you through a telescope. I didn't think you were going to guess that I wa-watch you through a telescope on the fa-first guess, anyway. Not on the *first guess*.

Rosalie: Well, it was just a guess.

Jonathan: [*Hopefully*]. Do you watch *me* through a telescope?

Rosalie: I never knew where your room was.

Jonathan: Now you know. Now will you watch me?

Rosalie: Well I . . . don't have a telescope.

Jonathan: [*Getting more elated and excited*]. You can make one. That's how I got mine. I made it. Out of lenses and tubing. That's all you need. Lenses and tubing. Do you have any lenses?

Rosalie: No.

Jonathan: Do you have any tubing?

Rosalie: No.

Jonathan: Oh. [*Pause*]. Well, would you like me to tell you how I made mine in case you find some lenses and tubing? Would you like that?

Rosalie: [*Disinterestedly*]. Sure, Jonathan. I think that would be nice.

Scene from
   Rhinoceros by Eugene Ionesco, translated by Derek Prouse

From Act II, Scene 2

For 2 men

Characters: **Berenger,** office worker in the production department of a firm of
         law publishers.
              Jean, Berenger's close friend, also an office worker.

Setting: A small provincial town. Jean's house.

Situation: At a cafe, Berenger and Jean have observed rhinos running in the street.
         Gradually, as the play progresses, more and more rhinos are observed. The
         inhabitants of the town are changing into rhinos, many because they want
         to. At the end of the play, Berenger is the only human left; all the others
         have changed. In this scene, Berenger has come to visit his friend, Jean.

Script Notations

Berenger: You're probably still angry with me over our silly quarrel yesterday. I admit it was my fault. That's why I came to say I was sorry . . .

Jean: What quarrel are you talking about?

Berenger: I told you just now. You know, about the rhinoceros.

Jean: [*not listening to* **Berenger**] It's not that I hate people. I'm just indifferent to them—or rather, they disgust me; and they'd better keep out of my way, or I'll run them down.

Berenger: You know very well that I shall never stand in your way.

Jean: I've got one aim in life. And I'm making straight for it.

Berenger: I'm sure you're right. But I feel you're passing through a moral crisis.

[**Jean** *has been pacing the room like a wild beast in a cage, from one wall to the other.* **Berenger** *watches him, occasionally stepping aside to avoid him.* **Jean's** *voice has become more and more hoarse.*]

You mustn't excite yourself, it's bad for you.

Jean: I felt uncomfortable in my clothes; now my pyjamas irritate me as well. [*He undoes his pyjama jacket and does it up again.*]

Berenger: But whatever's the matter with your skin?

Jean: Can't you leave my skin alone? I certainly wouldn't want to change it for yours.

Berenger: It's gone like leather.

Jean: That makes it more solid. It's weatherproof.

Berenger: You're getting greener and greener.

Jean: You've got colour mania today. You're seeing things, you've been drinking again.

Berenger: I did yesterday, but not today.

Jean: It's the result of all your past debauches.

Berenger: I promised you to turn over a new leaf. I take notice when friends like you give me advice. And I never feel humiliated—on the contrary!

Jean: I don't care what you feel. Brrr . . .

Berenger: What did you say?

Jean: I didn't say anything. I just went Brrr . . . because I felt like it.

Berenger: [*looking fixedly at* **Jean**] Do you know what's happened to Boeuf? He's turned into a rhinoceros.

Jean: What happened to Boeuf?

Berenger: He's turned into a rhinoceros.

Jean: [*fanning himself with the flaps of his jacket*] Brrr . . .

Berenger: Come on now, stop joking.

Jean: I can puff if I want to, can't I? I've every right . . . I'm in my own house.

Berenger: I didn't say you couldn't.

Jean: And I shouldn't if I were you. I feel hot, I feel hot. Brrr . . . Just a moment. I must cool myself down.

Berenger: [*whilst* **Jean** *darts to the bathroom*] He must have a fever. [Jean *is in the bathroom, one hears him puffing, and also the sound of a running tap.*]

Jean: [*off*] Brrr . . .

Berenger: He's got the shivers. I'm jolly well going to 'phone the doctor. [*He goes to the telephone again then comes back quickly when he hears* Jean's *voice.*]

Jean: [*off*] So old Boeuf turned into a rhinoceros, did he? Ah, ah, ah . . . ! He was just having you on, he'd disguised himself. [*He pokes his head around the bathroom door. He is very green. The bump over his nose is slightly larger.*] He was just disguised.

Berenger: [*walking about the room, without seeing* Jean] He looked very serious about it, I assure you.

Jean: Oh well, that's his business.

Berenger: [*turning to* Jean *who disappears again into the bathroom*] I'm sure he didn't do it on purpose. He didn't want to change.

Jean: [*off*] How do you know?

Berenger: Well, everything led one to suppose so.

Jean: And what if he did do it on purpose? Eh? What if he did it on purpose?

Berenger: I'd be very surprised. At any rate, Mrs. Boeuf didn't seem to know about it . . .

Jean: [*in a very hoarse voice*] Ah, ah, ah! Fat old Mrs. Boeuf. She's just a fool!

Berenger: Well fool or no fool . . .

Jean: [*he enters swiftly, takes off his jacket, and throws it on the bed.* **Berenger** *discreetly averts his gaze.* **Jean,** *whose back and chest are now green, goes back into the bathroom. As he walks in and out:*] Boeuf never let his wife know what he was up to . . .

Berenger: You're wrong there, Jean—it was a very united family.

Jean: Very united, was it? Are you sure? Hum, hum, Brr . . .

Berenger: [*moving to the bathroom, where* **Jean** *slams the door in his face*] Very united. And the proof is that . . .

Jean: [*from within*] Boeuf led his own private life. He had a secret side to him deep down which he kept to himself.

Berenger: I shouldn't make you talk, it seems to upset you.

Jean: On the contrary, it relaxes me.

Berenger: Even so, let me call the doctor, I beg you.

Jean: I absolutely forbid it. I can't stand obstinate people.

[Jean *comes back into the bedroom.* **Berenger** *backs away a little scared, for* **Jean** *is greener than ever and speaks only with difficulty. His voice is unrecognizable.*]

Well, whether he changes into a rhinoceros on purpose or against his will, he's probably all the better for it.

Berenger: How can you say a thing like that? Surely you don't think . . .

Jean: You always see the black side of everything. It obviously gave him great pleasure to turn into a rhinoceros. There's nothing extraordinary in that.

Berenger: There's nothing extraordinary in it, but I doubt if it gave him much pleasure.

Jean: And why not, pray?

Berenger: It's hard to say exactly why; it's just something you feel.

Jean: I tell you it's not as bad as all that. After all, rhinoceroses are living creatures the same as us; they've got as much right to life as we have!

Berenger: As long as they don't destroy ours in the process. You must admit the difference in mentality.

Jean: [*pacing up and down the room, and in and out of the bathroom*] Are you under the impression that our way of life is superior?

Berenger: Well at any rate, we have our own moral standards which I consider incompatible with the standards of these animals.

Jean: Moral standards! I'm sick of moral standards! We need to go beyond moral standards!

Berenger: What would you put in their place?

Jean: [*still pacing*] Nature!

Berenger: Nature?

Jean: Nature has its own laws. Morality's against Nature.

Berenger: Are you suggesting we replace our moral laws by the law of the jungle?

Jean: It would suit me, suit me fine.

Berenger: You say that. But deep down, no one . . .

Jean: [*interrupting him, pacing up and down*] We've got to build our life on new foundations. We must get back to primeval integrity.

Berenger: I don't agree with you at all.

Jean: [*breathing noisily*] I can't breathe.

Berenger: Just think a moment. You must admit that we have a philosophy that animals don't share, and an irreplaceable set of values, which it's taken centuries of human civilization to build up . . .

Jean: [*in the bathroom*] When we've demolished all that, we'll be better off!

Berenger: I know you don't mean that seriously. You're joking! It's just a poetic fancy.

Jean: Brrr. [*He almost trumpets.*]

Berenger: I'd never realized you were a poet.

Jean: [*comes out of the bathroom*] Brrr. [*He trumpets again.*]

Berenger: That's not what you believe fundamentally—I know you too well. You know as well as I do that mankind . . .

Jean: [*interrupting him*] Don't talk to me about mankind!

Berenger: I mean the human individual, humanism . . .

Jean: Humanism is all washed up! You're a ridiculous old sentimentalist. [*He goes into the bathroom.*]

Berenger: But you must admit that the mind . . .

Jean: [*from the bathroom*] Just clichés! You're talking rubbish!

Berenger: Rubbish!

Jean: [*from the bathroom in a very hoarse voice, difficult to understand*] Utter rubbish!

Berenger: I'm amazed to hear you say that, Jean, really! You must be out of your mind. You wouldn't like to be a rhinoceros yourself, now would you?

Jean: Why not? I'm not a victim of prejudice like you.

Berenger: Can you speak more clearly? I didn't catch what you said. You swallowed the words.

Jean: [*still in the bathroom*] Then keep your ears open.

Berenger: What?

Jean: Keep your ears open. I said what's wrong with being a rhinoceros? I'm all for change.

Berenger: It's not like you to say a thing like that . . .

[**Berenger** *stops short, for* **Jean's** *appearance is truly alarming.* **Jean** *has become, in fact, completely green. The bump on his forehead is practically a rhinoceros horn.*]

Oh! You really must be out of your mind!

[**Jean** *dashes to his bed, throws the covers on the floor, talking in a fast and furious gabble, and making very weird sounds.*]

You mustn't get into such a state—calm down! I hardly recognize you any more.

Jean: [*hardly distinguishable*] Hot . . . far too hot! Demolish the lot, clothes itch, they itch! [*He drops his pyjama trousers.*]

Berenger: What are you doing? You're not yourself! You're generally so modest!

Jean: The swamps! The swamps!

Berenger: Look at me! Can't you see me any longer? Can't you hear me?

Jean: I can hear you perfectly well! I can see you perfectly well!

[*He lunges towards* **Berenger**, *head down.* **Berenger** *gets out of the way.*]

Berenger: Watch out!

Jean: [*puffing noisily*] Sorry! [*He darts at great speed into the bathroom.*]

Berenger: [*makes as if to escape by the door left, then comes back and goes into the bathroom after* **Jean**, *saying*] I really can't leave him like that—after all he is a friend. [*From the bathroom:*] I'm going to get the doctor! It's absolutely necessary, believe me!

Jean: [*from the bathroom*] No!

Berenger: [*from the bathroom*] Calm down, Jean, you're being ridiculous! Oh, your horn's getting longer and longer—you're a rhinoceros!

Jean: [*from the bathroom*] I'll trample you, I'll trample you down! [*A lot of noise comes from the bathroom, trumpetings, objects falling, the sound of a shattered mirror; then* **Berenger** *reappears, very frightened; he closes the bathroom door with difficulty against the resistance that is being made from inside.*]

Berenger: [*pushing against the door*] He's a rhinoceros, he's a rhinoceros!

[**Berenger** *manages to close the door. As he does so, his coat is pierced by a rhinoceros horn. The door shakes under the animal's constant pressure and the din continues in the bathroom; trumpetings are heard, interspersed with indistinct phrases such as: 'I'm furious! The swine!' etc.* **Berenger** *rushes to the door right.*]

I never would have thought it of him—never!

Scene from
   Rosencrantz & Guildenstern Are Dead by Tom Stoppard

From Act I

For 2 men

Characters and Setting: **Rosencrantz and Guildenstern,** "two Elizabethans passing the time in a place without any visible character."

Situation: As this is the opening scene of the play, it needs little introduction. Although we intermittently glimpse Hamlet going about the business of his life as we know it from Shakespeare's play, we are primarily concerned with the minor characters of his two fellow students who here become the principal focus of Stoppard's play.

Script Notations

*Two **Elizabethans** passing the time in a place without any visible character.*
They are well dressed—hats, cloaks, sticks and all.
Each of them has a large leather money bag.
***Guildenstern's** bag is nearly empty.*
***Rosencrantz's** bag is nearly full.*
*The reason being: they are betting on the toss of a coin, in the following manner: **Guildenstern** (hereafter ''**Guil**'') takes a coin out of his bag, spins it, letting it fall. **Rosencrantz** (hereafter ''**Ros**'') studies it, announces it as ''heads'' (as it happens) and puts it into his own bag. Then they repeat the process. They have apparently been doing this for some time.*
*The run of ''heads'' is impossible, yet **Ros** betrays no surprise at all—he feels none. However, he is nice enough to feel a little embarrassed at taking so much money off his friend. Let that be his character note.*
***Guil** is well alive to the oddity of it. He is not worried about the money, but he is worried by the implications; aware but not going to panic about it— his character note.*
***Guil** sits. **Ros** stands (he does the moving, retrieving coins).*
***Guil** spins. **Ros** studies coin.*
Ros: Heads.
He picks it up and puts it in his bag. The process is repeated.
Heads.
Again.
Heads.
Again.
Heads.
Again.
Heads.
Guil (*flipping a coin*): There is an art to the building up of suspense.
Ros: Heads.
Guil (*flipping another*): Though it can be done by luck alone.
Ros: Heads.
Guil: If that's the word I'm after.
Ros (*raises his head at **Guil***): Seventy-six—love.
***Guil** gets up but has nowhere to go. He spins another coin over his shoulder without looking at it, his attention being directed at his environment or lack of it.*
Heads.
Guil: A weaker man might be moved to re-examine his faith, if in nothing else at least in the law of probability. (*He flips a coin over his shoulder as he goes to look upstage.*)
Ros: Heads.
***Guil**, examining the confines of the stage, flips over two more coins as he does so, one by one of course.*
***Ros** announces each of them as ''heads.''*

Guil (*musing*): The law of probability, it has been oddly asserted, is something to do with the proposition that if six monkeys (*he has surprised himself*) . . . if six monkeys were . . .

Ros: Game?

Guil: Were they?

Ros: Are you?

Guil (*understanding*): Game. (*Flips a coin.*) The law of averages, if I have got this right, means that if six monkeys were thrown up in the air for long enough they would land on their tails about as often as they would land on their——

Ros: Heads. (*He picks up the coin.*)

Guil: Which even at first glance does not strike one as a particularly rewarding speculation, in either sense, even without the monkeys. I mean you wouldn't *bet* on it. I mean *I* would, but *you* wouldn't. . . . (*As he flips a coin.*)

Ros: Heads.

Guil: Would you? (*Flips a coin.*)

Ros: Heads.

Repeat.

Heads. (*He looks up at* **Guil**—*embarrassed laugh.*) Getting a bit of a bore, isn't it?

Guil (*coldly*): A bore?

Ros: Well . . .

Guil: What about the suspense?

Ros (*innocently*): What suspense?

Small pause.

Guil: It must be the law of diminishing returns. . . . I feel the spell about to be broken. (*Energizing himself somewhat. He takes out a coin, spins it high, catches it, turns it over on to the back of his other hand, studies the coin—and tosses it to* **Ros.** *His energy deflates and he sits.*)

Well, it was an even chance . . . if my calculations are correct.

Ros: Eighty-five in a row—beaten the record!

Guil: Don't be absurd.

Ros: Easily!

Guil (*angry*): Is that *it*, then? Is that all?

Ros: What?

Guil: A new record? Is that as far as you are prepared to go?

Ros: Well . . .

Guil: No questions? Not even a pause?

Ros: You spun them yourself.

Guil: Not a flicker of doubt?

Ros (*aggrieved, aggressive*): Well, I won—didn't I?

Guil (*approaches him—quieter*): And if you'd lost? If they'd come down against you, eighty-five times, one after another, just like that?

Ros (*dumbly*): Eighty-five in a row? *Tails?*

Guil: Yes! What would you think?

Ros (*doubtfully*): Well . . . (*Jocularly.*) Well, I'd have a good look at your coins for a start!

Guil (*retiring*): I'm relieved. At least we can still count on self-interest as a predictable factor. . . . I suppose it's the last to go. Your capacity for trust made me wonder if perhaps . . . you, alone . . . (*He turns on him suddenly, reaches out a hand.*) Touch.

Ros *clasps his hand.* **Guil** *pulls him up to him.*

Guil (*more intensely*): We have been spinning coins together since—— (*He releases him almost as violently.*) This is not the first time we have spun coins!

Ros: Oh no—we've been spinning coins for as long as I remember.

Guil: How long is that?

Ros: I forget. Mind you—eighty-five times!

Guil: Yes?

Ros: It'll take some beating, I imagine.

Guil: Is *that* what you imagine? Is that it? No *fear*?

Ros: Fear?

Guil (*in fury—flings a coin on the ground*): Fear! The crack that might flood your brain with light!

Ros: Heads. . . . (*He puts it in his bag.*)

Guil *sits despondently. He takes a coin, spins it, lets it fall between his feet. He looks at it, picks it up, throws it to* **Ros,** *who puts it in his bag.*

Guil *takes another coin, spins it, catches it, turns it over on to his other hand, looks at it, and throws it to* **Ros,** *who puts it in his bag.*

Guil *takes a third coin, spins it, catches it in his right hand, turns it over onto his left wrist, lobs it in the air, catches it with his left hand, raises his left leg, throws the coin up under it, catches it and turns it over on the top of his head, where it sits.* **Ros** *comes, looks at it, puts it in his bag.*

Ros: I'm afraid——

Guil: So am I.

Ros: I'm afraid it isn't your day.

Guil: I'm afraid it is.

Small pause.

Ros: Eighty-nine.

Guil: It must be indicative of something, besides the redistribution of wealth. (*He muses.*) List of possible explanations. One: I'm willing it. Inside where nothing shows, I am the essence of a man spinning double-headed coins, and betting against himself in private atonement for an unremembered past. (*He spins a coin at* **Ros.**)

Ros: Heads.

Guil: Two: time has stopped dead, and the single experience of one coin being spun once has been repeated ninety times. . . . (*He flips a coin, looks at it, tosses it to* **Ros.**) On the whole, doubtful. Three: divine intervention, that is to say, a good turn from above concerning him, cf. children of Israel, or retribution from above concerning me, cf. Lot's wife. Four: a spectacular vindication of the principle that each individual coin spun individually (*he spins one*) is as likely to come down heads as tails and therefore should cause no surprise each individual time it does. (*It does. He tosses it to* **Ros.**)

Ros: I've never known anything like it!

Guil: And a syllogism: One, he has never known anything like it. Two, he has never known anything to write home about. Three, it is nothing to write home about. . . . Home . . . What's the first thing you remember?

Ros: Oh, let's see. . . . The first thing that comes into my head, you mean?

Guil: No—the first thing you remember.

Ros: Ah. (*Pause.*) No, it's no good, it's gone. It was a long time ago.

Guil (*patient but edged*): You don't get my meaning. What is the first thing after all the things you've forgotten?

Ros: Oh I see. (*Pause.*) I've forgotten the question.

Scene from
  A Slight Ache by Harold Pinter

For 1 man, 1 woman

Characters: **Flora,** his wife.
  Edward, her husband.

Setting: Their home. The breakfast table.

Situation: As this is the opening scene of the play, it needs little explanation other
  than this fact: during Flora and Edward's breakfast chatter they are aware of
  a strange matchseller who has mysteriously been standing by their back gate
  for many weeks.

Script Notations

Flora: Do you know what today is?

Edward: Saturday.

Flora: It's the longest day of the year.

Edward: Really?

Flora: It's the height of summer today.

Edward: Cover the marmalade.

Flora: What?

Edward: Cover the pot. There's a wasp. [*He puts the paper down on the table.*] Don't move. Keep still. What are you doing?

Flora: Covering the pot.

Edward: Don't move. Leave it. Keep still.

[*Pause.*]

Give me the 'Telegraph'.

Flora: Don't hit it. It'll bite.

Edward: Bite? What do you mean, bite? Keep still. It's landing.

Flora: It's going in the pot.

Edward: Give me the lid.

Flora: It's in.

Edward: Give me the lid.

Flora: I'll do it.

Edward: Give it to me! Now . . . Slowly . . .

Flora: What are you doing?

Edward: Be quiet. Slowly . . . carefully . . . on . . . the . . . pot! Ha-ha-ha. Very good.

Flora: Now he's in the marmalade.

Edward: Precisely.

[*Pause. She . . . reads the 'Telegraph'.*]

Flora: Can you hear him?

Edward: Hear him?

Flora: Buzzing.

Edward: Nonsense. How can you hear him? It's an earthenware lid.

Flora: He's becoming frantic.

Edward: Rubbish. Take it away from the table.

Flora: What shall I do with it?

Edward: Put it in the sink and drown it.

Flora: It'll fly out and bite me.

Edward: It will not bite you! Wasps don't bite. Anyway, it won't fly out. It's stuck. It'll drown where it is, in the marmalade.

Flora: What a horrible death.

Edward: On the contrary.

Flora: Have you got something in your eyes?

Edward: No. Why do you ask?

Flora: You keep clenching them, blinking them.

Edward: I have a slight ache in them.

Flora: Oh, dear.

Edward: Yes, a slight ache. As if I hadn't slept.

Flora: Did you sleep, Edward?

Edward: Of course I slept. Uninterrupted. As always.

Flora: And yet you feel tired.

Edward: I didn't say I felt tired. I merely said I had a slight ache in my eyes.

Flora: Why is that, then?

Edward: I really don't know.

Flora: Oh goodness!

Edward: What is it?

Flora: I can see it. It's trying to come out.

Edward: How can it?

Flora: Through the hole. It's trying to crawl out, through the spoon-hole.

Edward: Mmmnn, yes. Can't do it, of course. Well, let's kill it, for goodness' sake.

Flora: Yes, let's. But how?

Edward: Bring it out on the spoon and squash it on a plate.

Flora: It'll fly away. It'll bite.

Edward: If you don't stop saying that word I shall leave this table.

Flora: But wasps do bite.

Edward: They don't bite. They sting. It's snakes . . . that bite.

Flora: What about horseflies?

Edward: [*to himself*] Horseflies suck.

Flora: If we . . . if we wait long enough, I suppose it'll choke to death. It'll suffocate in the marmalade.

Edward: You do know I've got work to do this morning, don't you? I can't spend the whole day worrying about a wasp.

Flora: Well, kill it.

Edward: You want to kill it?

Flora: Yes.

Edward: Very well. Pass me the hot water jug.

Flora: What are you going to do?

Edward: Scald it. Give it to me.

[*She hands him the jug.*]

Now . . .

Flora: Do you want me to lift the lid?

Edward: No, no, no. I'll pour down the spoon-hole. Right . . . down the spoon-hole.

Flora: Listen!

Edward: What?

Flora: It's buzzing.

Edward: Vicious creatures.

Curious, but I don't remember seeing any wasps at all, all summer, until now. I'm sure I don't know why. I mean, there must have been wasps.

Flora: Please.

Edward: This couldn't be the first wasp, could it?

Flora: Please.

Edward: The first wasp of summer? No. It's not possible.

Flora: Edward.

Edward: Mmmmnnn?

Flora: Kill it.

Edward: Ah, yes. Tilt the pot. Tilt. Aah . . . down

here . . . right down . . . blinding him . . . that's
. . . it.
Flora: Is it?
Edward: Lift the lid. All right, I will. There he is!
Dead. What a monster. [*He squashes it on a plate.*]
Flora: What an awful experience.

Scene from
  A Thurber Carnival by James Thurber

From the scene "Mr. Preble Gets Rid of His Wife"

For 1 man, 1 woman

Characters: **Mr. Preble,** a middle-aged business man.
              Mrs. Preble, his wife.

Setting: The living room and cellar of the Prebles' home.

Situation: This satirical sketch from Thurber's full-length musical revue is almost completely presented here. One needs only to be aware that, prior to the action of this scene, Mr. Preble has asked his attractive secretary to run away with him. Her response was, "You'd have to get rid of your wife."

Script Notations

Mr. Preble: Let's go down in the cellar.

Mrs. Preble: (*Not looking up from her reading.*) What for?

Mr. Preble: Oh, I don't know. We never go down in the cellar any more.

Mrs. Preble: We never did go down in the cellar that I remember. I could rest easy the balance of my life if I never went down in the cellar.

Mr. Preble: Supposing I said it meant a whole lot to me.

Mrs. Preble: What's come over you? It's cold down there and there is absolutely nothing to do.

Mr. Preble: (*Rises.*) We could pick up pieces of coal. We could get up some kind of a game with pieces of coal.

Mrs. Preble: I don't want to. Anyway I'm reading.

Mr. Preble: (*Crossing left, looking off at the cellar.*) Listen, I wish you'd come down in the cellar with me. You can read down there, as far as that goes.

Mrs. Preble: There isn't a good enough light down there, and anyway, I'm not going to go down in the cellar. You may as well make up your mind to that.

Mr. Preble: (*Turns front and kicks the carpet, like a small boy.*) Gee whiz! Other people's wives go down in the cellar. Why is it you never want to do anything together? I come home worn out from the office and you won't even go down in the cellar with me. God knows it isn't very far—it isn't as if I was asking to go to the movies or some place.

Mrs. Preble: I don't want to *go!*

Mr. Preble: All right, all *right.* (*He sits on the sofa to her left.*)

Mrs. Preble: (*A long pause.*) You probably want to get me down there to bury me. (*Laughs.*)

Mr. Preble: All right. I might as well tell you the truth. I want to get rid of you so I can marry my stenographer. Is there anything especially wrong about that? People do it every day. Love is something you can't control.

Mrs. Preble: (*Patting his hand absentmindedly.*) We've been all over that. I'm not going to go all over that again. I suppose this filing person put you up to it.

Mr. Preble: You needn't get sarcastic. Miss Daley's my secretary. I have plenty of people to file without having her file. She doesn't know anything about this. She isn't in on it. I was going to tell her you had gone to visit some friends and fell over a cliff. She wants me to get a divorce.

Mrs. Preble: *That's* a laugh. (*Right to him.*) You may bury me, but you'll never get a divorce.

Mr. Preble: I told her that. I mean—I told her I'd never get a divorce.

Mrs. Preble: Oh, you probably told her about burying me too.

Mr. Preble: That's not true. That's between you and me. I was never going to tell a soul.

Mrs. Preble: You'd blab it to the whole world; don't tell me. I know you.

Mr. Preble: I wish you were buried now and it was all over with.

Mrs. Preble: Don't you suppose you would get caught, you crazy thing? They always get caught. Why don't you go to bed? (*She tweaks his nose, pats his cheek and pinches his chin in rhythm with her words. Her tone is cajoling; as though she were talking to a recalcitrant four-year-old.*) You're just getting yourself all worked up over nothing.

Mr. Preble: (*Looks at her, then jumps up.*) I'm not going to bed. I'm going to bury you in the cellar. I've got my mind made up to it. I don't know how I could make it any plainer.

Mrs. Preble: (*Putting her book down.*) Listen, will you be satisfied and shut up if I go down in the cellar? Can I have a little peace if I go down in the cellar? Will you let me alone then?

Mr. Preble: Yes, but you spoil it by taking that attitude.

Mrs. Preble: Sure, sure, I always spoil everything. Have you got an envelope?

Mr. Preble: What do you want an envelope for?

Mrs. Preble: I want to mark my place in this book.

Mr. Preble: Why? You're not going to have a chance to finish it. (*She puts the book on the couch and rises.*) You go first.

Mrs. Preble. All right, you lead the way. (**Preble** *nods, and starts off left. She follows. The lights go to black and the revolves turn. Their voices are heard off left immediately.* **Mrs. Preble** *enters first, in the black. The three panels are black with white drawings of ominous-looking cellar fixtures. A furnace and its pipes and a naked light bulb seem to leap out of the dark. This is accomplished by using a strobe light. Crossing slowly up right.*) You *would* think of this, at this time of year! Any other husband would have buried his wife in the summer.

Mr. Preble: (*Following, but staying behind.*) You can't arrange these things just whenever you want to. I didn't fall in love with this girl till late Fall.

Mrs. Preble: Mercy, but it's cold down here, and I can never find the light. (*She reaches up for the light cord, and the lights come on. On the right revolve is a crate, on top of which is a strange wrench. Two steps behind the left portal shows the entrance,* **Mr. Preble** *stands with a shovel concealed behind his back.*) What have you got there?

Mr. Preble: (*Shows her.*) I was going to hit you over the head with this shovel.

Mrs. Preble: You were, huh? Well, get that out of your mind. Do you want to leave a great big clue right here in the middle of everything where the first detective that comes snooping around will find

EXECUTION

External   *Internal*

it? Go out in the street and find some piece of iron or something.

Mr. Preble: Like what, for instance? It's just like you to think there's always a piece of iron lying around in the streets.

Mrs. Preble: (*Looking around; spots the wrench.*) Well, let me see now. (*Crosses, picks up the wrench, hefts it.*) Oh, here's the perfect thing. It's what they call a heavy blunt instrument.

Mr. Preble: That isn't ours. We don't have a monkey wrench like that in this house.

Mrs. Preble: No. That's what I'm trying to tell you. The plumber left this last week after he fixed the sink in the kitchen. And it doesn't belong to either one of us.

Mr. Preble: What's it doing down here? Why didn't you give it back to him? Didn't he find out he had left it here?

Mrs. Preble: Well, you see it was this way. He *did* call up about it, but I told him he hadn't left it here. So then I brought it down to the cellar. (*She reaches into her bodice and pulls out a long white glove which she pulls onto her right hand.*)

Mr. Preble: Where did you get that glove?

Mrs. Preble: Oh, I had stuck it in my bodice, absentmindedly. I guess I was thinking about something else. (*With her gloved hand she polishes the tip of the wrench, presumably removing fingerprints.*)

Mr. Preble: Are you going to give it to me? (*She smiles at him.*) That's why you were so willing to come down here. (*He is backing away from her toward the steps; glancing back of him he sees a hole in the corner.*) Hey! Who's been digging here in this corner?

Mrs. Preble: Well, if I were a cop, I'd want to know whose fingerprints were on that shovel.

Mr. Preble: (*He looks at her, then at the shovel. He casts it from him, then runs up onto the steps.*) Don't you come near me!

Mrs. Preble: (*She takes a quick step toward him.*) Where are you going, dear?

Mr. Preble: First I'm going up and call the plumber and tell him you've got his wrench. And then—let's go to bed. (*He exits left.*)

Mrs. Preble: (*Starts removing her glove; smiles.*) All righty!

BLACKOUT

Scene from
   Waiting for Godot by Samuel Beckett

From Act I

For 3 men

Characters: **Vladimir (Didi)**, a tramp or a clown.
            Estragon (Gogo), a tramp or a clown.
            A shepherd boy.

Setting: An empty place, near sundown.

Situation: Beckett's play tells the story of the seemingly endless wait for someone
   or something Didi and Gogo call Godot. Although never identified, Godot
   may represent the object of humanity's continual hope that something is waiting at the end of a random existence.
       In this scene, Didi and Gogo have just encountered two travellers, Pozzo
   and Lucky, who passed by as the two tramps tried to find a means of occu-
   pying themselves while waiting for Godot. As Pozzo and Lucky leave, the two
   tramps turn to each other, wondering what to do next now that they are alone
   again.

Script Notations

Estragon: What do we do now?
Vladimir: I don't know.
Estragon: Let's go.
Vladimir: We can't.
Estragon: Why not?
Vladimir: We're waiting for Godot.
Estragon: (*despairingly*). Ah!
Pause.
Vladimir: How they've changed!
Estragon: Who?
Vladimir: Those two.
Estragon: That's the idea, let's make a little conversation.
Vladimir: Haven't they?
Estragon: What?
Vladimir: Changed.
Estragon: Very likely. They all change. Only we can't.
Vladimir: Likely! It's certain. Didn't you see them?
Estragon: I suppose I did. But I don't know them.
Vladimir: Yes you do know them.
Estragon: No I don't know them.
Vladimir: We know them, I tell you. You forget everything. (*Pause. To himself.*) Unless they're not the same . . .
Estragon: Why didn't they recognize us then?
Vladimir: That means nothing. I too pretended not to recognize them. And then nobody ever recognizes us.
Estragon: Forget it. What we need—ow! (**Vladimir** *does not react.*) Ow!
Vladimir: (*to himself*). Unless they're not the same . . .
Estragon: Didi! It's the other foot!
He goes hobbling towards the mound.
Vladimir: Unless they're not the same . . .
Boy: (*off*). Mister!
Estragon *halts. Both look towards the voice.*
Estragon: Off we go again.
Vladimir: Approach, my child.
Enter **Boy,** *timidly. He halts.*
Boy: Mister Albert . . . ?
Vladimir: Yes.
Estragon: What do you want?
Vladimir: Approach!
The **Boy** *does not move.*
Estragon: (*forcibly*). Approach when you're told, can't you?
The **Boy** *advances timidly, halts.*
Vladimir: What is it?
Boy: Mr. Godot . . .
Vladimir: Obviously . . . (*Pause.*) Approach.
Estragon: (*violently*). Will you approach! (*The* **Boy** *advances timidly.*) What kept you so late?
Vladimir: You have a message from Mr. Godot?

Boy: Yes Sir.

Vladimir: Well, what is it?

Estragon: What kept you so late?

The **Boy** *looks at them in turn, not knowing to which he should reply.*

Vladimir: (*to* **Estragon**) Let him alone.

Estragon: (*violently*). You let me alone. (*Advancing, to the* **Boy**.) Do you know what time it is?

Boy: (*recoiling*). It's not my fault, Sir.

Estragon: And whose is it? Mine?

Boy: I was afraid, Sir.

Estragon: Afraid of what? Of us? (*Pause.*) Answer me!

Vladimir: I know what it is, he was afraid of the others.

Estragon: How long have you been here?

Boy: A good while, Sir.

Vladimir: You were afraid of the whip?

Boy: Yes Sir.

Vladimir: The roars?

Boy: Yes Sir.

Vladimir: The two big men.

Boy: Yes Sir.

Vladimir: Do you know them?

Boy: No Sir.

Vladimir: Are you a native of these parts? (*Silence.*) Do you belong to these parts?

Boy: Yes Sir.

Estragon: That's all a pack of lies. (*Shaking the* **Boy** *by the arm.*) Tell us the truth!

Boy: (*trembling*). But it is the truth, Sir!

Vladimir: Will you let him alone! What's the matter with you? (**Estragon** *releases the* **Boy**, *moves away, covering his face with his hands.* **Vladimir** *and the* **Boy** *observe him.* **Estragon** *drops his hands. His face is convulsed.*) What's the matter with you?

Estragon: I'm unhappy.

Vladimir: Not really! Since when?

Estragon: I'd forgotten.

Vladimir: Extraordinary the tricks that memory plays! (**Estragon** *tries to speak, renounces, limps to his place, sits down and begins to take off his boots. To* **Boy**.) Well?

Boy: Mr. Godot—

Vladimir: I've seen you before, haven't I?

Boy: I don't know, Sir.

Vladimir: You don't know me?

Boy: No Sir.

Vladimir: It wasn't you came yesterday?

Boy: No Sir.

Vladimir: This is your first time?

Boy: Yes Sir.

Silence.

Vladimir: Word words. (*Pause.*) Speak.

Boy: (*in a rush*). Mr. Godot told me to tell you he won't come this evening but surely to-morrow.

Silence.

Vladimir: Is that all?

Boy: Yes Sir.

Silence.

Vladimir: You work for Mr. Godot?

Boy: Yes Sir.

Vladimir: What do you do?

Boy: I mind the goats, Sir.

Vladimir: Is he good to you?

Boy: Yes Sir.

Vladimir: He doesn't beat you?

Boy: No Sir, not me.

Vladimir: Whom does he beat?

Boy: He beats my brother, Sir.

Vladimir: Ah, you have a brother?

Boy: Yes Sir.

Vladimir: What does he do?

Boy: He minds the sheep, Sir.

Vladimir: And why doesn't he beat you?

Boy: I don't know, Sir.

Vladimir: He must be fond of you.

Boy: I don't know, Sir.

Silence.

Vladimir: Does he give you enough to eat? (*The* **Boy** *hesitates.*) Does he feed you well?

Boy: Fairly well, Sir.

Vladimir: You're not unhappy? (*The* **Boy** *hesitates.*) Do you hear me?

Boy: Yes Sir.

Vladimir: Well?

Boy: I don't know, Sir.

Vladimir: You don't know if you're unhappy or not?

Boy: No Sir.

Vladimir: You're as bad as myself. (*Silence.*) Where do you sleep?

Boy: In the loft, Sir.

Vladimir: With your brother?

Boy: Yes Sir.

Vladimir: In the hay?

Boy: Yes Sir.

Silence.

Vladimir: All right, you may go.

Boy: What am I to tell Mr. Godot, Sir?

Vladimir: Tell him . . . (*he hesitates*) . . . tell him you saw us. (*Pause.*) You did see us, didn't you?

Boy: Yes Sir.

He steps back, hesitates, turns and exits running. The light suddenly fails. In a moment it is night. The moon rises at back, mounts in the sky, stands still, shedding a pale light on the scene.

Vladimir: At last! (**Estragon** *gets up and goes towards* **Vladimir**, *a boot in each hand. He puts them down at edge of stage, straightens and contemplates the moon.*) What are you doing?

Estragon: Pale for weariness.

Vladimir: Eh?

Estragon: Of climbing heaven and gazing on the likes of us.

Vladimir: Your boots, what are you doing with your boots?

Estragon: (*turning to look at the boots*). I'm leaving them there. (*Pause.*) Another will come, just as . . . as . . . as me, but with smaller feet, and they'll make him happy.

Vladimir: But you can't go barefoot!

Estragon: Christ did.

Vladimir: Christ! What has Christ got to do with it? You're not going to compare yourself to Christ!

Estragon: All my life I've compared myself to him.

Vladimir: But where he lived it was warm, it was dry!

Estragon: Yes. And they crucified quick.

Silence.

Vladimir: We've nothing more to do here.

Estragon: Nor anywhere else.

Vladimir: Ah Gogo, don't go on like that. To-morrow everything will be better.

Estragon: How do you make that out?

Vladimir: Did you not hear what the child said?

Estragon: No.

Vladimir: He said that Godot was sure to come tomorrow. (*Pause.*) What do you say to that?

Estragon: Then all we have to do is to wait on here.

Vladimir: Are you mad? We must take cover. (*He takes* Estragon *by the arm.*) Come on.

He draws Estragon *after him.* Estragon *yields, then resists. They halt.*

Estragon: (*looking at the tree*). Pity we haven't got a bit of rope.

Vladimir: Come on. It's cold.

He draws Estragon *after him. As before.*

Estragon: Remind me to bring a bit of rope to-morrow.

Vladimir: Yes. Come on.

He draws him after him. As before.

Estragon: How long have we been together all the time now?

Vladimir: I don't know. Fifty years maybe.

Estragon: Do you remember the day I threw myself into the Rhone?

Vladimir: We were grape harvesting.

Estragon: You fished me out.

Vladimir: That's all dead and buried.

Estragon: My clothes dried in the sun.

Vladimir: There's no good harking back on that. Come on.

He draws him after him. As before.

Estragon: Wait!

Vladimir: I'm cold!

Estragon: Wait! (*He moves away from* Vladimir.) I sometimes wonder if we wouldn't have been better off all alone, each one for himself. (*He crosses the*

stage and sits down on the mound.) We weren't
made for the same road.

Vladimir: (*without anger*). It's not certain.

Estragon: No, nothing is certain.

Vladimir *slowly crosses the stage and sits down beside* **Estragon.**

Vladimir: We can still part, if you think it would
be better.

Estragon: It's not worth while now.

Silence.

Vladimir: No, it's not worth while now.

Silence.

Estragon: Well, shall we go?

Vladimir: Yes, let's go.

They do not move.

CURTAIN

PRE-TWENTIETH CENTURY PERIOD SCENES

Scene from
    Antigone by Sophocles, translated by Dudley Fitts and Robert Fitzgerald

For 2 women

Characters: **Antigone,** the daughter of Oedipus.
                Ismene, her sister.

Setting: Before the palace of Creon, King of Thebes, in ancient Greece.

Situation: Following the exile and death of Antigone's father Oedipus, who unknowingly murdered his father and married his mother, Antigone's uncle Creon assumed the kingship of Thebes. In the civil war that followed, her two brothers Eteocles and Polyneices were both killed. Eteocles died fighting for Thebes, but Polyneices perished as a traitor against the state. Creon has ordered that Eteocles be buried with full military honors but that Polyneices be left out on the field to rot. Antigone now faces the moral dilemma of whether to bury her brother even though he is a traitor, in contradiction to the order of Creon the king. In this scene from the beginning of the play, the two sisters review the events leading up to the present moment and their current difficult position.

Script Notations

Antig.: Ismenê, dear sister,
You would think that we had already suffered enough
For the curse on Oedipus:
I cannot imagine any grief
That you and I have not gone through.
And now—
Have they told you the new decree of our
King Creon?

Ismene: I have heard nothing: I know
That two sisters lost two brothers, a double death
In a single hour; and I know that the Argive army
Fled in the night; but beyond this, nothing.

Antig.: I thought so. And that is why I wanted you
To come out here with me. There is something we must do.

Ismene: Why do you speak so strangely?

Antig.: Listen, Ismenê:
Creon buried our brother Eteoclês
With military honours, gave him a soldier's funeral,
And it was right that he should; but Polyneicês,
Who fought as bravely and died as miserably,—
They say that Creon has sworn
No one shall bury him, no one mourn for him,
But his body must lie in the fields, a sweet treasure
For carrion birds to find as they search for food.
That is what they say, and our good Creon is coming here
To announce it publicly; and the penalty—
Stoning to death in the public square!
                                        There it is,
And now you can prove what you are:
A true sister, or a traitor to your family.

Ismene: Antigonê, you are mad! What could I possibly do?

Antig.: You must decide whether you will help me or not.

Ismene: I do not understand you. Help you in what?

Antig.: Ismenê, I am going to bury him. Will you come?

Ismene: Bury him! You have just said the new law forbids it.

Antig.: He is my brother. And he is your brother, too.

Ismene: But think of the danger! Think what Creon will do!

Antig.: Creon is not strong enough to stand in my way.

Ismene: Ah sister!
Oedipus died, everyone hating him
For what his own search brought to light, his eyes
Ripped out by his own hand; and Iocastê died,
His mother and wife at once: she twisted the cords
That strangled her life; and our two brothers died,
Each killed by the other's sword. And we are left:
But oh, Antigonê,
Think how much more terrible than these
Our own death would be if we should go against Creon
And do what he has forbidden! We are only women,
We cannot fight with men, Antigonê!
The law is strong, we must give in to the law
In this thing, and in worse. I beg the Dead
To forgive me, but I am helpless: I must yield
To those in authority. And I think it is dangerous business
To be always meddling.

Antig.:   If that is what you think,
I should not want you, even if you asked to come.
You have made your choice, you can be what you want to be.
But I will bury him; and if I must die,
I say that this crime is holy: I shall lie down
With him in death, and I shall be as dear
To him as he to me.
                    It is the dead,
Not the living, who make the longest demands:
We die for ever . . .
                    You may do as you like,
Since apparently the laws of the gods mean nothing to you.

Ismene: They mean a great deal to me; but I have no strength
To break laws that were made for the public good.

Antig.: That must be your excuse, I suppose. But as for me,
I will bury the brother I love.

Ismene: Antigonê,
I am so afraid for you!

Antig.:   You need not be:
You have yourself to consider, after all.

Ismene: But no one must hear of this, you must
tell no one!
I will keep it a secret, I promise!

Antig.:   Oh tell it! Tell everyone!
Think how they'll hate you when it all
comes out
If they learn that you knew about it all the
time!

Ismene: So fiery! You should be cold with fear.

Antig.: Perhaps. But I am doing only what I must.

Ismene: But can you do it? I say that you cannot.

Antig.: Very well: when my strength gives out, I
shall do no more.

Ismene: Impossible things should not be tried at
all.

Antig.: Go away, Ismenê:
I shall be hating you soon, and the dead
will too,
For your words are hateful. Leave me my
foolish plan:
I am not afraid of the danger; if it means
death,
It will not be the worst of deaths—death
without honour.

Ismene: Go then, if you feel that you must.
You are unwise,
But a loyal friend indeed to those who love
you.

Scene from

> *The Doctor in Spite of Himself* by Molière, translated and adapted by Stanley
> Kahan

From Act I

Scene: For 2 men, 1 woman

Characters: **Sganarelle,** a drunken woodcutter.
Martine, his wife.
Monsieur Robert, a gentleman.

Setting: A forest in France. A day during the mid-seventeenth century.

Situation: This is the opening scene of the play. Sganarelle and Martine are continuing an argument which they started offstage. They are low-comedy characters, endowed with little of the gentility found in the other characters in
the play.

Script Notations

(Sganarelle *and* Martine *appear on the stage quarreling*)

Sganarelle: Absolutely not. I tell you I will do nothing of the kind. It is up to me to decide when to speak, and I will be master here.

Martine: And I am telling you that I will live as I wish, and I am not married to you to put up with all of your foolishness.

Sganarelle: Good grief . . . what a pain in the . . . to have a wife! Aristotle was perfectly right in stating that a woman is worse than the devil.

Martine: Look at Mister Smark-Aleck—and his Greek friend Aristotle.·

Sganarelle: That's right. Mister Smark-Aleck. You go and find a better wood chopper who can debate the way I can.—I, who have served a great physician for six years, and who, when only a little boy, knew his grammar by heart!

Martine: A plague on this idiot!

Sganarelle: A plague on this slut of a wife.

Martine: Cursed be the hour and the day when I took it in my poor head to say yes to this lout!

Sganarelle: Cursed be the notary who made me put my mark on that vile contract.

Martine: So . . . it is very nice of you to complain about that matter. Shouldn't you rather thank Heaven every second you breathe that you have me for a wife? How did you ever deserve a woman like me?

Sganarelle: Oh, my sweet, you are much too kind—and I must admit I have had occasions to remember our wedding night with great warmth! Heavens!—Don't make me open my mouth too wide. I might say certain things I shouldn't.

Martine: Eh! What? Say? What could you say?

Sganarelle: Enough of that! Let us drop the matter. It is enough that we know what we know, and that you were very fortunate to meet me at all.

Martine: What do you mean—fortunate to meet you. A slob who will send me to a hospital?—a drunken, lying wretch who gobbles up every penny I have?

Sganarelle: That is a lie: I don't gobble—I drink every penny of it!

Martine: A wretch who sells all the furniture in the house?

Sganarelle: That is called living off one's means.

Martine: A fiend who has taken the very bed from under me?

Sganarelle: That is simply to help you get up earlier in the morning.

Martine: An idiot who doesn't leave a stick of furniture in the house.

Sganarelle: It is just a way to make moving that much easier.

Martine: A lout who does nothing from morning till night but gamble and drink.

Sganarelle: I do that simply to keep from becoming too depressed.

Martine: And what am I supposed to do with our family?

Sganarelle: You can do whatever you like.

Martine: I have four poor children on my hands.

Sganarelle: Then drop them.

Martine: They keep asking for a little bread!

Sganarelle: So then—beat them. When I've had enough to eat and drink everyone in the house should be satisfied.

Martine: Do you mean to tell me, you drunken sot, that things can go on as they have been all this time?

Sganarelle: My dear wife, let us not get excited, pretty-please?

Martine: And that I must bear forever your drunkenness and insults?

Sganarelle: Let us not get upset, my little pigeon.

Martine: And that I don't know how to bring you back to a sense of responsibility?

Sganarelle: My little canary—you know I am not a patient man—and my arm is beginning to get a little excited!

Martine: I give that for your threats. (*snaps her fingers*)

Sganarelle: My bird, my parrot, my canary—your skin is itching for a good hiding!

Martine: You had better observe that I couldn't care less for your threats!

Sganarelle: My dear little rib—you have set your heart upon a good beating.

Martine: Do you think I am frightened of all your talk?

Sganarelle: Sweet little barbecued chop, I shall belt you in the ears.

Martine: Drunken lout!

Sganarelle: I'll beat you!

Martine: Walking wine-cask.

Sganarelle: I'll pummel you.

Martine: Infamous wretch.

Sganarelle: I'll tan your hide so that you won't forget it.

Martine: Lout! villain! scoundrel! drunkard! wretch! dog's meat! horse's tail! liar! deceiver! . . .

Sganarelle: So you really want it, eh? Very well then. (*He picks up a stick and starts to beat her*)

Martine: (*Yelling*) Help! Oh, help! Please help! Help!

Sganarelle: And this my pet is the best way to shut you up!

M. Robert: Hello there! I say, Hello. Good Heavens. What is this? How revolting. The plague take this villain for beating the poor woman so.

Martine: (*Her arms crossed, she speaks to* **M. Robert,** *forcing him back, and then slaps him across the face*) Maybe I enjoy him beating me. In fact, I do!

M. Robert: Really! If that is the case, please continue.

Martine: Why are you interfering?

M. Robert: I must be wrong.—Pray forgive me.

Martine: Is this any of your business?

M. Robert: You are absolutely correct!

Martine: Look at this fancy peacock, who wants to stop a husband from beating his poor wife.

M. Robert: I said I was sorry!

Martine: What do you have to say about it—eh?

M. Robert: Not another word!

Martine: Who asked you to stick your nose in this business?

M. Robert: Mum's the word! I won't say anything else!

Martine: Mind your own business.

M. Robert: I'll be as quiet as the grave!

Martine: I enjoy being beaten.

M. Robert: Good for you.

Martine: It doesn't hurt you, does it?

M. Robert: You are right. It doesn't.

Martine: And you are a first-class ass, who interferes in matters that don't concern you.

M. Robert: (*to* **Sganarelle**) My good friend, I earnestly beg your pardon. Go ahead and beat your wife as much as you wish. As a matter of fact, if you like, I'll lend a hand. Two hands are better than one! (*He moves over to* **Sganarelle** *who begins to beat him with the stick he has been using on* **Martine.**)

Sganarelle: No thank you, I'm quite able to do the job by myself.

M. Robert: Ah—Well then, that is quite a different matter.

Sganarelle: If I feel like beating her, I'll beat her; and if I don't feel like it, I won't.

M. Robert: That's wonderful.

Sganarelle: She happens to be my wife, not yours!

M. Robert: I am certainly pleased about that!

Sganarelle: No one told you to tell me how to deal with my wife.

M. Robert: Quite right.

Sganarelle: I can beat her without your help, understand!

M. Robert: Evidently.

Sganarelle: And it is just your busy-body attitude that makes you meddle in other people's business. Remember what Cicero said: Between the tree and the finger you must not place the bark. (*He beats him and drives him off-stage. He returns to his wife and takes her hand.*) Come my dear, let us make up. Let us shake hands.

Martine: That's fine now, after you have beaten me!

Sganarelle: That doesn't bother me. Let's shake hands.

Martine: I won't shake hands.

Sganarelle: What?

Martine: No!

Sganarelle: Come, my little canary.

Martine: I won't shake hands.

Sganarelle: Come, my little porcupine, let's shake hands.

Martine: I will do nothing of the kind!

Sganarelle: Come now. Come, come on.

Martine: I have said no, and I mean it.

Sganarelle: It's just a trifle. Please do, my little mackerel.

Martine: Leave me alone.

Sganarelle: I said "Shake hands!"

Martine: You have treated me too cruelly.

Sganarelle: All right then! I beg your pardon; put your hand right there.

Martine: I forgive you. (*aside, very softly*) I shall see that you pay ten fold for this little escapade.

Sganarelle: You are silly to take this matter too seriously. These are minor matters that are necessary now and then to show that we love each other. Five or six solid blows only strengthen our bond of affection. There—that's done. Now I'm going into the woods, and I promise that I will return with several full loads today.

Scene from
   Fashion by Anna Cora Mowatt

From Act III, Scene 2

For 1 man, 2 women

Characters: **Millinette,** a French lady's maid,
             Count Jolimaitre, a fashionable European importation.
             Gertrude, an attractive young governess.

Setting: Housekeeper's room in the house of Mrs. Tiffany. The 1840s in New York.

Situation: Mrs. Tiffany would like to be a "lady of fashion" and has surrounded
         herself with European importations, especially from France. Among these
         people is a phony count, Jolimaitre, a fortune hunter, who has plotted to get
         the hand of Seraphina, Mrs. Tiffany's daughter. Prior to this scene, he has
         also made advances to Gertrude but was discovered by Millinette, who has
         told him to meet her or else she will reveal his true identity.

Script Notations

Scene 2. *Housekeeper's room.*
(*Enter* **Millinette.**)

Mil.: I have set dat bête, Adolph, to vatch for him. He say he would come back so soon as Madame's voiture drive from de door. If he not come—but he vill—he vill—he *bien etourdi*, but he have *bon coeur*.

(*Enter* **Count.**)

Count: Ah! Millinette, my dear, you see what a good-natured dog I am to fly at your bidding—

Mil.: Fly? Ah! *trompeur!* Vat for you fly from Paris? Vat for you leave me—and I love you so much? Ven you sick—you almost die—did I not stay by you— take care of you—and you have no else friend? Vat for you leave Paris?

Count: Never allude to disagreeable subjects, *mon enfant!* I was forced by uncontrollable circumstances to fly to the land of liberty—

Mil.: Vat you do vid all de money I give you? The last sou I had—did I not give you?

Count: I dare say you did, ma petite—wish you'd been better supplied! (*Aside.*) Don't ask any questions here—can't explain now—the next time we meet—

Mil.: But, ah! ven shall ve meet—ven? You not deceive me, not any more.

Count: Deceive you! I'd rather deceive myself—I wish I could! I'd persuade myself you were once more washing linen in the Seine! (*Aside.*)

Mil.: I vil tell you ven ve shall meet—On Friday night Madame give one grand ball—you come *sans doute*—den ven de supper is served—de Americans tink of noting else ven de supper come—den you steal out of de room, and you find me here—and you give me one grand *explanation!*

(*Enter* **Gertrude,** *unperceived.*)

Count: Friday night—while supper is serving—*parole d'honneur* I will be here—I will explain every thing—my sudden departure from Paris—my— demme, my courtship—every thing! Now let me go—if any of the family should discover us—

Ger.: (*Who during the last speech has gradually advanced.*) They might discover more than you think it advisable for them to know!

Count: The devil!

Mil.: *Mon Dieu!* Mademoiselle Gertrude!

Count: (*Recovering himself.*) My dear Miss Gertrude, let me explain—aw—aw—nothing is more natural than the situation in which you find me—

Ger.: I am inclined to believe that, Sir.

Count: Now—'pon my honor, that's not fair. Here is Millinette will bear witness to what I am about to say—

Ger.: Oh, I have not the slightest doubt of that, Sir.

Count: You see, Millinette happened to be lady's-maid in the family of—of—the Duchess Chateau D'Espagne—and I chanced to be a particular friend of the Duchess—*very particular* I assure you! Of course I saw Millinette, and she, demme, she saw me! Didn't you, Millinette?

Mil.: Oh! *oui*—Mademoiselle, I knew him ver vell.

Count: Well, it is a remarkable fact that—being in correspondence with this very Duchess—at this very time—

Ger.: That is sufficient, Sir—I am already so well acquainted with your extraordinary talents for improvisation, that I will not further tax your invention—

Mil.: Ah! Mademoiselle Gertrude do not betray us—have pity!

Count: (*Assuming an air of dignity.*) Silence, Millinette! My word has been doubted—the word of a nobleman! I will inform my friend, Mrs. Tiffany, of this young person's audacity. (*Going.*)

Ger.: His own weapons alone can foil this villain! (*Aside.*) Sir—Sir—Count! (*At the last word the Count turns.*) Perhaps, Sir, the least said about this matter the better!

Count: (*Delightedly.*) The least said? We won't say anything at all. She's coming round—couldn't resist me. (*Aside.*) Charming Gertrude—

Mil.: *Quoi?* Vat that you say?

Count: My sweet, adorable Millinette, hold your tongue, will you? (*Aside to her.*)

Mil.: (*Aloud.*) No, I vill not! If you do look so from out your eyes at her again, I vill tell all!

Count: Oh, I never could manage two women at once,—jealousy makes the dear creatures so spiteful. The only valor is in flight! (*Aside.*) Miss Gertrude, I wish you good morning. Millinette, *mon enfant*, adieu. (*Exit.*)

Mil.: But I have one word more to say. Stop, Stop! (*Exit after him.*)

Ger.: (*Musingly.*) Friday night while supper is serving, he is to meet Millinette here and explain—what? This man is an impostor! His insulting me—his familiarity with Millinette—his whole conduct—prove it. If I tell Mrs. Tiffany this she will disbelieve me, and one word may place this so-called Count on his guard. To convince Seraphina would be equally difficult, and her rashness and infatuation may render her miserable for life. No—she shall be saved! I must devise some plan for opening their eyes. Truly, if I *cannot* invent one, I shall be the first woman who was ever at a loss for a stratagem—especially to punish a villain or to shield a friend. (*Exit.*)

END OF ACT THIRD

Scene from
The Importance of Being Earnest by Oscar Wilde

From Act I

For 1 man, 1 woman

Characters: **Jack Worthing,** a gentleman about town, in his late twenties.
Lady Bracknell, Gwendolen's mother and Algernon's aunt.

Setting: The morning room. Algernon Moncrieff's flat in Halfmoon Street, London. An afternoon in the 1890s.

Situation: Jack is in love with Gwendolen in a passionately trivial manner. He has taken the opportunity to propose marriage to her while her mother, Lady Bracknell, was out of the room. Gwendolen does not know that her suitor's real name is Jack; she believes it to be Ernest, the name Jack assumes while carrying on his bachelor escapades. His name is "Ernest in town and Jack in the country."

Lady Bracknell has entered the room as Jack is kneeling before Gwendolen. She assumes that Jack wishes to propose to her daughter, and she dismisses Gwendolen in order to talk to him to determine if he will be a suitable husband. Gwendolen has just left the room as Lady Bracknell begins the interview.

Script Notations

Lady Bracknell: (*sitting down*) You can take a seat, Mr. Worthing. (*looks in her pocket for note-book and pencil*)

Jack: Thank you, Lady Bracknell, I prefer standing.

Lady Bracknell: (*pencil and note-book in hand*) I feel bound to tell you that you are not down on my list of eligible young men, although I have the same list as the dear Duchess of Bolton has. We work together, in fact. However, I am quite ready to enter your name, should your answers be what a really affectionate mother requires. Do you smoke?

Jack: Well, yes, I must admit I smoke.

Lady Bracknell: I am glad to hear it. A man should always have an occupation of some kind. There are far too many idle men in London as it is. How old are you?

Jack: Twenty-nine.

Lady Bracknell: A very good age to be married at. I have always been of opinion that a man who desires to get married should know either everything or nothing. Which do you know?

Jack: (*after some hesitation*) I know nothing, Lady Bracknell.

Lady Bracknell: I am pleased to hear it. I do not approve of anything that tampers with natural ignorance. Ignorance is like a delicate exotic fruit; touch it and the bloom is gone. The whole theory of modern education is radically unsound. Fortunately in England, at any rate, education produces no effect whatsoever. If it did, it would prove a serious danger to the upper classes, and probably lead to acts of violence in Grosvenor Square. What is your income?

Jack: Between seven and eight thousand a year.

Lady Bracknell: (*makes a note in her book*) In land, or in investments?

Jack: In investments, chiefly.

Lady Bracknell: That is satisfactory. What between the duties expected of one during one's lifetime, and the duties exacted from one after one's death, land has ceased to be either a profit or a pleasure. It gives one position, and prevents one from keeping it up. That's all that can be said about land.

Jack: I have a country house with some land, of course, attached to it, about fifteen hundred acres, I believe; but I don't depend on that for my real income. In fact, as far as I can make out, the poachers are the only people who make anything out of it.

Lady Bracknell: A country house! How many bedrooms? Well, that point can be cleared up afterwards. You have a town house, I hope? A girl with a simple, unspoiled nature, like Gwendolen, could hardly be expected to reside in the country.

Jack: Well, I own a house in Belgrave Square, but

it is let by the year to Lady Bloxham. Of course, I can get it back whenever I like, at six months' notice.

Lady Bracknell: Lady Bloxham? I don't know her.

Jack: Oh, she goes about very little. She is a lady considerably advanced in years.

Lady Bracknell: Ah, now-a-days that is no guarantee of respectability of character. What number in Belgrave Square?

Jack: 149.

Lady Bracknell: (*shaking her head*) The unfashionable side. I thought there was something. However, that could easily be altered.

Jack: Do you mean the fashion, or the side?

Lady Bracknell: (*sternly*) Both, if necessary, I presume. What are your politics?

Jack: Well, I am afraid I really have none. I am a Liberal Unionist.

Lady Bracknell: Oh, they count as Tories. They dine with us. Or come in the evening, at any rate. Now to minor matters. Are your parents living?

Jack: I have lost both my parents.

Lady Bracknell: To lose one parent, Mr. Worthing, may be regarded as a misfortune; to lose both looks like carelessness. Who was your father? He was evidently a man of some wealth. Was he born in what the Radical papers call the purple of commerce, or did he rise from the ranks of the aristocracy?

Jack: I am afraid I really don't know. The fact is, Lady Bracknell, I said I had lost my parents. It would be nearer the truth to say that my parents seem to have lost me . . . I don't actually know who I am by birth. I was . . . well, I was found.

Lady Bracknell: Found!

Jack: The late Mr. Thomas Cardew, an old gentleman of a very charitable and kindly disposition, found me, and gave me the name of Worthing, because he happened to have a first-class ticket for Worthing in his pocket at the time. Worthing is a place in Sussex. It is a seaside resort.

Lady Bracknell: Where did the charitable gentleman who had a first-class ticket for this seaside resort find you?

Jack: (*gravely*) In a hand-bag.

Lady Bracknell: A hand-bag?

Jack: (*very seriously*) Yes, Lady Bracknell. I was in a hand-bag—a somewhat large, black leather handbag, with handles to it—an ordinary hand-bag in fact.

Lady Bracknell: In what locality did this Mr. James, or Thomas, Cardew come across this ordinary handbag?

Jack: In the cloak-room at Victoria Station. It was given to him in mistake for his own.

Lady Bracknell: The cloak-room at Victoria Station?

Jack: Yes. The Brighton line.

Lady Bracknell: The line is immaterial. Mr. Worthing, I confess I feel somewhat bewildered by what you have just told me. To be born, or at any rate bred, in a hand-bag, whether it had handles or not, seems to me to display a contempt for the ordinary decencies of family life that remind one of the worst excesses of the French Revolution. And I presume you know what that unfortunate movement led to? As for the particular locality in which the hand-bag was found, a cloak-room at a railway station might serve to conceal a social indiscretion—has probably, indeed, been used for that purpose before now— but it could hardly be regarded as an assured basis for a recognized position in good society.

Jack: May I ask you then what you would advise me to do? I need hardly say I would do anything in the world to ensure Gwendolen's happiness.

Lady Bracknell: I would strongly advise you, Mr. Worthing, to try and acquire some relations as soon as possible, and to make a definite effort to produce at any rate one parent, of either sex, before the season is quite over.

Jack: Well, I don't see how I could possibly manage to do that. I can produce the hand-bag at any moment. It is in my dressing-room at home. I really think that should satisfy you, Lady Bracknell.

Lady Bracknell: Me, sir! What has it to do with me? You can hardly imagine that I and Lord Bracknell would dream of allowing our only daughter—a girl brought up with the utmost care—to marry into a cloak-room, and form an alliance with a parcel? Good morning, Mr. Worthing!

[**Lady Bracknell** *sweeps out in majestic indignation.*]

Jack: Good morning!

Scene from

    King Oedipus by Sophocles, translated by William Butler Yeats

For 1 man, 1 woman

Characters: **Oedipus,** the king of Thebes.
                Jocasta, the queen.

Setting: In front of the palace of Oedipus in Thebes in ancient Greece.

Situation: A plague has broken out in the city of Thebes, and King Oedipus has pledged that he will find the cause of the disaster, visited on the city by the gods. He does not realize that he himself is the guilty party, having unknowingly killed his father (Laius) and married his mother (Jocasta). In the previous scenes, Creon and the soothsayer Tiresias have strongly suggested that Oedipus is guilty of the deeds which he refuses to acknowledge. Clearly Oedipus is deeply upset, and Jocasta comes to him to find out why he is in such a rage. (The following scene includes one line by the leader of the chorus which may be easily eliminated.)

Script Notations

Jocas.: In the name of the gods, King, what put you in this anger?

Oedip.: I will tell you; for I honor you more than these men do. The cause is Creon and his plots against me.

Jocas.: Speak on, if you can tell clearly how this quarrel arose.

Oedip.: He says that I am guilty of the blood of Laius.

Jocas.: On his own knowledge, or on hearsay?

Oedip.: He has made a rascal of a seer his mouthpiece.

Jocas.: Do not fear that there is truth in what he says. Listen to me, and learn to your comfort that nothing born of woman can know what is to come. I will give you proof of that. An oracle came to Laius once, I will not say from Phoebus, but from his ministers, that he was doomed to die by the hand of his own child sprung from him and me. When his child was but three days old, Laius bound its feet together and had it thrown by sure hands upon a trackless mountain; and when Laius was murdered at the place where three highways meet, it was, or so at least the rumor says, by foreign robbers. So Apollo did not bring it about that the child should kill its father, nor did Laius die in the dreadful way he feared by his child's hand. Yet that was how the message of the seers mapped out the future. Pay no attention to such things. What the God would show he will need no help to show it, but bring it to light himself.

Oedip.: What restlessness of soul, lady, has come upon me since I heard you speak, what a tumult of the mind!

Jocas.: What is this new anxiety? What has startled you?

Oedip.: You said that Laius was killed where three highways meet.

Jocas.: Yes: that was the story.

Oedip.: And where is the place?

Jocas.: In Phocis where the road divides branching off to Delphi and to Daulis.

Oedip.: And when did it happen? How many years ago?

Jocas.: News was published in this town just before you came into power.

Oedip.: O Zeus! What have you planned to do unto me?

Jocas.: He was tall; the silver had just come into his hair; and in shape not greatly unlike to you.

Oedip.: Unhappy that I am! It seems that I have laid a dreadful curse upon myself, and did not know it.

Jocas.: What do you say? I tremble when I look on you, my King.

Oedip.: And I have a misgiving that the seer can see indeed. But I will know it all more clearly, if you tell me one thing more.

Jocas.: Indeed, though I tremble I will answer whatever you ask.

Oedip.: Had he but a small troop with him; or did he travel like a great man with many followers?

Jocas.: There were but five in all—one of them a herald; and there was one carriage with Laius in it.

Oedip.: Alas! It is now clear indeed. Who was it brought the news, lady?

Jocas.: A servant—the one survivor.

Oedip.: Is he by chance in the house now?

Jocas.: No; for when he found you reigning instead of Laius he besought me, his hand clasped in mine, to send him to the fields among the cattle that he might be far from the sight of this town; and I sent him. He was a worthy man for a slave and might have asked a bigger thing.

Oedip.: I would have him return to us without delay.

Jocas.: Oedipus, it is easy. But why do you ask this?

Oedip.: I fear that I have said too much, and therefore I would question him.

Jocas.: He shall come, but I too have a right to know what lies so heavy upon your heart, my King.

Oedip.: Yes: and it shall not be kept from you now that my fear has grown so heavy. Nobody is more to me than you, nobody has the same right to learn my good or evil luck. My father was Polybus of Corinth, my mother the Dorian Merope, and I was held the foremost man in all that town until a thing happened—a thing to startle a man, though not to make him angry as it made me. We were sitting at the table, and a man who had drunk too much cried out that I was not my father's son—and I, though angry, restrained my anger for that day; but the next day went to my father and my mother and questioned them. They were indignant at the taunt and that comforted me—and yet the man's words rankled, for they had spread a rumor through the town. Without consulting my father or my mother I went to Delphi, but Phoebus told me nothing of the thing for which I came, but much of other things— things of sorrow and of terror: that I should live in incest with my mother, and beget a brood that men would shudder to look upon; that I should be my father's murderer. Hearing those words I fled out of Corinth, and from that day have but known where it lies when I have found its direction by the stars. I sought where I might escape those infamous things—the doom that was laid upon me. I came in my flight to that very spot where you tell me this king perished. Now, lady, I will tell you the truth. When I had come close up to those three roads, I came upon a herald, and a man like him you have described seated in a carriage. The man who held the reins and the old man himself would not give me room, but thought to force me from the path, and I struck the driver in my anger. The old man, seeing what I had done, waited till I was passing him and then struck me upon the head. I paid him back in full, for I knocked him out of the carriage with a blow of my stick. He rolled on his back, and after that I killed them all. If this stranger were indeed Laius, is there a more miserable man in the world than the man before you? Is there a man more hated of Heaven? No stranger, no citizen, may receive him into his house, not a soul may speak to him, and no mouth but my own mouth has laid this curse upon me. Am I not wretched? May I be swept from this world before I have endured this doom!

Scene from
    Lysistrata by Aristophanes, translated by Charles T. Murphy

For 1 man, 1 woman

Characters: **Myrrhine,** an Athenian woman.
                Cinesias, her Athenian husband.

Setting: In Athens, Greece, beneath the Acropolis, in the fifth century B.C.

Situation: Led by Lysistrata, the women of Athens have agreed to go on a sex strike
        against their warrior husbands and thus, they hope, end the Peloponnesian
        War. The women seize the war treasury from the Parthenon to keep it from
        their men and set themselves up to be alluring, while refusing to grant the
        men any sexual pleasures. This scene follows the entrance of Cinesias, "mad
        with passion" for his wife, whom Lysistrata has instructed to tease him. (The
        very brief appearance of the slave and the baby need not be included in the
        scene.)

Script Notations

Myrrhine: Oh, what it is to be a mother! I've got to come down, I suppose. (*She leaves the wall and shortly reappears at the gate.*)

Cinesias (*to himself*): She seems much younger, and she has such a sweet look about her. Oh, the way she teases me! And her pretty, provoking ways make me burn with longing.

Myrrhine (*coming out of the gate and taking the baby*): O my sweet little angel. Naughty papa! Here, let Mummy kiss you, Mamma's little sweetheart! (*She fondles the baby lovingly.*)

Cinesias (*in despair*): You heartless creature, why do you do this? Why follow these other women and make both of us suffer so? (*He tries to embrace her.*)

Myrrhine: Don't touch me!

Cinesias: You're letting all our things at home go to wrack and ruin.

Myrrhine: I don't care.

Cinesias: You don't care that your wool is being plucked to pieces by the chickens?

Myrrhine: Not in the least.

Cinesias: And you haven't celebrated the rites of Aphrodite for ever so long. Won't you come home?

Myrrhine: Not on your life, unless you men make a truce and stop the war.

Cinesias: Well then, if that pleases you, we'll do it.

Myrrhine: Well then, if that pleases *you*, I'll come home—afterwards! Right now I'm on oath not to.

Cinesias: Then just lie down here with me for a moment.

Myrrhine: No—(*in a teasing voice*) and yet, I won't say I don't love you.

Cinesias: You love me? Oh, do lie down here, Myrrhine dear!

Myrrhine: What, you silly fool! in front of the baby?

Cinesias (*hastily thrusting the baby at the slave*): Of course not. Here—home! Take him, Manes! (*The slave goes off with the baby.*) See, the baby's out of the way. Now won't you lie down?

Myrrhine: But where, my dear?

Cinesias: Where? The grotto of Pan's a lovely spot.

Myrrhine: How could I purify myself before returning to the shrine?

Cinesias: Easily: just wash here in the Clepsydra.

Myrrhine: And then, shall I go back on my oath?

Cinesias: On my head be it! Don't worry about the oath.

Myrrhine: All right, then. Just let me bring out a bed.

Cinesias: No, don't. The ground's all right.

Myrrhine: Heavens, no! Bad as you are, I won't let you lie on the bare ground. (*She goes into the Acropolis.*)

Cinesias: Why, she really loves me; it's plain to see.

Myrrhine (*returning with a bed*): There! Now hurry up and lie down. I'll just slip off this dress. But— let's see: oh yes, I must fetch a mattress.

Cinesias: Nonsense! No mattress for me.

Myrrhine: Yes indeed! It's not nice on the bare springs.

Cinesias: Give me a kiss.

Myrrhine (*giving him a hasty kiss*): There! (*She goes.*)

Cinesias (*in mingled distress and delight*): Oh-h! Hurry back!

Myrrhine (*returning with a mattress*): Here's the mattress; lie down on it. I'm taking my things off now—but—let's see: you have no pillow.

Cinesias: I don't *want* a pillow!

Myrrhine: But I do. (*She goes.*)

Cinesias: Cheated again, just like Heracles and his dinner!

Myrrhine (*returning with a pillow*): Here, lift your head. (*to herself, wondering how else to tease him*) Is that all?

Cinesias: Surely that's all! Do come here, precious!

Myrrhine: I'm taking off my girdle. But remember: don't go back on your promise about the truce.

Cinesias: Hope to die, if I do.

Myrrhine: You don't have a blanket.

Cinesias (*shouting in exasperation*): *I don't want one!* I WANT TO—

Myrrhine: Sh-h! There, there, I'll be back in a minute. (*She goes.*)

Cinesias: She'll be the death of me with these bed-clothes.

Myrrhine (*returning with a blanket*): Here, get up.

Cinesias: I've got *this* up!

Myrrhine: Would you like some perfume?

Cinesias: Good heavens, no! I won't have it!

Myrrhine: Yes, you shall, whether you want it or not. (*She goes.*)

Cinesias: O lord! Confound all perfumes anyway!

Myrrhine (*returning with a flask*): Stretch out your hand and put some on.

Cinesias (*suspiciously*): By God, I don't much like this perfume. It smacks of shilly-shallying, and has no scent of the marriage-bed.

Myrrhine: Oh dear! This is Rhodian perfume I've brought.

Cinesias: It's quite all right, dear. Never mind.

Myrrhine: Don't be silly! (*She goes out with the flask.*)

Cinesias: Damn the man who first concocted perfumes!

Myrrhine (*returning with another flask*): Here, try this flask.

Cinesias: I've got another one all ready for you. Come, you wretch, lie down and stop bringing me things.

Myrrhine: All right; I'm taking off my shoes. But, my dear, see that you vote for peace.

Cinesias (*absently*): I'll consider it. (**Myrrhine** *runs away to the Acropolis.*) I'm ruined! The wench has skinned me and run away! (*chanting, in tragic style*) Alas! Alas! Deceived, deserted by this fairest of women, whom shall I—lay?

Scene from
   Macbeth by William Shakespeare

From Act II, Scene 2

For 1 man, 1 woman

Characters: **Macbeth,** a Scottish nobleman, later King of Scotland.
   Lady Macbeth, his wife.

Setting: A courtyard of Macbeth's castle at Inverness, Scotland. An evening in the eleventh century.

Situation: Macbeth, a Scottish nobleman, stands on the threshold of seizing the crown of Scotland. Earlier in the evening, King Duncan and his retinue paid a visit to Macbeth's castle. Duncan has now retired and is guarded only by two grooms. Macbeth and his wife have decided to take this opportunity to murder him. Lady Macbeth has drugged Duncan's two guards so that Macbeth's path to Duncan's bedside will be clear. But despite their ambition and their preparations, the enormity of the Macbeths' deed weighs heavily on them. As the scene opens, Lady Macbeth enters the courtyard to wait for Macbeth, who has just left for Duncan's bedchamber to commit the murder.

Script Notations

[*Enter* Lady Macbeth.]

Lady Macbeth: That which hath made them drunk
hath made me bold;

What hath quench'd them hath given me fire.
Hark! Peace!

It was the owl that shriek'd, the fatal bellman,

Which gives the stern'st good-night. He is about
it:

The doors are open; and the surfeited grooms

Do mock their charge with snores: I have drugg'd
their possets,

That death and nature do contend about them,

Whether they live or die.

Macbeth: (*within*) Who's there? what, ho!

Lady Macbeth: Alack, I am afraid they have
awaked,

And 'tis not done. The attempt and not the deed

Confounds us. Hark! I laid their daggers ready;

He could not miss 'em. Had he not resembled

My father as he slept, I had done't.

[*Enter* Macbeth.]

My husband!

Macbeth: I have done the deed. Didst thou not
hear a noise?

Lady Macbeth: I heard the owl scream and the
crickets cry.

Did not you speak?

Macbeth: When?

Lady Macbeth: Now.

Macbeth: As I descended?

Lady Macbeth: Aye.

Macbeth: Hark!

Who lies i' the second chamber?

Lady Macbeth: Donalbain.

Macbeth: This is a sorry sight.

(*looking on his hands*)

Lady Macbeth: A foolish thought, to say a sorry
sight.

Macbeth: There's one did laugh in's sleep, and one
cried "Murder!"

That they did wake each other: I stood and heard
them:

But they did say their prayers, and address'd them
Again to sleep.

Lady Macbeth: There are two lodged together.

Macbeth: One cried "God bless us!" and "Amen"
the other;

As they had seen me with these hangman's hands.

Listening their fear, I could not say "Amen,"

When they did say "God bless us!"

Lady Macbeth: Consider it not so deeply.

Macbeth: But wherefore could not I pronounce
"Amen"?

I had most need of blessing, and "Amen"
Stuck in my throat.

Lady Macbeth:　　These deeds must not be thought
After these ways; so, it will make us mad.

Macbeth: Methought I heard a voice cry ''Sleep no
more!

Macbeth does murder sleep,'' the innocent sleep,
Sleep that knits up the ravell'd sleave of care,
The death of each day's life, sore labour's bath,
Balm of hurt minds, great nature's second course,
Chief nourisher in life's feast—

Lady Macbeth:　　　　　　　What do you mean?

Macbeth: Still it cried ''Sleep no more!'' to all the
house:

''Glamis hath murder'd sleep, and therefore
Cawdor

Shall sleep no more; Macbeth shall sleep no
more.''

Lady Macbeth: Who was it that thus cried? Why,
worthy thane,

You do unbend your noble strength, to think
So brainsickly of things. Go get some water,
And wash this filthy witness from your hand.
Why did you bring these daggers from the place?
They must lie there: go carry them; and smear
The sleepy grooms with blood.

Macbeth:　　　　　　　　I'll go no more:
I am afraid to think what I have done;
Look on 't again I dare not.

Lady Macbeth:　　　　　Infirm of purpose!
Give me the daggers: the sleeping and the dead
Are but as pictures: 'tis the eye of childhood
That fears a painted devil. If he do bleed,
I'll gild the faces of the grooms withal;
For it must seem their guilt.

[*Exit.*]

Macbeth:　　　　　　Whence is that knocking?
How is 't with me, when every noise appals me?
What hands are here? Ha! they pluck out mine
eyes.

Will all great Neptune's ocean wash this blood
Clean from my hand? No, this my hand will
rather

The multitudinous seas incarnadine,
Making the green one red.

[*Re-enter* **Lady Macbeth.**]

Lady Macbeth: My hands are of your colour; but I
shame

To wear a heart so white.

　　　　　　　　　I hear a knocking
At the south entry: retire we to our chamber:
A little water clears us of this deed:
How easy is it, then! Your constancy
Hath left you unattended.

　　　　　　　　　Hark! more knocking.
Get on your nightgown, lest occasion call us,
And show us to be watchers. Be not lost
So poorly in your thoughts.

Macbeth: To know my deed, 'twere best not know
myself.
Wake Duncan with thy knocking! I would thou
couldst!
[*Exeunt.*]

Scene from
> *Medea* by Euripides, translated by Frederic Prokosch and shaped into verse by
> Randolph Goodman

For 1 man, 1 woman

Characters: **Medea,** daughter of the king of Colchis, ex-wife of Jason, possessing
supernatural powers.

>   **Jason,** now married to Creon's daughter, thus successor to the throne
of Corinth.

Setting: Corinth, before the house of Medea in ancient Greece.

Situation: In quest of the Golden Fleece, Jason went to Colchis where he and Medea fell passionately in love. Through her supernatural powers, she aided him,
slaying her own brother and others, and fled with him to Corinth where they
received sanctuary and had two sons. The king of Corinth, Creon, without
heir, offered Jason his daughter in marriage in return for Jason's becoming
his successor. Because Jason accepts, Medea's passion, rage, and sorcery lead
her to seek revenge. In this, the final scene in the play, she has just killed
their two sons in order to punish Jason. The scene may be performed without
actually using bodies for the children.

>   (Note: It should be an interesting challenge to deal with two quite dif-
ferent versions of what is essentially the same scene. Please see the contemporary version by Jeffers in Section C.)

Script Notations

External   *Internal*

Medea: Why do you batter at the doors?
Why do you shake these bolts,
In quest of the dead and their
Murderess? You may cease your trouble,
Jason; and if there is anything you
Want to say, then say it! Never
Again shall you lay your hand on me;
So swift is the chariot which my
Father's father gave me, the Sun God
Helios, to save me from my foes!

Jason: Horrible woman! Now you are utterly
Loathed by the gods, and by me, and
By all mankind. You had the heart
To stab your children; you,
Their own mother, and to leave me
Childless; you have done these fearful
Things, and still you dare to gaze
As ever at the sun and the earth! O
I wish you were dead! Now at last
I see clearly what I did not see
On the day I brought you, loaded
With doom, from your barbarous home
To live in Hellas—a traitress
To your father and your native land.
On me too the gods have hurled
The curse which has haunted you. For
You killed your own brother at his
Fireside, and then came aboard our
Beautiful ship the Argo. And that
Was how it started. And then you
Married me, and slept with me, and
Out of your passion bore me children;
And now, out of your passion, you have
Killed them. There is no woman in all
Of Greece who would dare to do this. And
Yet I passed them over, and chose you
Instead; and chose to marry my own
Doom! I married not a woman,
But a monster, wilder of heart than
Scylla in the Tyrrhenian Sea!
But even if I hurled a thousand
Insults at you, Medea, I know
I could not wound you: your heart
Is so hard, so utterly hard. Go,
You wicked sorceress; I see
The stains of your children's blood
Upon you! Go; all that is left
To me now is to mourn. I shall never
Lie beside my newly wedded love;
I shall never have my sons, whom
I bred and brought up, alive
Beside me to say a last farewell!
I have lost them forever,
And my life is ended.

Medea: O Jason, to these words of yours
    I could make a long reply; but
    Zeus, the father, himself well knows
    All that I did for you, and what
    You did to me. Destiny has
    Refused to let you scorn my love,
    And lead a life of pleasure,
    And mock at me; nor were the royal
    Princess and the matchmaker
    Kreon destined to drive me into exile,
    And then go untormented! Call me
    A monster if you wish; call me
    The Scylla in the Tyrrhenian Sea.
    For now I have torn your heart:
    And this indeed was destined, Jason!

Jason: You too must feel the pain; you will share
    my grief, Medea.

Medea: Yes; but the pain is milder, since you can-
    not mock me!

Jason: O my sons, it was an unspeakable mother
    who bore you!

Medea: O my sons, it was really your father who
    destroyed you!

Jason: But I tell you: it was not my hand that slew
    them!

Medea: No; but your insolence, and your new wed-
    ding slew them!

Jason: And you thought this wedding cause enough
    to kill them?

Medea: And you think the anguish of love is tri-
    fling for a woman?

Jason: Yes, if her heart is sound: but yours makes
    all things evil.

Medea: Your sons are dead, Jason! Does it hurt you
    when I say this?

Jason: They will live on, Medea, by bringing suf-
    fering on you.

Medea: The gods are well aware who caused all this
    suffering.

Jason: Yes, the gods are well aware. They know your
    brutal heart.

Medea: You too are brutal. And I am sick of your
    bitter words!

Jason: And I am sick of yours. Oh Medea, it will
    be easy to leave you.

Medea: Easy! Yes! And for me too! What, then, do
    you want?

Jason: Give me those bodies to bury, and to mourn.

Medea: Never! I will bury them myself.
    I will take them myself to Hera's
    Temple, which hangs over the Cape,
    Where none of their enemies can
    Insult them, and where none can defile
    Their graves! And in this land
    Of Corinth I shall ordain a holy
    Feast and sacrifice, forever after,
    To atone for this guilt of killing.

And I shall go myself to Athens,
To live in the House of Aegeus,
The son of Pandion. And I predict
That you, as you deserve, will die
Without honor; and your head crushed
By a beam of the shattered Argo;
And then you will know the bitter
End of all my love for you!

Jason: May the avenging fury of our sons
Destroy you! May Justice destroy
You, and repay blood with blood!

Medea: What god, what heavenly power
Would listen to you? To a breaker
Of oaths? To a betrayer of love?

Jason: Oh, you are vile! You sorceress!
Murderess!

Medea: Go to your house. Go, and bury your bride.

Jason: Yes, I shall go; and mourn for my murdered
sons.

Medea: Wait; do not weep yet, Jason!
Wait till age has sharpened your grief!

Jason: Oh my sons, whom I loved! My sons!

Medea: It was I, not you, who truly loved them.

Jason: You say you loved them; yet you killed them.

Medea: Yes. I killed them to make you suffer.

Jason: Medea, I only long to kiss them one last time.

Medea: Now, now, you long to kiss them!
Now you long to say farewell:
But before, you cast them from you!

Jason: Medea, I beg you, let me touch the little
bodies of my boys!

Medea: No. Never. You speak in vain.

Jason: O Zeus, high in your heaven,
Have you heard these words?
Have you heard this unutterable
Cruelty? Have you heard this
Woman, this monster, this murderess?
And now I shall do the only
Thing I still can do! Yes!
I shall cry, I shall cry
Aloud to heaven, and call on
The gods to witness how you
Killed my sons, and refused
To let me kiss them farewell,
Or touch them, or give them burial!
Oh, I'd rather never have seen them live,
Than have seen them slaughtered so!

Scene from
    A Midsummer Night's Dream by William Shakespeare

"Pyramus and Thisbe" from Act V

For 6 men (women may play some of the roles)

Characters: **Prologue Tradesmen** who perform a play within the play in the roles
            of:
            Pyramus (played by Bottom, a weaver).
            Thisbe (played by Flute, a bellows-mender).
            Prologue (played by Quince, a carpenter).
            Wall (played by Snout, a tinker).
            Moonshine (played by Starvling, a tailor).
            Lion (played by Snug, a joiner).

Setting: An acting area before the palace of Theseus, Athens. The actual setting
            and period of the play are variable.

Situation: As part of the wedding festivities which serve to bring the various lovers
            happily together at the end of the play, the "most lamentable comedy" of
            Pyramus and Thisbe is performed for the wedding party. Written and per-
            formed by the rustics of Athens, the play is an over-blown farcical treatment
            of a theme Shakespeare himself was to handle much more seriously in *Romeo
            and Juliet.* The amateur actors are quite serious in the performance of their
            home-made play, which comes across more as a burlesque or a travesty than
            the tragedy they actually intend. (The lines of the wedding party, which in-
            terrupt the performance, have been deleted so as to make the *Pyramus and
            Thisbe* segment a self-contained piece.)

Script Notations

Enter [Quince *for*] *the* **Prologue.**

Pro.: If we offend, it is with our good will.
   That you should think, we come not to offend,
But with good will. To show our simple skill,
   That is the true beginning of our end.
Consider then we come but in despite.
   We do not come as minding to content you,
Our true intent is. All for your delight
   We are not here. That you should here repent
   you,
The actors are at hand, and by their show
You shall know all that you are like to know.

Enter with a trumpet before them, **Pyramus** *and*
Thisbe, Wall, Moonshine, *and* **Lion.**

Pro.: Gentles, perchance you wonder at this show;
   But wonder on till truth make all things plain.
This man is Pyramus, if you would know;
   This beauteous lady Thisby is certain.
This man, with lime and rough-cast, doth present
   Wall, that vile Wall which did these lovers sun-
   der;
And through Wall's chink, poor souls, they are
   content
   To whisper. At the which let no man wonder.
This man, with lantern, dog, and bush of thorn,
   Presenteth Moonshine; for, if you will know,
By moonshine did these lovers think no scorn
   To meet at Ninus' tomb, there, there to woo.
This grisly beast, which Lion hight by name,
   The trusty Thisby, coming first by night,
Did scare away, or rather did affright;
   And, as she fled, her mantle she did fall,
   Which Lion vile with bloody mouth did stain.
Anon comes Pyramus, sweet youth and tall,
   And finds his trusty Thisby's mantle slain;
Whereat, with blade, with bloody blameful
   blade,
   He bravely broach'd his boiling bloody breast;
And Thisby, tarrying in mulberry shade,
   His dagger drew, and died. For all the rest,
Let Lion, Moonshine, Wall, and lovers twain
At large discourse, while here they do remain.

[*Exeunt* **Prologue, Thisbe, Lion,** *and* **Moonshine.**]

Wall: In this same interlude it doth befall
   That I, one Snout by name, present a wall;
And such a wall, as I would have you think,
   That had in it a crannied hole or chink,
Through which the lovers, Pyramus and Thisby,
   Did whisper often very secretly.
This loam, this rough-cast, and this stone doth
   show
   That I am that same wall; the truth is so;
And this the cranny is, right and sinister,
   Through which the fearful lovers are to whisper.

Enter **Pyramus.**

Pyr.: O grim-look'd night! O night with hue so
  black!
   O night, which ever art when day is not!
  O night, O night! alack, alack, alack,
   I fear my Thisby's promise is forgot!
  And thou, O wall, O sweet, O lovely wall,
   That stand'st between her father's ground and
   mine!
  Thou wall, O wall, O sweet and lovely wall,
   Show me thy chink, to blink through with mine
   eyne! [**Wall** *holds up his fingers.*]
  Thanks, courteous wall; Jove shield thee well for
   this!
   But what see I? No Thisby do I see.
  O wicked wall, through whom I see no bliss!
   Curs'd be thy stones for thus deceiving me!

          . . .

   Enter **Thisbe.**
This.: O wall, full often hast thou heard my moans,
   For parting my fair Pyramus and me!
  My cherry lips have often kiss'd thy stones,
   Thy stones with lime and hair knit up in thee.
Pyr.: I see a voice! Now will I to the chink,
   To spy an I can hear my Thisby's face.
  Thisby!
This.: My love, thou art my love, I think.
Pyr.: Think what thou wilt, I am thy lover's grace;
   And, like Limander, am I trusty still.
This.: And I like Helen, till the Fates me kill.
Pyr.: Not Shafalus to Procrus was so true.
This.: As Shafalus to Procrus, I to you.
Pyr.: O, kiss me through the hole of this vile wall!
This.: I kiss the wall's hole, not your lips at all.
Pyr.: Wilt thou at Ninny's tomb meet me straight-
   way?
This.: 'Tide life, 'tide death, I come without
   delay.   [*Exeunt* **Pyramus** *and* **Thisbe.**]
Wall: Thus have I, Wall, my part discharged so;
   And, being done, thus Wall away doth
   go. [*Exit.*]
          Enter **Lion** *and* **Moonshine.**
Lion: You, ladies, you, whose gentle hearts do fear
   The smallest monstrous mouse that creeps on
   floor,
  May now perchance both quake and tremble here,
   When lion rough in wildest rage doth roar.
  Then know that I, as Snug the joiner, am
  A lion fell, nor else no lion's dam;
  For, if I should as lion come in strife
  Into this place, 'twere pity on my life.
Moon: This lantern doth the horned moon present;
  Myself the man i' th' moon do seem to be.
  All that I have to say, is, to tell you that the lan-
   tern is the moon; I, the man i' th' moon; this
   thorn-bush, my thorn-bush; and this dog, my
   dog.

Re-enter **Thisbe.**
This.: This is old Ninny's tomb. Where is my love?
Lion (*Roaring.*) Oh——   [**Thisbe** *runs off.*]
[*The* **Lion** *shakes* **Thisbe's** *mantle and exit.*]

        .   .   .

Re-enter **Pyramus.**
Pyr.: Sweet Moon, I thank thee for thy sunny
  beams;
  I thank thee, Moon, for shining now so bright;
For, by thy gracious, golden, glittering gleams,
  I trust to take of truest Thisby sight.
    But stay, O spite!
    But mark, poor knight,
What dreadful dole is here!
    Eyes, do you see?
    How can it be?
O dainty duck! O dear!
    Thy mantle good,
    What, stain'd with blood!
Approach, ye Furies fell!
    O Fates, come, come,
    Cut thread and thrum;
    Quail, crush, conclude, and quell!
    O wherefore, Nature, didst thou lions frame?
Since lion vile hath here deflow'r'd my dear;
Which is—no, no—which was the fairest dame
  That liv'd, that lov'd, that lik'd, that look'd
  with cheer.
    Come, tears, confound;
    Out, sword, and wound
The pap of Pyramus;
    Ay, that left pap,
    Where heart doth hop.   [*Stabs himself.*]
Thus die I, thus, thus, thus.
    Now am I dead,
    Now am I fled;
My soul is in the sky.
    Tongue, lose thy light;
    Moon, take thy flight.   [*Exit* **Moonshine.**]
Now die, die, die, die, die.   [*Dies.*]
Re-enter **Thisbe.**

        .   .   .

This.:   Asleep, my love?
    What, dead, my dove?
  O Pyramus, arise!
    Speak, speak! Quite dumb?
    Dead, dead? A tomb
Must cover thy sweet eyes.
    These lily lips,
    This cherry nose,
These yellow cowslip cheeks,
    Are gone, are gone!
    Lovers, make moan.
His eyes were green as leeks.
    O Sisters Three,
    Come, come to me,

EXECUTION

External   *Internal*

With hands as pale as milk;
    Lay them in gore,
    Since you have shore
With shears his thread of silk.
    Tongue, not a word!
    Come, trusty sword;
Come, blade, my breast imbrue!
                          [Stabs herself.]
    And, farewell friends;
    Thus, Thisby ends.
Adieu, adieu, adieu.   *[Dies.]*

Scene from
  Othello by William Shakespeare

From Act V, Scene 2

For 1 man, 2 women

Characters: **Othello,** a Moor in the service of the Venetian state.
  Desdemona, wife of Othello.
  Emilia, friend to Desdemona and wife of Iago.

Setting: Desdemona's bedchamber in a castle on the island of Cyprus. An evening
  in the sixteenth century.

Situation: Othello has fallen prey to Iago's scheme to convince him that Desdemona has been unfaithful. Although Desdemona is well aware of Othello's
  recent distraught behavior, she does not know that Iago has told Othello that
  she has been having an illicit affair with Othello's lieutenant, Cassio. An
  exceptionally jealous man, Othello is enraged by Iago's news and decides he
  must kill the wife he loves in order to defend his honor.

Script Notations

External   *Internal*

[*A bedchamber in the castle:* **Desdemona** *in bed asleep; a light burning. Enter* **Othello.**]

Othello: It is the cause, it is the cause, my soul,—
Let me not name it to you, you chaste stars!—
It is the cause. Yet I'll not shed her blood;
Nor scar that whiter skin of hers than snow,
And smooth as monumental alabaster.
Yet she must die, else she'll betray more men.
Put out the light, and then put out the light.
If I quench thee, thou flaming minister,
I can again thy former light restore,
Should I repent me: but once put out thy light,
Thou cunning'st pattern of excelling nature,
I know not where is that Promethean heat
That can thy light relume. When I have pluck'd
   the rose,
I cannot give it vital growth again,
It needs must wither: I'll smell it on the tree.
   (*kissing her*)
Ah, balmy breath, that doth almost persuade
Justice to break her sword! One more, one more.
Be thus when thou art dead, and I will kill thee,
And love thee after. One more, and this the last:
So sweet was ne'er so fatal. I must weep,
But they are cruel tears: this sorrow's heavenly;
It strikes where it doth love. She wakes.

Desdemona: Who's there? Othello?

Othello: Aye, Desdemona.

Desdemona: Will you come to bed, my lord?

Othello: Have you pray'd to-night, Desdemona?

Desdemona: Aye, my lord.

Othello: If you bethink yourself of any crime
Unreconciled as yet to heaven and grace,
Solicit for it straight.

Desdemona: Alas, my lord, what do you mean by
   that?

Othello: Well, do it, and be brief; I will walk by:
I would not kill thy unprepared spirit;
No; heaven forfend! I would not kill thy soul.

Desdemona: Talk you of killing?

Othello: Aye, I do.

Desdemona: Then heaven
Have mercy on me!

Othello: Amen, with all my heart!

Desdemona: If you say so, I hope you will not kill
   me.

Othello: Hum!

Desdemona: And yet I fear you; for you are fatal
   then
When your eyes roll so: why I should fear I know
   not,
Since guiltiness I know not; but yet I feel I fear.

Othello: Think on thy sins.

Desdemona: They are loves I bear to you.

Othello: Aye, and for that thou diest.

Desdemona: That death's unnatural that kills for
    loving.
    Alas, why gnaw you so your nether lip?
    Some bloody passion shakes your very frame:
    These are portents; but yet I hope, I hope,
    They do not point on me.
Othello: Peace, and be still!
Desdemona: I will so. What's the matter?
Othello: That handkerchief which I so loved and
    gave thee
    Thou gavest to Cassio.
Desdemona: No, by my life and soul!
    Send for the man, and ask him.
Othello: Sweet soul, take heed,
    Take heed of perjury; thou art on thy deathbed.
Desdemona: Aye, but not yet to die.
Othello: Yes, presently:
    Therefore confess thee freely of thy sin;
    For to deny each article with oath
    Cannot remove nor choke the strong conception
    That I do groan withal. Thou art to die.
Desdemona: Then Lord have mercy on me!
Othello: I say, amen.
Desdemona: And have you mercy too! I never did
    Offend you in my life; never loved Cassio
    But with such general warranty of heaven
    As I might love; I never gave him token.
Othello: By heaven, I saw my handkerchief in's
    hand.
    O perjured woman! thou dost stone my heart,
    And makest me call what I intend to do
    A murder, which I thought a sacrifice:
    I saw the handkerchief.
Desdemona: He found it then;
    I never gave it him: send for him hither;
    Let him confess a truth.
Othello: He hath confess'd.
Desdemona: What, my lord?
Othello: That he hath used thee.
Desdemona: How? unlawfully?
Othello: Aye.
Desdemona: He will not say so.
Othello: No, his mouth is stopp'd;
    Honest Iago hath ta'en order for 't.
Desdemona: O! my fear interprets: what, is he
    dead?
Othello: Had all his hairs been lives, my great re-
    venge
    Had stomach for them all.
Desdemona: Alas! he is betray'd and I undone.
Othello: Out, strumpet! weep'st thou for him to
    my face?
Desdemona: O, banish me, my lord, but kill me
    not!
Othello: Down, strumpet!
Desdemona: Kill me to-morrow: let me live to-
    night!

Othello: Nay, if you strive,—

Desdemona: But half an hour!

Othello: Being done, there is no pause.

Desdemona: But while I say one prayer!

Othello: It is too late.

[He stifles her.]

Emilia: (*within*)

My lord, my lord! what, ho! my lord, my lord!

Othello: What noise is this? Not dead? not yet
    quite dead?

I that am cruel am yet merciful;

I would not have thee linger in thy pain:

So, so.

Emilia: (*within*)

What, ho! my lord, my lord!

Othello: Who's there?

Emilia: (*within*)

O, good my lord, I would speak a word with you!

Othello: Yes: 'tis Emilia. By and by. She's dead.

'Tis like she comes to speak of Cassio's death.—

The noise was here. Ha! no more moving?

Still as the grave. Shall she come in? were 't
    good?—

I think she stirs again:—no. What's best to do?

If she come in, she'll sure speak to my wife:

My wife! my wife! what wife! I have no wife.

O, insupportable! O heavy hour!

Methinks it should be now a huge eclipse

Of sun and moon, and that the affrighted globe

Should yawn at alteration.

Emilia: (*within*)

                                        I do beseech you

That I may speak with you, O, good my lord!

Othello: I had forgot thee: O, come in, Emilia:

Soft; by and by. Let me the curtains draw.

Where art thou?

        (*unlocks the door. Enter* **Emilia.**)

                        What's the matter with thee now?

Emilia: O, my good lord, yonder's foul murders
    done!

Othello: What, now?

Emilia: But now, my lord.

Othello: It is the very error of the moon;

She comes more nearer earth than she was wont,

And makes men mad.

Emilia: Cassio, my lord, hath kill'd a young Vene-
    tian

Call'd Roderigo.

Othello: Roderigo kill'd!

And Cassio kill'd!

Emilia: No, Cassio is not kill'd.

Othello: Not Cassio kill'd! then murder's out of
    tune,

And sweet revenge grows harsh.

Desdemona: O, falsely, falsely murder'd!

Emilia: Alas, what cry is that?

Othello: That! What?

Emilia: Out, and alas! that was my lady's voice.
   Help! help, ho! help! O lady, speak again!
   Sweet Desdemona! O sweet mistress, speak!
Desdemona: A guiltless death I die.
Emilia: O, who hath done this deed?
Desdemona: Nobody; I myself. Farewell:
   Commend me to my kind lord: O, farewell!
      [*dies*]
Othello: Why, how should she be murder'd?
Emilia: Alas, who knows?
Othello: You heard her say herself, it was not I.
Emilia: She said so: I must needs report the truth.
Othello: She's like a liar gone to burning hell:
   'Twas I that kill'd her.
Emilia: O, the more angel she,
   And you the blacker devil!
Othello: She turn'd to folly, and she was a whore.
Emilia: Thou dost belie her, and thou art a devil.
Othello: She was false as water.
Emilia: Thou art rash as fire, to say
   That she was false: O, she was heavenly true!
Othello: Cassio did top her; ask thy husband else.
   O, I were damn'd beneath all depth in hell,
   But that I did proceed upon just grounds
   To this extremity. Thy husband knew it all.
Emilia: My husband!
Othello: Thy husband.
Emilia: That she was false to wedlock?
Othello: Aye, with Cassio. Nay, had she been true,
   If heaven would make me such another world
   Of one entire and perfect chrysolite,
   I'd not have sold her for it.
Emilia: My husband!
Othello: Aye, 'twas he that told me first:
   An honest man he is, and hates the slime
   That sticks on filthy deeds.
Emilia: My husband!
Othello: What needs this iteration, woman? I say
   thy husband.
Emilia: O mistress, villainy hath made mocks with
   love!
   My husband says that she was false!
Othello: He, woman;
   I say thy husband: dost understand the word?
   My friend, thy husband, honest, honest Iago.
Emilia: If he say so, may his pernicious soul
   Rot half a grain a day! he lies to the heart:
   She was too fond of her most filthy bargain.
Othello: Ha!
Emilia: Do thy worst:
   This deed of thine is no more worthy heaven
   Than thou wast worthy her.
Othello: Peace, you were best.
Emilia: Thou hast not half that power to do me
   harm
   As I have to be hurt. O gull! O dolt!

As ignorant as dirt! thou hast done a deed—
I care not for thy sword: I'll make thee known,
Though I lost twenty lives.—Help! help, ho!
   help!
The Moor hath kill'd my mistress! Murder! mur-
   der!

Scene from
The School for Scandal by Richard Brinsley Sheridan

From Act V, Scene 2

For 2 men, 2 women

Characters: **Mrs. Candour**
        Sir Benjamin Backbite ⎫
        Lady Sneerwell ⎬ a group of scandalmongers.
        Crabtree ⎭

Setting: The house of Sir Peter Teazle. London in the 1770s.

Situation: Lady Sneerwell heads a group of scandalmongers whose *forte* is gossiping and ruining the reputations of anyone who happens to provide a juicy morsel for their regular intrigues. Mrs. Candour is particularly excited, as are all the members of the school for scandal, for she has heard that Charles Surface has been caught in a compromising situation with the wife of Sir Peter Teazle. As each member of the infamous "school" comes into the scene, he or she adds a particularly vivid piece of misinformation about the tryst and the discovery of the alleged affair by the unhappy husband, Sir Peter Teazle. Actually Lady Teazle was found by her husband with Charles's elder brother, Sir Joseph Surface (Mr. Surface), but the scandalmongers are not certain who the guilty party really was. Consequently, they contrive only to confuse each other more than they were confused before

Script Notations

Mrs. Candour: Dear heart, how provoking! I'm not mistress of half the circumstances! We shall have the whole affair in the newspapers, with the names of the parties at length, before I have dropped the story at a dozen houses.

[*Enter* **Sir Benjamin Backbite**]

Oh, dear Sir Benjamin! you have heard, I suppose—

Sir Benjamin: Of Lady Teazle and Mr. Surface—

Mrs. Candour: And Sir Peter's discovery—

Sir Benjamin: Oh, the strangest piece of business, to be sure!

Mrs. Candour: Well, I never was so surprised in my life. I am so sorry for all parties, indeed.

Sir Benjamin: Now, I don't pity Sir Peter at all: he was so extravagantly partial to Mr. Surface.

Mrs. Candour: Mr. Surface! Why, 'twas with Charles Lady Teazle was detected.

Sir Benjamin: No, no, I tell you: Mr. Surface is the gallant.

Mrs. Candour: No such thing! Charles is the man. 'Twas Mr. Surface brought Sir Peter on purpose to discover them.

Sir Benjamin: I tell you I had it from one—

Mrs. Candour: And I have it from one—

Sir Benjamin: Who had it from one, who had it—

Mrs. Candour: From one immediately—But here comes Lady Sneerwell; perhaps she knows the whole affair.

[*Enter* **Lady Sneerwell**]

Lady Sneerwell: So, my dear Mrs. Candour, here's a sad affair of our friend Lady Teazle!

Mrs. Candour: Ay, my dear friend, who would have thought—

Lady Sneerwell: Well, there is no trusting to appearances; though indeed, she was always too lively for me.

Mrs. Candour: To be sure, her manners were a little too free; but then she was so young!

Lady Sneerwell: And had, indeed, some good qualities.

Mrs. Candour: So she had, indeed. But have you heard the particulars?

Lady Sneerwell: No; but everybody says that Mr. Surface—

Sir Benjamin: Ay, there; I told you Mr. Surface was the man.

Mrs. Candour: No, no: indeed the assignation was with Charles.

Lady Sneerwell: With Charles! You alarm me, Mrs. Candour.

Mrs. Candour: Yes, yes: he was the lover. Mr. Surface, to do him justice, was only the informer.

Sir Benjamin: Well, I'll not dispute with you, Mrs. Candour; but, be it which it may, I hope that Sir Peter's wound will not—

Mrs. Candour: Sir Peter's wound! Oh, mercy! I didn't hear a word of their fighting.

Lady Sneerwell: Nor I, a syllable.

Sir Benjamin: No! what, no mention of the duel?

Mrs. Candour: Not a word.

Sir Benjamin: Oh, yes: they fought before they left the room.

Lady Sneerwell: Pray let us hear.

Mrs. Candour: Ay, do oblige us with the duel.

Sir Benjamin: *"Sir,"* says Sir Peter, immediately after the discovery, *"you are a most ungrateful fellow."*

Mrs. Candour: Ay, to Charles—

Sir Benjamin: No, no—to Mr. Surface—*"a most ungrateful fellow; and old as I am, sir,"* says he, *"I insist on immediate satisfaction."*

Mrs. Candour: Ay, that must have been to Charles; for 'tis very unlikely Mr. Surface should fight in his own house.

Sir Benjamin: 'Gad's life, ma'am, not at all—*"giving me immediate satisfaction."*—On this, ma'am, Lady Teazle, seeing Sir Peter in such danger, ran out of the room in strong hysterics, and Charles after her, calling out for hartshorn and water; then, madam, they began to fight with swords—

[*Enter* **Crabtree**]

Crabtree: With pistols, nephew—pistols! I have it from undoubted authority.

Mrs. Candour: Oh, Mr. Crabtree, then it is all true!

Crabtree: Too true, indeed, madam, and Sir Peter is dangerously wounded—

Sir Benjamin: By a thrust in second quite through his left side—

Crabtree: By a bullet lodged in the thorax.

Mrs. Candour: Mercy on me! Poor Sir Peter!

Crabtree: Yes, madam; though Charles would have avoided the matter, if he could.

Mrs. Candour: I knew Charles was the person.

Sir Benjamin: My uncle, I see, knows nothing of the matter.

Crabtree: But Sir Peter taxed him with the basest ingratitude—

Sir Benjamin· That I told you, you know—

Crabtree: Do, nephew, let me speak!—and insisted on immediate—

Sir Benjamin: Just as I said—

Crabtree: Odds life, nephew, allow others to know something too! A pair of pistols lay on the bureau (for Mr. Surface, it seems, had come home the night before late from Salthill, where he had been to see the Montem with a friend, who has a son at Eton), so, unluckily, the pistols were left charged.

Sir Benjamin: I heard nothing of this.

Crabtree: Sir Peter forced Charles to take one, and they fired, it seems, pretty nearly together. Charles's shot took effect, as I tell you, and Sir Peter's missed;

but, what is very extraordinary, the ball struck against a little bronze Shakespeare that stood over the fireplace, grazed out of the window at a right angle, and wounded the postman, who was just coming to the door with a double letter from Northamptonshire.

Sir Benjamin: My uncle's account is more circumstantial, I confess; but I believe mine is the true one for all that.

Lady Sneerwell: [*Aside*] I am more interested in this affair than they imagine, and must have better information. [*Exit*]

Sir Benjamin: Ah! Lady Sneerwell's alarm is very easily accounted for.

Crabtree: Yes, yes, they certainly do say—but that's neither here nor there.

Mrs. Candour: But, pray, where is Sir Peter at present?

Crabtree: Oh! they brought him home, and he is now in the house, though the servants are ordered to deny him.

Mrs. Candour: I believe so, and Lady Teazle, I suppose, attending him.

Crabtree: Yes, yes; and I saw one of the faculty enter just before me.

Sir Benjamin: Hey! who comes here?

Crabtree: Oh, this is he: the physician, depend on't.

Mrs. Candour: Oh, certainly! it must be the physician; and now we shall know.

Scene from
   Ten Nights in a Bar-room by William W. Pratt

From Act III, Scene 3

For 1 man, 2 women

Characters: **Joe Morgan**, a drunkard.
            Mrs. Morgan, the drunkard's wife.
            Mary Morgan, the drunkard's daughter.
            (The role of Mrs. Slade has been cut from this scene.)

Setting: A bedroom in the Morgans' dilapidated house. An evening in the mid-nineteenth century.

Situation: This temperance play, very popular over one hundred years ago, is now normally played as an example of nineteenth-century "camp." At the time, it tried to depict the evils of alcoholism seriously and to further the temperance movement and the cause of prohibition.

   Through a series of misfortunes and temptations, Joe Morgan has become an uncontrollable alcoholic. In an accident in Slade's bar-room, the "Sickle and Sheaf," little Mary Morgan was struck in the head by a glass thrown by Slade at Morgan. Now lying on her cot, dying, poor Mary pleads with her father not to leave her alone and return to the bar-room, for she cannot go after him as she has on so many other countless evenings, when she begged her "father, dear father [to] come home with me now." Gradually, as the scene progresses, poor Joe Morgan sinks into a nineteenth-century case of *delirium tremens*.

Script Notations

Room in **Morgan's** *house.*—**Morgan** *discovered* L. H. *putting on his coat.*—**Mary** *on couch—head bound up.*—**Mrs. M.** *trying to restrain* **Morgan** *from going out.*

Mrs. Morgan: Don't go out to-night, Joe. Please don't go.

Mary: Father! father! Don't leave little Mary and poor mother alone to-night, will you? You know I can't come after you now.

Mor.: Well, well, I won't go out.

Mary: Come and sit near me, dear father.

Mor.: [*Goes to couch*] Yes, dear Mary.

Mary: I am so glad you won't go out to-night.

Mrs. M.: How very hot your hand is! Does your head ache?

Mary: A little, but it will soon be better. Dear father—

Mor.: Well, love?

Mary: I wish you would promise me something.

Mor.: What is it?

Mary: That you will never go into Simon Slade's bar-room any more.

Mor.: I won't go there to-night, dear; so let your heart be at rest.

Mary: Oh, thank you! I'll be well enough to get out in two or three days. You know the doctor said I must keep very still.

Mrs. M.: Yes, my dear. That is to avoid your having a fever. Husband, you feel better for the promise you have given our darling child, I know you do.

Mor.: Yes, Fanny. But my constitution is broken, as well as my heart. I feel now each moment, as I stand near that suffering child, as though my reason was leaving me. It is now five hours since I have tasted liquor, and I have been the slave so long of unnatural stimulants, that all vitality is lost without them.

Mrs. M.: [*Takes cup from table*] Here—here—drink this. It is coffee. I cannot, dare not give you rum, even though you should die for the want of it! [*Gives him cup—his hand trembles as he drinks*]

Mor.: Thank you, dear one! O God, what a wretched slave have I become! Fanny, I could not blame you were you to leave me to die alone!

Mrs. M.: Leave you—no! Though you have banished relatives and friends from your door, though you have drawn the contempt of the world upon your wretched head, though you are a mark for the good to grieve at, and the vain to scoff at, still, still I will never desert you. The name of husband is not lost, though it be coupled with that of—

Mor.: Drunkard! Yes, end the sentence—'tis too true.

Mrs. M.: Oh, think how I have suffered, to see you day by day sink from your once exalted station, until you have reached the wretched footing of the out-cast, your temper broken by that infatuation which my heart sickens to think of and my lips refuse to name.

. . .

Mary: [*Delirious*] Remember, you have promised me, father. I'm not well yet, you know. Oh, don't—go!—don't! There, he has gone! [*Sits up again.*] Well, I'll go after him again! I'll try and walk there! I can sit down and rest by the way! Oh dear, how tired I am! Father, father! Oh dear!

Mor.: Here I am. Lie down, my child. I have not gone and left you.

Mary: Oh, I know you, now! It is my father! Stoop down to me. I want to whisper something to you—not to mother. I don't want her to hear it—it will make her feel so bad.

Mor.: Well, what is it, my child?

Mary: I shall never get well, father; I am going to die.

Mrs. M.: What does she say, husband?

Mary: Hush! father. Don't tell her; I only said it to *you*. There, mother; you go away—you've got trouble enough. I only told him, because he promised not to go to the tavern any more until I get well—and I'm not going to get well. Oh! Mr. Slade threw it so hard; but it didn't strike father, and I'm so glad! How it would have hurt him! But he'll never go there any more, and that will be so good, won't it, mother?   [*Sleeps.*]

Mrs. M.: Do you hear what she says, Joe?

Mor.: Yes. Her mind wanders; and yet she may have spoken the truth.

Mrs. M.: If she should die, Joe?

Mor.: Don't! oh, don't talk so, Fanny! She's not going to die; it's only because she's a little light-headed.

Mrs. M.: Yes; why is she light-headed? It was the cruel blow that caused this delirium. I'm afraid, husband, the worst is before us. I've borne and suffered much. I pray Heaven to give me strength to bear this trial, also. She is better fitted for heaven than for earth. She has been a great comfort to me and to you, Joe, too—more like an angel than a child. Joe, if Mary should die, you cannot forget the cause of her death, nor the hand that struck the cruel blow?

Mor.: Forget it?—never! And if I ever forgive Simon Slade—   [*Excitedly.*]

Mrs. M.: You'll not forget where the blow was struck, nor your promise given to our dying child?

Mor.: [*In delirium*] No, no! Wife, wife! My brain is on fire! Hideous visions are before my eyes! Look! look!—see!—what's there?—there—in the corner?
                              [*Points.*]

Mrs. M.: Oh, heavens! 'Tis another symptom of that

terrible mania from which he has twice escaped. There's nothing there, Joe.

Mor.: There is, I tell you! I can see as well as you. Look—a huge snake is twining himself around my arms! Take him off! Take him off!—quick! quick!

Mrs. M.: It's only fancy, Joe. Try and lie down and get some rest; I will get you a cup of strong tea; you're only a little nervous. Mary's trouble has disturbed you—there—I'll return in a minute.

[*Exit* R.]

Mor.: There! look for yourself! Don't go!—don't go! Oh, you've come for me, have you? Well, I'm ready! Quick! Quick! How bright they look!—their eyes are glaring at me! And now they are leaping, dancing, and shouting with joy, to think the drunkard's hour has come. Keep them off! keep them off! Oh, horror! horror!

[*Rushes, throws himself behind couch.*]

Mary: [*Awaking*] Oh, father! is it you? I'm so glad you're here.

Enter **Mrs. Morgan,** *hastily,* R. *with cup.*

Mrs. M.: Not here? Gone? Joe! husband!—where are you?

Mary: Here he is, dear mother.

Mor.: Keep them off, I say! Keep them off! You won't let them hurt me, will you? [*Clings to* **Mary.**] There they are, creeping along the floor! Quick! jump out of bed, Mary! See, now—there—right over your head!

Mary: Nothing can hurt you here, dear father.

Mor.: No, no; that's true. Pray for me, my child; they can't come in here, for this is your room. Yes, this is my Mary's room, and she is an angel. There— I knew you wouldn't dare to come in here. Keep off! keep off! Ha! ha! ha! ha!

[*Falls* C. **Mrs. Morgan** *kneels over him.* **Mary** *sits in bed with her hands raised in prayer. Soft music. Tableau.*]

Scene from
   Twelfth Night by William Shakespeare

From Act I, Scene 5

For 2 women

Characters: **Viola,** Sebastian's twin sister, disguised page of Duke Orsino and also
      in love with him.
         Olivia, a rich, beautiful countess beloved by Duke Orsino.

Setting: Olivia's home in Illyria.

Situation: Viola, a shipwrecked gentlewoman in disguise, has been employed by
      Orsino, Duke of Illyria, as his male page. The sentimental Duke has decided
      to send his page to court the beautiful Countess Olivia, who is in mourning
      over the loss of her dead brother and therefore has refused to allow any man
      to approach her amorously. In this scene, the veiled Countess has finally ad-
      mitted Viola.

Script Notations

Vio.: The honourable lady of the house, which is she?

Oli.: Speak to me; I shall answer for her. Your will?

Vio.: Most radiant, exquisite, and unmatchable beauty,—I pray you, tell me if this be the lady of the house, for I never saw her. I would be loath to cast away my speech, for besides that it is excellently well penn'd, I have taken great pains to con it. Good beauties, let me sustain no scorn. I am very comptible, even to the least sinister usage.

Oli.: Whence came you, sir?

Vio.: I can say little more than I have studied, and that question's out of my part. Good gentle one, give me modest assurance if you be the lady of the house, that I may proceed in my speech.

Oli.: Are you a comedian?

Vio.: No, my profound heart; and yet, by the very fangs of malice I swear, I am not that I play. Are you the lady of the house?

Oli.: If I do not usurp myself, I am.

Vio.: Most certain, if you are she, you do usurp yourself; for what is yours to bestow is not yours to reserve. But this is from my commission. I will on with my speech in your praise, and then show you the heart of my message.

Oli.: Come to what is important in't. I forgive you the praise.

Vio.: Alas, I took great pains to study it, and 'tis poetical.

Oli.: It is the more like to be feigned. I pray you, keep it in. I heard you were saucy at my gates, and allow'd your approach rather to wonder at you than to hear you. If you be not mad, be gone. If you have reason, be brief. 'Tis not that time of moon with me to make one in so skipping a dialogue.

. . .

Vio.: Tell me your mind. I am a messenger.

Oli.: Sure, you have some hideous matter to deliver, when the courtesy of it is so fearful. Speak your office.

Vio.: It alone concerns your ear. I bring no overture of war, no taxation of homage. I hold the olive in my hand. My words are as full of peace as matter.

Oli.: Yet you began rudely. What are you? What would you?

Vio.: The rudeness that hath appear'd in me have I learn'd from my entertainment. What I am, and what I would, are as secret as maidenhead; to your ears, divinity, to any others, profanation.

Oli.: . . . We will hear this divinity. . . . What is your text?

Vio.: Most sweet lady,—

Oli.: A comfortable doctrine, and much may be said of it. Where lies your text?

Vio.: In Orsino's bosom.

Oli.: In his bosom! In what chapter of his bosom?

Vio.: To answer by the method, in the first of his heart.

Oli.: O, I have read it; it is heresy. Have you no more to say?

Vio.: Good madam, let me see your face.

Oli.: Have you any commission from your lord to negotiate with my face? You are now out of your text, but we will draw the curtain and show you the picture. Look you, sir, such a one I was—this present. Is't not well done? [*Unveiling.*]

Vio.: Excellently done, if God did all.

Oli.: 'Tis in grain, sir; 'twill endure wind and weather.

Vio.: 'Tis beauty truly blent, whose red and white
Nature's own sweet and cunning hand laid on.
Lady, you are the cruell'st she alive
If you will lead these graces to the grave
And leave the world no copy.

Oli.: O, sir, I will not be so hard-hearted; I will give out divers schedules of my beauty. It shall be inventoried, and every particle and utensil labell'd to my will: as, item, two lips, indifferent red; item, two grey eyes, with lids to them; item, one neck, one chin, and so forth. Were you sent hither to praise me?

Vio.: I see you what you are, you are too proud;
But, if you were the devil, you are fair.
My lord and master loves you. O, such love
Could be but recompens'd, though you were crown'd
The nonpareil of beauty!

Oli.:   How does he love me?

Vio.: With adorations, with fertile tears,
With groans that thunder love, with sighs of fire.

Oli.: Your lord does know my mind; I cannot love him.
Yet I suppose him virtuous, know him noble;
Of great estate, of fresh and stainless youth,
In voices well divulg'd, free, learn'd, and valiant
And in dimension and the shape of nature
A gracious person. But yet I cannot love him
He might have took his answer long ago.

Vio.: If I did love you in my master's flame,
With such a suff'ring, such a deadly life,
In your denial I would find no sense.
I would not understand it.

Oli.:   Why, what would you?

Vio.: Make me a willow cabin at your gate,
And call upon my soul within the house;
Write loyal cantons of contemned love
And sing them loud even in the dead of night;
Halloo your name to the reverberate hills
And make the babbling gossip of the air
Cry out "Olivia!" O, you should not rest
Between the elements of air and earth,
But you should pity me!

Oli.:   You might do much.
What is your parentage?
Vio.: Above my fortunes, yet my state is well.
I am a gentlemen.
Oli.:   Get you to your lord.
I cannot love him. Let him send no more,—
Unless, perchance, you come to me again
To tell me how he takes it. Fare you well!
I thank you for your pains. Spend this for me.
Vio.: I am no fee'd post, lady. Keep your purse.
My master, not myself, lacks recompense.
Love makes his heart of flint that you shall love;
And let your fervour, like my master's, be
Plac'd in contempt! Farewell, fair cruelty. [*Exit.*]
Oli.: "What is your parentage?"
"Above my fortunes, yet my state is well.
I am a gentleman." I'll be sworn thou art.
Thy tongue, thy face, thy limbs, actions, and
    spirit
Do give thee five-fold blazon. Not too fast! Soft,
    soft!
Unless the master were the man. How now!
Even so quickly may one catch the plague?
Methinks I feel this youth's perfections
With an invisible and subtle stealth
To creep in at mine eyes. Well, let it be.

PART THREE

APPENDICES

A EXERCISE IN DEVELOPING A REHEARSAL SCHEDULE

The following exercises are provided in order to help the director plan a typical rehearsal schedule. Many factors come together when the director plans a rehearsal schedule. The length, difficulty or intricacy of certain scenes may require more intensive work than others. Hence it is vital that the director complete preparations (i.e., has done the necessary homework) before developing a rehearsal schedule.

Three standard rehearsal periods are included in this exercise section. They are (1) a six- to seven-week rehearsal schedule—35 rehearsal periods, (2) a somewhat briefer four- to five-week rehearsal schedule—25 rehearsal periods, and (3) a typical and compressed summer stock schedule of 15 rehearsal periods. Obviously the amount of time devoted to each part of the play during rehearsal will depend upon the number of available rehearsal periods. Some typical entries in a projected rehearsal schedule might resemble the following for a 35-period rehearsal schedule and a three-act play, each with two scenes.

REHEARSAL PERIOD	REHEARSAL UNITS
1	Discussion with full cast
5	Run Act II for blocking
10	Act I, scene 2, principals only
15	Special problems in Act I
20	Run Act II—no books—lines learned
25	Polish Act III, Scene 1
30	Run-through with props
35	FINAL DRESS REHEARSAL

Be sure to consider the play carefully before developing a rehearsal schedule. Such planning will be useful in helping to avoid multiple adjustments which may be necessary even in the best-planned productions.

The exercises may be extracted without damage to the book.

REHEARSAL SCHEDULE: 35 REHEARSAL PERIOD SCHEDULE
(3 HOURS EACH PERIOD)

DIRECTOR'S NAME _____

PLAY TITLE _____

AUTHOR _____ TRANSLATION _____

NUMBER OF ACTS_____ NUMBER OF SCENES (TOTAL) _____

ESTIMATED PLAYING TIME PER ACT

ACT   I _____ Scene 1 _____ Scene 2 _____

Scene 3 _____ Scene 4 _____

ACT II _____ Scene 1 _____ Scene 2 _____

Scene 3 _____ Scene 4 _____

ACT III _____ Scene 1 _____ Scene 2 _____

Scene 3 _____ Scene 4 _____

ACT IV _____ Scene 1 _____ Scene 2 _____

Scene 3 _____ Scene 4 _____

ACT V _____ Scene 1 _____ Scene 2 _____

Scene 3 _____ Scene 4 _____

TOTAL PLAYING TIME _____

PLANNED REHEARSAL SCHEDULE

REHEARSAL PERIOD   REHEARSAL UNITS

1 _____

2 _____

3 _____

4 _____

5 _____

6 _____

7 _____

8 _____

9 _____

10 _____

11 _____

12 _____

13 _____

14 _____
15 _____
16 _____
17 _____
18 _____
19 _____
20 _____
21 _____
22 _____
23 _____
24 _____
25 _____
26 _____
27 _____
28 _____
29 _____
30 _____
31 _____
32 _____
33 _____
34 _____
35 **FINAL DRESS REHEARSAL** _____
36 **OPENING NIGHT**

Name _____ Date _____

REHEARSAL SCHEDULE: 25 REHEARSAL PERIOD SCHEDULE
(3 HOURS EACH PERIOD)

DIRECTOR'S NAME _____

PLAY TITLE _____

AUTHOR _____ TRANSLATION _____

NUMBER OF ACTS _____ NUMBER OF SCENES (TOTAL) _____

ESTIMATED PLAYING TIME PER ACT

ACT I _____ Scene 1 _____ Scene 2 _____

Scene 3 _____ Scene 4 _____

ACT II _____ Scene 1 _____ Scene 2 _____

Scene 3 _____ Scene 4 _____

ACT III _____ Scene 1 _____ Scene 2 _____

Scene 3 _____ Scene 4 _____

ACT IV _____ Scene 1 _____ Scene 2 _____

Scene 3 _____ Scene 4 _____

ACT V _____ Scene 1 _____ Scene 2 _____

Scene 3 _____ Scene 4 _____

TOTAL PLAYING TIME _____

PLANNED REHEARSAL SCHEDULE

REHEARSAL PERIOD	REHEARSAL UNITS
1	_____
2	_____
3	_____
4	_____
5	_____
6	_____
7	_____
8	_____
9	_____
10	_____
11	_____
12	_____
13	_____

14 _____

15 _____

16 _____

17 _____

18 _____

19 _____

20 _____

21 _____

22 _____

23 _____

24 _____

25 FINAL DRESS REHEARSAL _____

26 OPENING NIGHT

REHEARSAL SCHEDULE: 15 REHEARSAL PERIOD SCHEDULE
(3 HOURS EACH PERIOD)
(NORMAL SUMMER STOCK SCHEDULE)

DIRECTOR'S NAME _____

PLAY TITLE _____

AUTHOR _____ TRANSLATION _____

NUMBER OF ACTS _____ **NUMBER OF SCENES (TOTAL)** _____

ESTIMATED PLAYING TIME PER ACT

    ACT I _____ Scene 1 _____ Scene 2 _____

                         Scene 3 _____ Scene 4 _____

    ACT II _____ Scene 1 _____ Scene 2 _____

                         Scene 3 _____ Scene 4 _____

    ACT III _____ Scene 1 _____ Scene 2 _____

                         Scene 3 _____ Scene 4 _____

    ACT IV _____ Scene 1 _____ Scene 2 _____

                         Scene 3 _____ Scene 4 _____

    ACT V _____ Scene 1 _____ Scene 2 _____

                         Scene 3 _____ Scene 4 _____

    TOTAL PLAYING TIME _____

PLANNED REHEARSAL SCHEDULE

REHEARSAL PERIOD   **REHEARSAL UNITS**

1 _____

2 _____

3 _____

4 _____

5 _____

6 _____

7 _____

8 _____

9 _____

10 _____

11 _____

12 _____

13 _____

B LIST OF RECOMMENDED PLAY COMPANIES

General
Samuel French, Inc.
7623 Sunset Boulevard
Hollywood, California 90046
or
25 West 45th Street
New York, New York 10036

Walter H. Baker Company
100 Summer Street
Boston, Massachusets 02110

Dramatists Play Service, Inc.
440 Park Avenue South
New York, New York 10016

The Dramatic Publishing Company
86 East Randolph Street
Chicago, Illinois 60601

Plays for Children
The Children's Theatre Press
Cloverlot
Anchorage, Kentucky 40223

The Coach House Press
53 West Jackson Boulevard
Chicago, Illinois 60604

C SUGGESTIONS FOR FURTHER READING

1. Acting

Albright, Hardie, and Albright, Anita. *Acting: The Creative Process,* 3rd ed. Belmont, Calif.: Wadsworth, 1980.

Benedetti, Robert L. *The Actor at Work.* rev. ed. Englewood Cliffs, N.J.: Prentice-Hall, 1976.

Blunt, Jerry. *The Composite Art of Acting.* New York: Macmillan, 1966.

Boleslavski, Richard. *Acting: The First Six Lessons.* New York: Theatre Arts Books, 1933.

Cole, Toby, and Chinoy, Helen Krich, eds. *Actors on Acting,* rev. ed. New York: Crown Publishers, 1970.

Crawford, Jerry L. *Acting: In Person and in Style.* 2nd ed. Dubuque, Iowa: Wm. C. Brown Co., 1980.

Eustis, Morton. *Players at Work.* New York: Theatre Arts Books, 1937.

Funke, Lewis, and Booth, John E. *Actors Talk About Acting.* New York: Random House, 1961.

Glenn, Stanley L. *The Complete Actor.* Boston: Allyn and Bacon, 1977.

Hethman, Robert H., ed. *Strasberg at the Actor's Studio.* New York: Viking Press, 1965.

Kahan, Stanley. *An Introduction to Acting,* 2d ed. Boston: Allyn and Bacon, 1985.

Kalter, Joanmarie. *Actors on Acting.* New York: Sterling Publishing Co., 1979.

Lewis, Robert. *Method or Madness.* New York: Samuel French, 1958.

Redgrave, Michael. *The Actor's Ways and Means.* London: William Heinemann; New York: Theatre Arts Books (HEB Paperback), 1979.

Rockwood, Jerome. *The Craftsmen of Dionysius: An Approach to Acting.* Glenview, Ill.: Scott, Foresman, 1966.

Ross, Lillian, and Ross, Helen. *The Player: A Profile of an Art.* New York: Simon and Schuster, 1962.

Stanislavski, Constantin. *An Actor Prepares.* Translated by Elizabeth Reynolds Hapgood. New York: Theatre Arts Books, 1936.

Stanislavski, Constantin. *Building a Character.* Translated by Elizabeth Reynolds Hapgood. New York: Theatre Arts Books, 1949.

Stanislavski, Constantin. *Creating a Role.* Translated by Elizabeth Reynolds Hapgood. Edited by Hermine Isaacs Popper. New York: Theatre Arts Books, 1961.

2. Directing

Brook, Peter. *The Empty Space.* New York: Atheneum, 1968.

Canfield, Curtis. *The Craft of Play Directing.* New York: Holt, Rinehart and Winston, 1963.

Clurman, Harold. *On Directing.* New York: Macmillan, 1972.

Cohen, Robert, and Harrop, John. *Creative Play Direction*. Englewood Cliffs, N.J.: Prentice-Hall, 1984.

Cole, Toby, and Chinoy, Helen Krich, eds. *Directors on Directing*. rev. ed. Indianapolis: Bobbs-Merrill, 1963.

Dean, Alexander. *Fundamentals of Play Directing*. Revised by Lawrence Carra. New York: Holt, Rinehart and Winston, 1974.

Dietrich, John, and Duckwall, Ralph. *Play Direction*. Englewood Cliffs, N.J.: Prentice-Hall, 1983.

Gallaway, Marian. *The Director in the Theatre*. New York: Macmillan, 1963.

Hodge, Francis. *Play Directing: Analysis, Communication and Style*. Englewood Cliffs, N.J.: Prentice-Hall, 1971.

Hunt, Hugh. *The Director in the Theatre*. London: Routledge & Kegan Paul, 1954.

Sievers, W. David, Stiver, Harry E., and Kahan, Stanley. *Directing for the Theatre*. Dubuque, Iowa: Wm. C. Brown Co., 1974.

Staub, August. *Creative Theatre: The Art of Theatrical Directing*. New York: Harper & Row 1973.

Welker, David. *Theatrical Direction*. Boston: Allyn and Bacon, 1971.

Wills, J. Robert, ed. *The Director in a Changing Theatre*. Palo Alto, Calif.: Mayfield Publishing Co., 1976.